Level 3

BRICKWORK

NVQ/SVQ and Diploma

9

www.pearsonschoolsandfe.co.uk

✓ Free online support
✓ Useful weblinks
✓ 24 hour online ordering

0845 630 44 44

Part of Pearson

Heinemann is an imprint of Pearson Education Limited, Edinburgh Gate, Harlow, Essex, CM20 2JE.

www.pearsonschoolsandfecolleges.co.uk

Heinemann is a registered trademark of Pearson Education Limited

Text © Carillion Construction Ltd 2011
Typeset by Tek-Art
Original illustrations © Pearson Education Ltd 2011
Cover design by Wooden Ark
Cover photo © Construction Photography: Buildpix

The right of Carillion to be identified as author of this work has been asserted by them in accordance with the Copyright, Designs and Patents Act 1988

First published 2011

14 13 12 11
10 9 8 7 6 5 4 3 2 1

British Library Cataloguing in Publication Data
A catalogue record for this book is available from the British Library

ISBN 978 0 435 047207

Printed and bound in Barcelona by Grafos

Websites
Pearson Education Limited is not responsible for the content of any external internet sites. It is essential for tutors to preview each website before using it in class so as to ensure that the URL is still accurate, relevant and appropriate. We suggest that tutors bookmark useful websites and consider enabling learners to access them through the school/college intranet.

The information and activities in this book have been prepared according to the standards reasonably to be expected of a competent trainer in the relevant subject matter. However, you should be aware that errors and omissions can be made and that different employers may adopt different standards and practices over time. Before doing any practical activity, you should always carry out your own risk assessment and make your own enquiries and investigations into appropriate standards and practices to be observed.

Acknowledgements

Every effort has been made to contact copyright holders of material reproduced in this book. Any omissions will be rectified in subsequent printings if notice is given to the publishers.

The author and publisher would like to thank the following individuals and organisations for permission to reproduce photographs:

(Key: b-bottom; c-centre; l-left; r-right; t-top)

Alamy Images: Ace Stock Limited 201, 201r, Adrian Sherratt 193, 211, Andrew Darrington 204, AT Willett 129, David Barton 93b, David J. Green 14, David Lawrence 100b, Eric Nathan 68, Justin Kase 101, 130, Kris Mercer 123, Leslie Garland Picture Library 158, Libby Welch 132, Macana 188, Mark Boulton 228, Niall McDiarmid 166, Nikreates 250, Paul Heinrich 225b, Pintail Pictures 69, Ros Drinkwater 247, Rubberball 145, Steve Walsh 30, Sue Heath 173, Tim Hurst 166cr, Tony Timmington 159, WIlliam S. Kuta 173r, Woodystock 152; **Construction Photography:** Buildpix 128, 233, David Burrows 93, David Potter 66, David Stewart-Smith 100, DIY Photolibrary 133, Grant Smith 90, Jean-Francois Cordella 181, Paul McMullin 92t, Xavier de Canto 135; **Creatas:** 62; **CSCS:** 4; **Getty Images:** PhotoDisc 129b, Taxi 61; **Robert Harding World Imagery:** age fotostock / Matz Sjoberg 209; **Pearson Education Ltd:** Gareth Boden 10, 82, 82r, 85, 85tr, 85bl, 86tl, 91, 92c, 92b, 133t, 151, 151t, 182, Ian Wedgewood 162tl, 162cl, 162cr, 164bl, 167, 228r, 230tl, 230tr, 230cl, 230cr, 230b, 231, 246l, 246r, Jules Selmes 225t; Naki Photography 86, 86tr; **Science Photo Library Ltd:** Alex Bartel 33, Carlos Dominguez 44, Garry Watson 7; **Shutterstock.com:** 1125089601 17, Andrey Bayda 7l, chrislofoto 227, David Hughes 139, David Lee 118, Frances A. Miller 11, K. Jakubowska 248, Kuzma 1, Stavklem 136, Yobidaba 7r, Yuri Arcurs 4b

All other images © Pearson Education Ltd

Every effort has been made to trace the copyright holders and we apologise in advance for any unintentional omissions. We would be pleased to insert the appropriate acknowledgement in any subsequent edition of this publication.

Contents

Introduction iv

Features of this book x

1001 Safe working practices in construction 1

3002 Knowledge of information, quantities and communicating with others 3 17

3003 Knowledge of building methods and construction technology 3 61

3027 Know how to carry out structural and decorative brickwork 145

3028 Know how to repair and maintain masonry structures 181

3029 Know how to erect complex masonry structures 209

Index 265

Introduction

Brickwork combines many different practical and visual skills with a knowledge of specialised materials and techniques. This book will introduce you to the construction trade and in the knowledge needed for you to begin constructing structural and decorative brickwork, repair masonry structures and erect more complex structures.

About this book

The information in this book covers the information you will need to attain your Level 3 qualification in Brickwork. Each chapter of the book relates to a particular unit of the CAA Diploma and provides the information needed to form the required knowledge and understanding of that area. The book is also designed to support those undertaking the NVQ at Level 3.

This book has been written based on a concept used with Carillion Training Centres for many years. The concept is about providing learners with the necessary information they need to support their studies and at the same time ensuring it is presented in a style which is both manageable and relevant.

This book will also be a useful reference tool for you in your professional life once you have gained your qualifications and are a practising painter and decorator.

Qualifications for the construction industry

There are many ways of entering the construction industry, but the most common method is as an apprentice.

Apprenticeships

You can become an apprentice by being employed:

- directly by a construction company who will send you to college
- by a training provider, such as Carillion, which combines construction training with practical work experience.
- Construction Skills is the national training organisation for construction in the UK and is responsible for setting training standards.
- The framework of an Apprenticeship is based around an NVQ (or SVQ in Scotland). These qualifications are developed and approved by industry experts and will measure your practical skills and job knowledge on site.
- You will also need to achieve:
- a technical certificate
- the Construction Skills health and safety test

- the appropriate level of Functional skills assessment
- an Employees Rights and Responsibilities briefing.
- You will also need to achieve the right qualifications to get on a construction site, including qualifying for the CSCS card scheme.

CAA Diploma

The CAA Diploma is a common testing strategy with knowledge tests for each unit, a practical assignment and the GOLA (Global Online Assessment) test. The Diploma meets the requirements of the new Qualifications and Credit Framework (QCF) which bases a qualification on the number of credits (with ten learning hours gaining one credit):

- Award (1 to 12 credits)
- Certificate (13 to 36 credits)
- Diploma (37+ credits)

As part of the CAA Diploma you will gain the skills needed for the NVQ as well as the functional skills knowledge you will need to complete your qualification.

National Vocational Qualifications (NVQs)

NVQs are available to anyone, with no restrictions on age, length or type of training, although learners below a certain age can only perform certain tasks. There are different levels of NVQ (for example 1, 2, 3), which in turn are broken down into units of competence. NVQs are not like traditional examinations in which someone sits an exam paper. An NVQ is a 'doing' qualification, which means it lets the industry know that you have the knowledge, skills and ability to actually 'do' something.

NVQs are made up of both mandatory and optional units and the number of units that you need to complete for an NVQ depends on the level and the occupation.

Acknowledgements

Carillion would like to thank Dave Whitten and Kevin Jarvis for their hard work and dedication in preparing the content of this book. Carillion would also like to thank John McLaughlin Harvie for preparing the functional skills content for this book.

Pearson would like to thank Kevin Diett, Bernard Dearle and Nigel Edwards of Sussex Downs College and John Spalding of Fareham College for their comprehensive review work. Pearson would also like to thank the staff and students at Carillion's Hull Training Centre for all their co-operation in helping to set up some of the photos used in this book.

Introduction

Functional skills

Functional skills are the skills needed to work independently in everyday life. The references are headed FM for mathematics and FE for English.

Features of this book

This book has been fully illustrated with artworks and photographs. These will help to give you more information about a concept or a procedure, as well as helping you to follow a step-by-step procedure or identify a particular tool or material.

This book also contains a number of different features to help your learning and development.

Key term

These are new or difficult words. They are picked out in **bold** in the text and then defined in the margin.

Did you know?

This feature gives you interesting facts about the building trade.

Safety tip

This feature gives you guidance for working safely on the tasks in this book.

Find out

These are short activities and research opportunities, designed to help you gain further information about, and understanding of, a topic area.

Working life

This feature gives you a chance to read about and debate a real-life work scenario or problem. Why has the situation occurred? What would you do?

Remember

This highlights key facts or concepts, sometimes from earlier in the text, to remind you of important things you will need to think about.

FAQ

These are frequently asked questions appearing at the end of most units to answer your questions with informative answers from the experts.

Check it out

A series of questions at the end of most units to check your understanding. Some of these questions may support the collecting of evidence for the NVQ.

Getting ready for assessment

This feature provides guidance for preparing for the practical assessment. It will give you advice on using the theory you have learned about in a practical way.

Check your knowledge

This is a series of multiple choice questions at the end of most units, in the style of the GOLA end-of-unit tests.

UNIT 1001

Safe working practices in construction

Health and safety is a vital part of all construction work. All work should be completed in a way that is safe not only for the individual worker, but also for the other workers on the site, people near by and the final users of the building. Health and safety is not optional in your career, but an essential part of working in the industry. Every year there are over 100 fatalities in the construction industry. Don't become one of them.

This unit will give you the key information you will need for safe working practice. It supports NVQ Units QCF 01 Conform to general workplace safety and QCF 03 Move and handle general resources. It also supports TAP Unit 1 Erect and dismantle working platforms and delivery of the five generic units.

This unit will cover the following learning outcomes:

- Health and safety regulations – roles and responsibilities
- Accident, first aid and emergency procedures and reporting
- Hazards on construction sites
- Health and hygiene
- Safe handling of materials and equipment
- Basic working platforms
- Working with electricity
- Use of appropriate personal protective equipment (PPE)
- Fire and emergency procedures
- Safety signs and notices.

K1. Health and safety regulations – roles and responsibilities

Health and safety **legislation** is there not just to protect you – it also states what you must and must not do to ensure that no workers are placed in a situation **hazardous** to themselves or others. You will also use codes of practice and guidance notes (produced by the HSE and by companies themselves).

The Health and Safety at Work Act 1974 (HASAWA)

HASAWA applies to all types and places of work and to employers, employees, self-employed people, **subcontractors** and even **suppliers**. The Act protects people at work and the general public. HASAWA is designed to ensure health, safety and welfare for all persons at work and the general public. It also controls the use, handling, storage and transportation of explosives and highly flammable substances and the release of noxious/offensive substances into the atmosphere.

Employer's duties	Provide a safe place to work with safe plant and machinery. Information, training and supervision supplied to all employees. A written safety policy supplied and risk assessments carried out. PPE provided to all employees free of charge. Health and safety assured when handling, storing and transporting materials and substances.
Employee's duties	Must take reasonable care for their own health and safety, and the health and safety of anyone who may be affected by their acts or **omissions**. Co-operate with employer and other persons to meet the law, (and not misuse) materials provided for their safety and report hazards or accidents.
Supplier's duties	Duty to make sure articles are designed and constructed safely, fully tested and safe to use, handle, transport and store. Information should be provided on all these to the user.

Health and Safety Executive (HSE)

The HSE is the government body responsible for the encouragement, regulation and enforcement of health, safety and welfare in the workplace in the UK and it enforces HASAWA and other laws through inspectors who can prosecute people or companies that break the law.

HSE inspectors have the authority to enter and examine any premises at any time, taking samples and possession of any dangerous article/substance. They can issue improvement notices, ordering a company to solve a problem in a certain time, or issue a prohibition notice stopping all work until the site is safe.

Construction (Design and Management) Regulations 2007

The Construction (Design and Management) Regulations 2007 are designed to help improve safety. Employers must plan, manage and monitor work, ensuring employees are competent and provided with training and information. They must also provide adequate welfare facilities for workers. There are also specific requirements relating to lighting, excavations and traffic etc.

Employees must check their own competence and co-operate to co-ordinate work safely, reporting any obvious risks.

Provision and Use of Work Equipment Regulations 1998 (PUWER)

These regulations cover all new or existing **work equipment**. PUWER covers starting, stopping, regular use, transport, repair, modification, servicing and cleaning of equipment.

The general duties of the Act require equipment to be used and maintained in suitable and safe conditions by a trained person. It should be fitted with appropriate warnings and be able to be isolated from sources of energy.

In addition, the Act also requires access to dangerous parts of machinery to be prevented or controlled. Suitable controls must be provided for stopping and starting of work equipment, in particular emergency stopping and braking systems should be installed. Sufficient lighting must be in place for operating equipment.

> **Did you know?**
>
> On large projects, a person is appointed as the CDM co-ordinator. This person has overall responsibility for compliance with CDM. There is a general expectation by the HSE that all parties involved in a project will co-operate and co-ordinate with each other.

> **Key term**
>
> **Work equipment** – any machinery, appliance, apparatus or tool and any assembly of components that are used in non-domestic premises

Other pieces of legislation

Legislation	Content
Reporting of Injuries, Diseases and Dangerous Occurrences Regulations 1995 (RIDDOR)	Employers have a duty to report accidents, diseases or dangerous occurrences. HSE uses this to identify where and how risks arise and to investigate serious accidents.
Control of Substances Hazardous to Health Regulations 2002 (COSHH)	State how employees and employers should work with, handle, store, transport and dispose of potentially hazardous substances. This includes substances used and generated during work (e.g. paints or dust), naturally occurring substances (e.g. sand) and biological elements (e.g. bacteria).

Legislation	Content
The Control of Noise at Work Regulations 2005	Employers must assess the risks to the employee and make sure legal limits are not exceeded, noise exposure is reduced, and hearing protection is provided along with information, instruction and training.
The Electricity at Work Regulations 1989	Cover work involving electricity. Employers must keep electrical systems safe and regularly maintained and reduce the risk of employees coming into contact with live electrical currents.
The Manual Handling Operations Regulations 1992	Cover all work activities involving a person lifting. Manual handling should be avoided wherever possible and a risk assessment must be carried out.
The Personal Protective Equipment at Work Regulations 1992 (PPER)	PPE must be checked by a trained and competent person and must be provided by the employer free of charge with a secure storage place. Employees must know how to use PPE, the risks it will help to protect against, its purpose, how to maintain it and its limitations.
The Work at Height Regulations 2005	Employers must avoid working at height and use equipment that prevents or minimises the danger of falls. Employees must follow training, report hazards and use safety equipment.

Find out

There are several sources for health and safety information. Use the Internet to find out more about each of the following:

- Construction Skills
- Royal Society for the Prevention of Accidents (RoSPA)
- Royal Society for the Promotion of Health (RPH).

Remember

As a trainee once you pass the health and safety test you will qualify for a trainee card and once you have achieved a Level 2 qualification you can then upgrade your card to an experienced worker card. Achieving a Level 3 qualification allows you to apply for a gold card.

Site inductions

Site inductions are the processes that an individual undergoes in order to accelerate their awareness of the potential health and safety hazards and risks they may face in their working environment; but excludes job-related skills training. Different site inductions will always cover operations on site, health and safety, welfare and emergency arrangements, reporting structure and the process for reporting near misses. Records must be kept to ensure all workers have received an induction.

Construction Skills Certification Scheme (CSCS)

The Construction Skills certification scheme requires all workers to obtain a CSCS card before working on a building site. There are various levels of cards which indicate your competence and skill background. This ensures that only skilled and safe tradespeople can work on site. To get a CSCS card all applicants must sit a health and safety test.

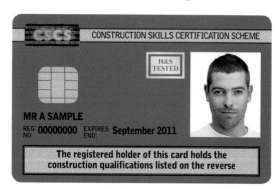

Figure 1.01 CSCS card

K2. Accident, first aid and emergency procedures and reporting

Major emergencies that could occur on site include not only accidents but also fires, security alerts and bomb alerts. Your site induction should make it clear to you what to do in the event of an emergency.

Reporting accidents

All accidents need to be reported and recorded in the accident book and the injured person must report to a trained first aider. An accident may result in an injury which may be minor (e.g. a cut or a bruise) or major (e.g. loss of a limb). Accidents can also be fatal. When an accident happens, the first thing to do is to be sure the victim is in no further danger, without putting yourself at risk.

As well as reporting accidents, 'near misses' must also be reported. A 'near miss' is when an accident nearly happened but did not actually occur. These might identify a problem and prevent accidents from happening in the future.

The accident book is completed by the person who had the accident or someone representing the injured person. You will need to enter some basic details, including:

- who was involved, what happened and where
- the date and time of the accident and any witnesses
- the address of the injured person
- what PPE was being worn and what first aid treatment was given.

K3. Hazards on construction sites

A major part of health and safety at work is being able to identify hazards and to help prevent them in the first place, therefore avoiding the risk of injury. Hazards include working at height (pages 11–13), electrical work (pages 13–14) and fires (pages 15–16).

Hazard	What to do
Tripping	Caused by poor **housekeeping**. Keep workplaces tidy and free from debris.
Chemical spills	Most are small with minimal risk and can be easily cleaned. If the spill is hazardous, take the correct action promptly.
Burns	From fires or chemical materials. You must be aware of the dangers and take the correct precautions.

> **Remember**
>
> Companies that have a lot of accidents will have a poor company image for health and safety and will find it increasingly difficult to gain future contracts. Unsafe companies with lots of accidents will also see injured people claiming against their insurance which will see their premiums rise. This will eventually make them uninsurable, meaning they will not get any work.

> **Remember**
>
> An accident that falls under RIDDOR should be reported by the safety officer or site manager and can be reported to the HSE by telephone (0845 3009923) or via the RIDDOR website (www.riddor.gov.uk).

> **Key term**
>
> **Housekeeping** – cleaning up after yourself and ensuring your work area is clean and tidy. Good housekeeping is vital on a construction site as an unclean work area is dangerous

Risk assessments and method statements

You must know how to carry out a risk assessment. You may be given direct responsibility for this, and the care and attention you take over it may have a direct impact on the safety of others. You must be aware of the dangers or hazards of any task, and know what can be done to prevent or reduce the risk.

There are five steps in a risk assessment:

- **Step 1** Identify the hazards
- **Step 2** Identify who is at risk
- **Step 3** Calculate the risk from the hazard against the likelihood of it taking place
- **Step 4** Introduce measures to reduce the risk
- **Step 5** Monitor the risk.

A method statement takes information about significant risks from risk assessments and combines them with the job specification to produce a practical and safe working method for the workers to follow for tasks on site. The hazard book can also be used to identify tasks and produce risk assessments.

K4. Health and hygiene

One of the easiest ways to stay healthy is to wash your hands on a regular basis to prevent hazardous substances from entering your body. You should always clean any cuts you may get to prevent infection. Broken skin can allow in bacteria, causing infections such as **leptospirosis**. Welfare facilities should be provided for employees. These include toilets, washing facilities, drinking water, storage and lunch areas.

Health effects of noise

Damage to hearing can be caused by one of two things:

- **Intensity** – you can be hurt in an instant from an explosive or very loud noise which can burst your ear drum.
- **Duration** – noise doesn't have to be deafening to harm you, it can be a quieter noise over a long period, e.g. a 12-hour shift.

Hazardous substances

Hazardous substances are a major health and safety risk on a construction site. They must be handled, stored, transported and disposed of in very specific ways.

Remember

Waste on site will need to be correctly identified and disposed of. Hazardous materials will need to be disposed of specially.

Key terms

Leptospirosis – an infectious disease that affects humans and animals. The human form is commonly called Weil's disease. The disease can cause fever, muscle pain and jaundice. In severe cases it can affect the liver and kidneys. Leptospirosis can often be caught from contaminated soil or water that has been urinated in by the carrier of the disease

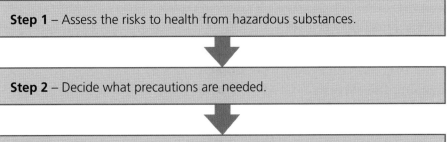

Step 1 – Assess the risks to health from hazardous substances.

Step 2 – Decide what precautions are needed.

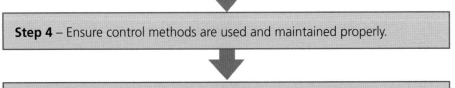

Step 3 – Prevent employees from being exposed to any hazardous substances. If prevention is impossible, the risk must be adequately controlled.

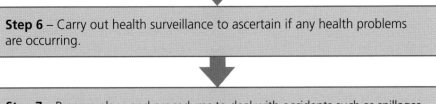

Step 4 – Ensure control methods are used and maintained properly.

Step 5 – Monitor the exposure of employees to hazardous substances.

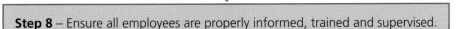

Step 6 – Carry out health surveillance to ascertain if any health problems are occurring.

Step 7 – Prepare plans and procedures to deal with accidents such as spillages.

Step 8 – Ensure all employees are properly informed, trained and supervised.

Figure 1.02 Process for dealing with hazardous substances

> **Safety tip**
>
> Not all substances are labelled, and sometimes the label may not match the contents. If you are in any doubt, don't use or touch the substance.

Ask the supplier or manufacturer for a COSHH data sheet, outlining the risks involved with a substance. Most substance containers carry a warning sign stating whether the contents are corrosive, harmful, toxic or bad for the environment. Exposure to chemicals can cause skin problems such as **dermatitis.**

> **Key terms**
>
> **Dermatitis** – a skin condition where the affected area is red, itchy and sore

Figure 1.03 Common safety signs for corrosive, toxic and explosive materials

Waste

You need to identify all the types of waste you create and the best way of disposing of them. The Controlled Waste Regulations 1992 state that only those authorised to dispose of waste may do so, keeping full records.

Several different types of waste are defined by these regulations:

* household waste – normal household rubbish
* commercial waste – for example, from shops or offices
* industrial waste – from factories and industrial sites.

K5. Safe handling of materials and equipment

Manual handling is the lifting and moving of a piece of equipment or material from one place to another without using machinery. This is one of the most common causes of injury at work and can cause injuries such as muscle strain, pulled ligaments and hernias. Spinal injury is the most common injury and is very serious because there is little doctors can do to correct it. When lifting a load the correct posture is:

* feet shoulder-width apart with one foot slightly in front of the other
* knees bent with the back straight and arms as close to the body as possible
* grip must be firm using the whole hand and not just the finger tips.

The correct technique when lifting is:

* approach the load squarely facing the direction of travel
* place hands under the load and pull it close to your body, lifting using your legs, not your back
* when lowering bend at the knees, not the back.

Safe storage and handling of tools and equipment

Tools

All tools need to be stored safely and securely in suitable bags or boxes to protect them from weather and rust. When not in use they should be safely locked away.

Did you know?

In 2004/2005 there were over 50,000 injuries while handling, lifting or carrying in the UK (Source: HSE).

Safety tip

Hand tools with sharp edges should be covered to prevent cuts.

Power tools should be carried by the handle.

Power tools that have gas-powered cartridges must be stored in an area that is safe and away from sources of ignition to prevent explosion. Used cartridges must be disposed of safely.

Bricks and blocks

Type	Storage and handling issues
Bricks and blocks	Largely pre-packed in shrink-wrapped plastic and banded using either plastic or metal bands with edges protected by plastic strips. Store on level ground close to where they are required and stack on edge in rows no more than two packs high. Take from a minimum of three packs and mix to prevent changes in colour in final brickwork.
Paving slabs	Normally delivered in wooden crates, covered in shrink-wrapped plastic, or banded and covered on pallets. Do not stack higher than two packs. Store outside and stack on edge to prevent lower slabs being damaged by the weight of the stack. Store on firm, level ground with timber bearers below to prevent damage to edges.

Aggregates, cement and plaster

Aggregates are delivered in tipper lorries or one-tonne bags. They should be stored on a concrete base, with a fall to allow for water to drain away. Cover aggregates with tarpaulin or plastic sheets.

Both cement and plaster are usually available in 25 kg bags. Bags are made from multi-wall layers of paper with a polythene liner. Do not puncture the bags before use. Store in a ventilated, waterproof shed, on a dry floor and stack no higher than five bags.

Wood and sheet materials

Type	Storage and handling issues
Carcassing timber	Store outside under a covered framework, on timber bearers clear of vegetation-free ground, to reduce ground moisture absorption. Use piling sticks between each layer of timber to provide support and allow air circulation.
Joinery grade and hardwoods	Store under full cover with ventilation to prevent build-up of moisture. Store on bearers on a well-prepared base.
Plywood and sheet materials	Store in a dry, well-ventilated environment. Stack flat on timber cross-bearers, spaced close together to prevent sagging. Do not lean against walls as this makes the plywood bow. For faces, place these against each other to minimise risk of damage. Keep different sizes, grades and qualities of sheet materials separate.
Joinery components	Doors, frames etc. should be stored flat on timber bearers under cover to protect from the weather. In limited space they can be stored upright in a rack, but do not lean against a wall. Wall and floor units must be stacked on a flat surface no more than two units high. Store inside and use protective sheeting to prevent damage and staining.
Plasterboard	Store in a flat waterproof area and do not lean against a wall.

Adhesives

All adhesives should be stored and used in line with the manufacturer's instructions. This is usually to store on shelves, with labels facing outwards, in a safe, secure area (preferably a lockable store room). It is important to keep the labels facing outwards so that the correct adhesive can be selected.

Paint and decorating materials

Type	Storage issues
Oil- and water-based materials	Store at a constant temperature in date order (new stock at the back) on clearly marked shelves with the labels turned to the front. Regularly **invert** to prevent settlement or separation of ingredients and keep tightly sealed to prevent **skinning**. Water-based paints should be protected from frost to prevent freezing.
Powdered materials	Heavy bags should be stored at ground level. Smaller items should be stored on shelves with loose materials in sealed containers. Protect from frost, moisture and high humidity.

Key terms

Invert – tip and turn upside down

Skinning – the formation of a skin which occurs when the top layer dries out

Remember

Decorating materials hazardous to health include spirits, turps, paint thinners and varnish removers. These should be stored on shelves to any COSHH requirements. Temperatures must be kept below 15°C to prevent storage containers expanding or blowing up.

Figure 1.04 Correct storage of paints

K6. Basic working platforms

Fall protection

With any task involving working at height, the main danger is falling. There are certain tasks where edge protection or scaffolding simply cannot be used. In these instances some form of fall protection must be used.

Remember

There is also a danger of objects falling from height and striking workers and people below. Barriers should be in place to prevent this.

Type of fall protection	Description
Harnesses and lanyards	Harness is attached to the worker and a lanyard to a secure beam/eyebolt. If the worker slips, they will fall only the length of the lanyard.
Safety netting	Used on the top floor where there is no point for a lanyard. Nets are attached to the joists to catch any falling workers.
Airbags	Made from interlinked modular air mattresses that expand together to form a soft fall surface. Ideal for short fall jobs.

Figure 1.05 A harness and lanyard can prevent a worker from falling to the ground

Stepladders and ladders

All types of ladders should only be set up on ground that is firm and level. All components should be checked fully before use. Don't use ladders to gain extra height on a working platform. There are some common safety checks for the materials that different types of ladder can be made from.

Type of ladder	Safety issues
Wood	Check for loose screws, nuts, bolts and hinges. Check tie ropes are in good condition. **Never** paint as this will hide defects.
Aluminium	Avoid working near live electricity supplies.
Fibreglass	Once damaged, **cannot be repaired** and must be replaced.

Using a stepladder

Stepladders should only be used for work that will take a few minutes to complete. When work is likely to take longer, use a sturdier alternative. Always open the steps fully and check for the Kitemark (Figure 1.06), which shows the ladder has been made to BSI standards.

Figure 1.06 British Standards Institution Kitemark

Using ladders

Ladders are not designed for work of a long duration and should be secured in place. One hand should always be free to hold the ladder and you should not have to stretch while using it.

You should also observe the following points when erecting a ladder.

- Ensure that there is at least a four-rung overlap on each extension section.
- Never rest on plastic guttering as it may break, causing the ladder to slip.
- If the base of the ladder is exposed, ensure it is guarded so it is not knocked.
- Secure the ladder at top and bottom. The bottom can be secured by a second person, but they must not leave while the ladder is in use.
- The angle of the ladder should be a ratio of 1:4 (or 75°) – see Figure 1.07.
- The top of the ladder must extend at least 1 m, or five rungs, above its landing point.

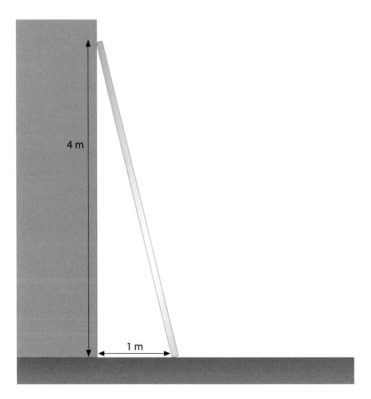

4 m

1 m

Figure 1.07 Correct angle for a ladder

Scaffolding

Tubular scaffold is the most commonly used type of scaffolding within the construction industry. There are two types of tubular scaffold:

- **Independent scaffold** – free-standing and does not rely on the building to support it.
- **Dependent scaffold** – attached to the building via putlogs into holes left in the brickwork. The putlogs stay in position until work is complete and give the scaffold extra support.

Mobile tower scaffolds

Mobile tower scaffolds can be moved without being dismantled. They have lockable wheels and are used extensively by many different trades. They are made from either traditional steel tubes and fittings or aluminium, which is lightweight and easy to move. The aluminium type of tower is normally specially designed and is referred to as a 'proprietary tower'. A 'low tower' scaffold is designed for use by one person at 2.5 m height.

Tower scaffolds must have a firm and level base. The stability of the tower depends on the height in relation to the size of the base:

- for use inside a building, the height should be no more than three and a half times the smaller base length
- for outside use the height should be no more than three times the smallest base length.

Working platforms at any height should be fitted with guard rails and toe boards on all four sides of the platform. Platforms over 9 m must be secured to the structure. Towers should not exceed 12 m unless specially designed to do so. Working platforms should be fully boarded and be at least 600 mm wide.

Safety tip

No one other than a qualified carded scaffolder is allowed to erect or alter scaffolding. Although you are not allowed to erect or alter this type of scaffold, you must be sure it is safe before you work on it.

Remember

The maximum height of platforms outside is three times the smallest width. Inside it is three and a half times.

Figure 1.08 Mobile tower scaffold

K7. Working with electricity

One of the main problems with electricity is that it is invisible. You don't even have to be working with an electric tool to be electrocuted. Working close to electrical supplies can put you at risk. There are two main types of voltage in the UK. These are 230 V and 110 V. The standard UK power supply is 230 V and this is what all the sockets in your house are.

Contained within the wiring there should be three wires: the live and neutral, which carry the alternating current, and the earth

Safety tip

When using a power tool, always check plugs and connections and be careful how you handle it. Don't pass it by the lead or allow it to get wet. Check the power is off when connecting leads and keep cables away from sharp edges to avoid damage.

wire, which acts as a safety device. The three wires are colour-coded as follows to make them easy to recognise:

- Live – Brown
- Neutral – Blue
- Earth – Yellow and green.

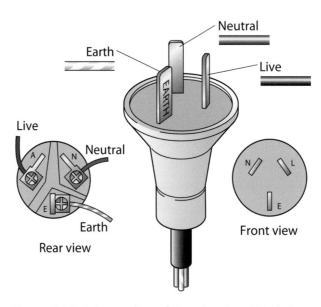

Figure 1.09 Colour coding of the wires in a 230 V plug

Figure 1.10 A 110 V plug

Safety tip

Don't attempt to go near a victim of an electric shock without wearing rubber or some form of insulated sole shoes; bare or socked feet will allow the current to flow through your body.

It is considered unsafe to use 230 V on construction sites so 110 V must be used. This is identified by a yellow cable and different style plug. A transformer converts the 230 V to 110 V. In domestic situations a portable transformer should be used.

Dealing with electric shocks

Always disconnect the power supply – if it is safe to do and will not take long to find. Touching the power source may put you in danger. If the victim is in contact with something portable (e.g. a drill), move it away using a non-conductive object such as a wooden broom. Don't attempt to touch the person until they are clear of the supply. Be especially careful in wet areas.

People 'hung up' in a live current flow may be unable to make a sound. Their muscles may also contract, preventing them from moving. Use a wooden object to swiftly and strongly knock the person free.

K8. Use of appropriate PPE

Personal protective equipment forms a defence against accidents or injury. PPE should be used with all the other methods of staying safe in the workplace. PPE must be regularly maintained otherwise its effectiveness will be affected. It will need cleaning, examining and replacement or repair. The cost of this is the responsibility of the employer. Storage facilities must be provided to protect PPE from contamination, loss, damage, damp or sunlight. PPE should be 'CE' marked to show it complies with the PPE Regulations 2002.

Find out

What are the most common forms of PPE on site? Find examples of each type.

K9. Fire and emergency procedures

Fires can start almost anywhere and at any time, but a fire needs all the ingredients of 'the triangle of fire' to burn. Remove one side of the triangle, and the fire will be extinguished. Fire moves by consuming all these ingredients and burns fuel as it moves.

Fires can be classified according to the type of material that is involved:

- Class A – wood, paper, textiles etc.
- Class B – flammable liquids, petrol, oil etc.
- Class C – flammable gases, liquefied petroleum gas (LPG), propane etc.
- Class D – metal, metal powder etc.
- Class E – electrical equipment.

There are several different types of fire extinguisher and it is important that you learn which type should be used on specific classes of fires.

Figure 1.11 The triangle of fire

Fire extinguisher	Colour band	Main use	Details
Water	Red	Class A fires	Never use for an electrical or burning fat/oil fire. Water will conduct electricity and 'explode' oil and fat fires.
Foam	Cream	Class A fires	Can be used on Class B if no liquid is flowing and on Class C if gas is in liquid form.
Carbon dioxide (CO_2)	Black	Class E fires	Can also be used on Class A, B and C.
Dry powder	Blue	All classes	Commonly used on electrical and liquid fires. Powder puts out the fire by smothering the flames.

Safety tip

For small fires a fire blanket can be used. These are made from fireproof material and work by smothering the fire and stopping any more oxygen from getting to it, thus putting it out. A fire blanket can also be used if a person is on fire.

What to do in the event of a fire

During your induction you will be made aware of the fire procedure and the location of fire assembly points. These should be clearly indicated by signs, and a map of their location displayed in the building. On hearing the alarm make your way calmly to the nearest muster point. This is so that everyone can be accounted for and prevents someone searching for you.

K10. Safety signs and notices

There are many different safety signs but each will usually fit into one of four categories. Figures 1.12–1.15 show an example of each. The colour and shape is always the same for each type of sign.

Figure 1.12 A prohibition sign

Figure 1.13 A mandatory sign

Figure 1.14 A warning sign

Figure 1.15 An information sign (safe conditions)

- **Prohibition signs** – these tell you that something **must not** be done.
- **Mandatory signs** – these tell you something **must** be done.
- **Warning signs** – these signs are there to alert you to a specific hazard.
- **Safe condition signs** (often called information signs) – these give you useful information like the location of things (e.g. a first aid point).

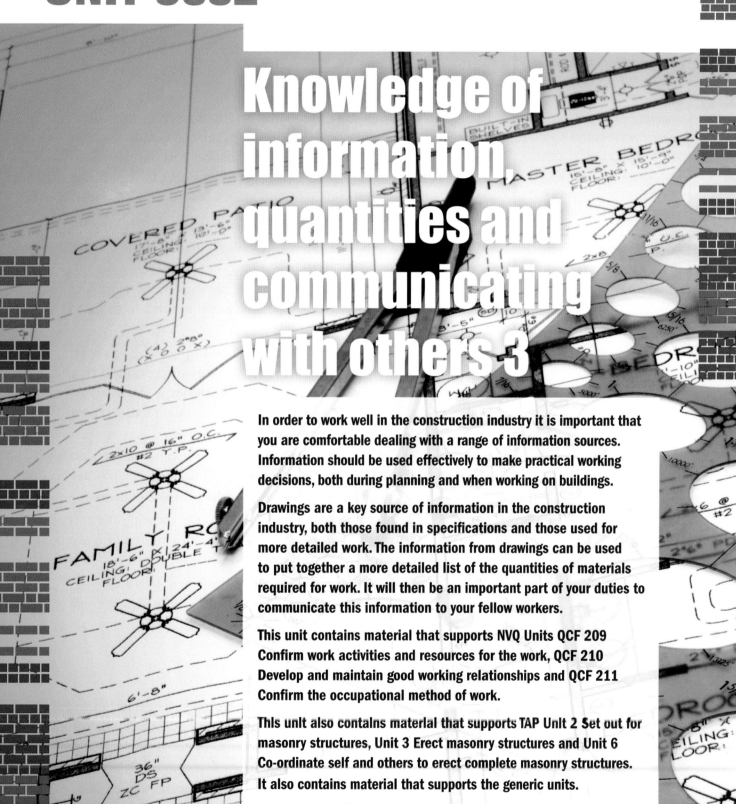

UNIT 3002

Knowledge of information, quantities and communicating with others 3

In order to work well in the construction industry it is important that you are comfortable dealing with a range of information sources. Information should be used effectively to make practical working decisions, both during planning and when working on buildings.

Drawings are a key source of information in the construction industry, both those found in specifications and those used for more detailed work. The information from drawings can be used to put together a more detailed list of the quantities of materials required for work. It will then be an important part of your duties to communicate this information to your fellow workers.

This unit contains material that supports NVQ Units QCF 209 Confirm work activities and resources for the work, QCF 210 Develop and maintain good working relationships and QCF 211 Confirm the occupational method of work.

This unit also contains material that supports TAP Unit 2 Set out for masonry structures, Unit 3 Erect masonry structures and Unit 6 Co-ordinate self and others to erect complete masonry structures. It also contains material that supports the generic units.

This unit will cover the following learning outcomes:

- Know about producing drawn information
- Know how to estimate quantities and price work
- Know how to ensure good working relationships.

Types of drawing

Before looking at producing types of drawing, it is worth revising the different types of drawing that can be used as well as the process followed to create drawings.

Plans and drawings are vital to any building work as a way of expressing the client's wishes. Drawings are the best way of communicating a lot of detailed information without the need for pages and pages of text. Drawings form part of the contract documents and go through several stages before they are given to tradespeople for use.

Stage 1   The client sits down with an architect and explains their requirements.

Stage 2   The architect produces drawings of the work and checks with the client to see if the drawings match what the client wants.

Stage 3   If required, the drawings go to planning to see if they can be allowed, and are also scrutinised by the Building Regulations Authority. It is at this stage that the drawings may need to be altered to meet Planning or Building Regulations.

Stage 4   Once passed, the drawings are given to contractors along with the other contract documents, so that they can prepare their tenders for the contract.

Stage 5   The winning contractor uses the drawings to carry out the job. At this point the drawings will be given to you to work from.

There are three main types of working drawings: location drawings, component drawings and assembly drawings. We will look at each of these in turn.

Location drawings

Location drawings include:

- **block plans,** which identify the proposed site in relation to the surrounding area (see Figure 2.01). These are usually drawn at a scale of 1:2500 or 1:1250
- **site plans,** which give the position of the proposed building and the general layout of things such as services and drainage (see Figure 2.02). These are usually drawn at a scale of 1:500 or 1:200
- **general location drawings,** which show different elevations and sections of the building (see Figure 2.03). These are usually drawn at a scale of 1:200, 1:100 or 1:50.

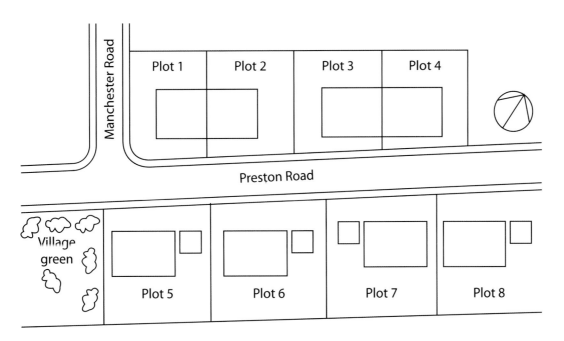

Figure 2.01 Block plan

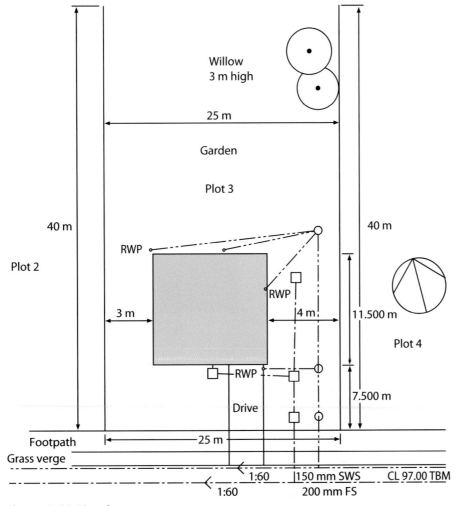

Figure 2.02 Site plan

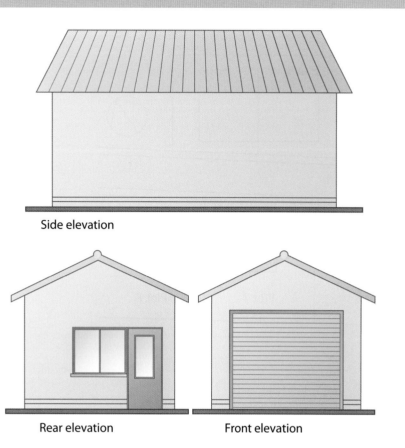

Side elevation

Rear elevation   Front elevation

Figure 2.03 General location drawing (of a one room per floor building)

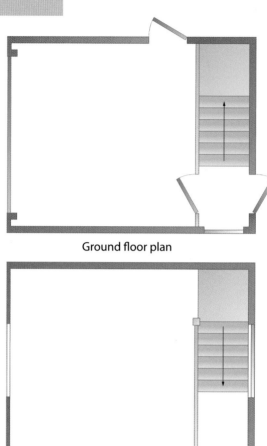

Ground floor plan

First floor plan

Figure 2.04 Floor plan (of a one room per floor building)

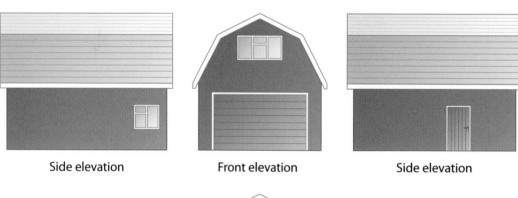

Side elevation   Front elevation   Side elevation

Rear elevation

Figure 2.05 Elevation

Component drawings

Component drawings include:

- range drawings, which show the different sizes and shapes of a particular range of components (see Figure 2.06). These are usually drawn at a scale of 1:50 or 1:20

- detailed drawings, which show all the information needed to complete or manufacture a component (see Figure 2.07). These are usually drawn at a scale of 1:10, 1:5 or 1:1.

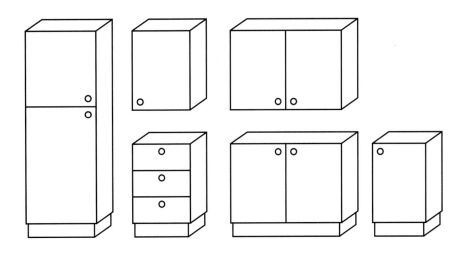

Figure 2.06 Range drawing

Assembly drawings

Assembly drawings are similar to detailed drawings (see Figure 2.08). They show in great detail the various joints and junctions in and between the various parts and components of a building. Assembly drawings are usually drawn at a scale of 1:20, 1:10 or 1:5.

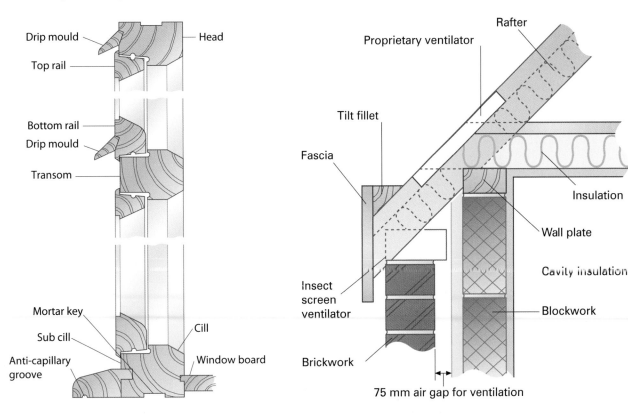

Figure 2.07 Detailed drawing

Figure 2.08 Assembly drawing

K1. Know about producing drawn information

When drawings are mentioned in the construction industry, people generally tend to think of the architect's drawings and plans that form part of the contract documents. These types of drawings are vital in the construction industry as they form part of the legal contract between client and contractor.

However, there are other forms of drawings that are just as important. Setting-out drawings are used to mark out for complex procedures such as constructing cut roofing, staircases or brick arches; and with advances in technology, CAD (computer-aided design) is being used more often.

Advantages of computer-aided design (CAD)

Computer-aided design (CAD) is a system in which a draftsperson uses computer technology to help design a part, product or whole building. It is both a visual and symbol-based method of communication, with conventions particular to a specific technical field.

CAD is used particularly at the drafting stage. Drafting can be done in two dimensions (2-D) and three dimensions (3-D).

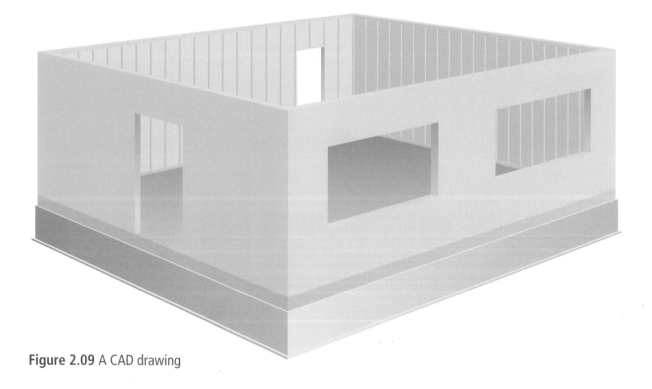

Figure 2.09 A CAD drawing

CAD is one of the many tools used by engineers and designers, and is used in many ways, depending on the profession of the user and the type of software in question.

There are several types of CAD. Each requires the operator to think differently about how they will use it, and they must design their virtual components in a different manner for each.

Many companies produce lower-end 2-D systems, and a number of free and open source programs are available. These make the drawing process easier, because there are no concerns about the scale and placement on the drawing sheet that accompanied hand drafting – these can simply be adjusted as required during the creation of the final draft.

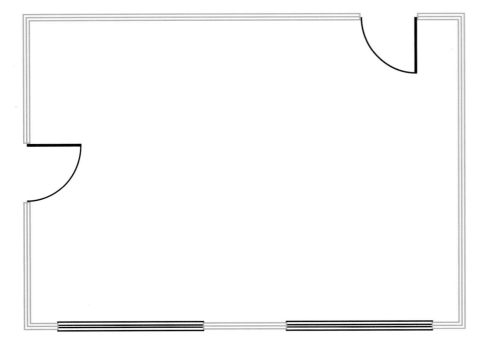

Figure 2.10 A simple 2-D CAD drawing

3-D wireframe

3-D wireframe is in essence an extension of 2-D drafting. Each line has to be manually inserted into the drawing. The final product has no mass properties associated with it, and cannot have features directly added to it, such as holes. The operator approaches these in a similar fashion to the 2-D systems, although many 3-D systems allow you to use the wireframe model to make the final engineering drawing views.

> **Did you know?**
>
> Google SketchUp is a simple, free 2-D CAD program, and IKEA and B&Q, among others, operate simple 2-D CAD programs for designing kitchens, etc.

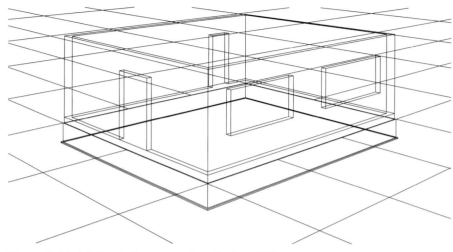

Figure 2.11 A 3-D wireframe produced using CAD

3-D dumb solids

3-D 'dumb' solids are created in a way corresponding to manipulations of real-world objects. Basic three-dimensional geometric forms (prisms, cylinders, spheres, and so on) have solid volumes added to or subtracted from them, as if assembling or cutting real-world objects. Two-dimensional projected views can easily be generated from the models. The sorts of basic 3-D solids that are created do not usually include tools to easily allow motion of components, set limits to their motion, or identify interference between components.

Figure 2.12 A 3-D view of a house produced using CAD

Top-end systems

Top-end systems offer the capabilities to incorporate more organic, aesthetic and ergonomic features into designs. Free-form surface modelling is often combined with solids to allow the designer to create products that fit the human form and visual requirements, as well as the interface with the machine.

Uses of CAD

CAD has become an especially important technology within the scope of computer-aided technologies, with benefits such as lower product development costs and a greatly shortened design cycle. CAD enables designers to lay out and develop work on screen, print it out and save it for future editing, saving time on their drawings.

Details required for floor plans

To complete floor plans you will need to use a range of different information sources. Some of the key pieces of information you will need to know about are covered below.

Sections

Sectional drawings are useful as they can show details of how certain aspects of a structure are constructed. They show a cross section of the build, using symbols to indicate what materials are used.

These drawings are particularly useful for showing how floors are constructed and also for types of walls, such as sleeper walls.

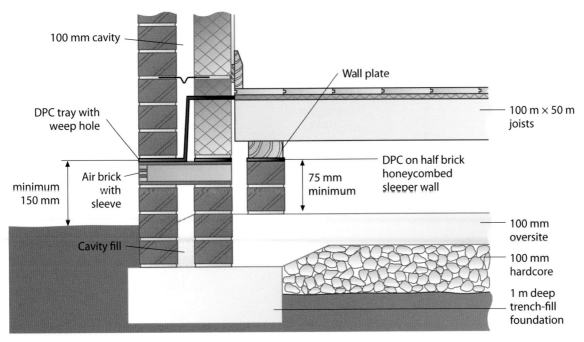

Figure 2.13 Section through floor and wall

Datum points

The need to apply levels is required at the beginning of the construction process and continues right up to the completion of the building. The whole country is mapped in detail and the Ordnance Survey place datum points (bench marks) at suitable locations from which all other levels can be taken.

Ordnance bench mark (OBM)

OBMs are found cut into locations such as walls of churches or public buildings. The height of the OBM can be found on the relevant Ordnance Survey map or by contacting the local authority planning office. Figure 2.14 shows the normal symbol used, although it can appear as shown in Figure 2.15.

Site datum

It is necessary to have a reference point on site to which all levels can be related. This is known as the site datum. The site datum is usually positioned at a convenient height, such as finished floor level (FFL), D.P.C. and ground level for a structural floor.

The site datum itself must be set in relation to some known point, preferably an OBM, and must be positioned where it cannot be moved.

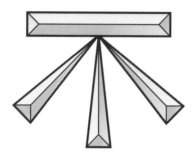

Figure 2.14 Ordnance bench mark

Figure 2.15 shows a site datum and OBM, illustrating the height relationship between them.

If no suitable position can be found a datum peg may be used, its accurate height transferred by surveyors from an OBM, as with the site datum. It is normally a piece of timber or steel rod positioned accurately to the required level and then set in concrete. However, it must be adequately protected and is generally surrounded by a small fence for protection, as shown in Figure 2.16.

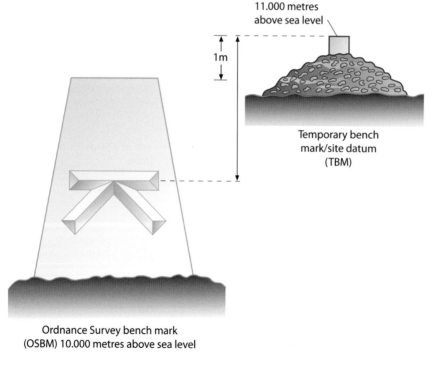

11.000 metres above sea level

1m

Temporary bench mark/site datum (TBM)

Ordnance Survey bench mark (OSBM) 10.000 metres above sea level

Figure 2.15 Site datum and OBM

Temporary bench mark (TBM)

When an OBM cannot be conveniently found near a site it is usual for a temporary bench mark (TBM) to be set up at a height suitable for the site. Its accurate height is transferred by surveyors from the nearest convenient OBM.

All other site datum points can now be set up from this TBM using datum points, which are shown on the site drawings. Figure 2.17 shows datum points on drawings.

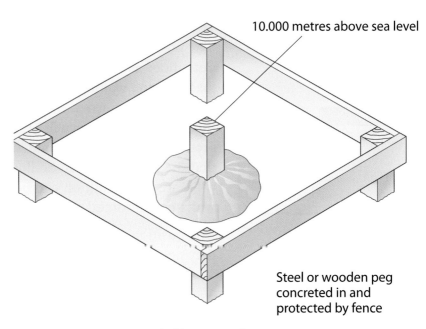

10.000 metres above sea level

Steel or wooden peg concreted in and protected by fence

Figure 2.16 Datum peg suitably protected

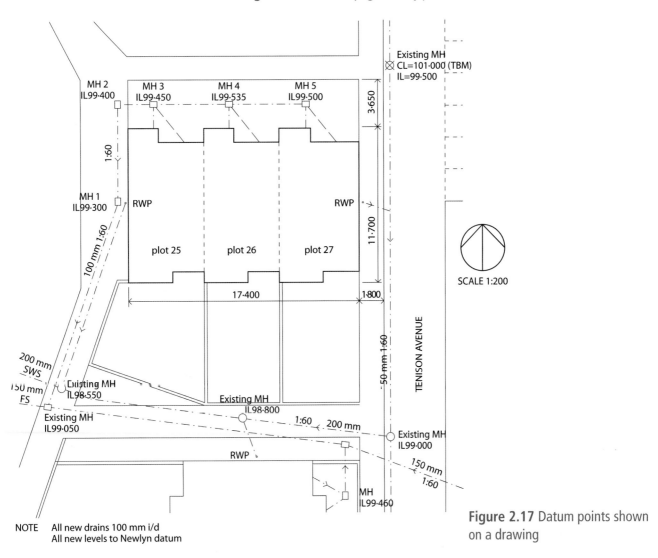

NOTE All new drains 100 mm i/d
All new levels to Newlyn datum

Figure 2.17 Datum points shown on a drawing

Wall constructions

The positioning of internal walling is important when planning out a floor as internal walling, particularly solid block walling or load-bearing walling, will place strain on the floor. This strain will have to be supported. Internal walling can be built directly onto the foundations. This will break the area of flooring into smaller sections and is usually done in larger buildings. The alternative is that the whole area can be floored and the area which the internal walls are to be built on can be reinforced with either **sleeper walls** or reinforced concrete or steel beams.

The position of the internal walling is also used by other trades, as they need to know where the services need to be run.

> **Key term**
>
> **Sleeper wall** – sometimes known as a dwarf wall this is a smaller wall built to support the ground floor joists

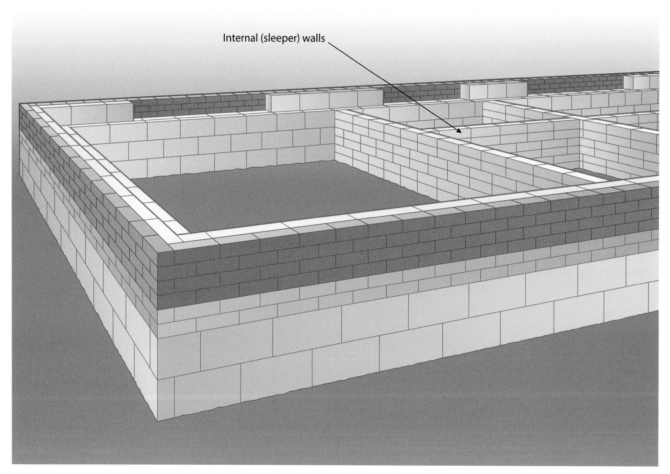

Figure 2.18 Internal (sleeper) walls being built into foundations

Material codes

Almost all the materials that are used in construction must adhere to British Standards. Each type of material must pass stringent tests so that it can be classified by the BSI and be used. With the move into European markets some of the codes will now be prefixed ISO (International Organization for Standardization).

The following is a list of BS ISO that relates to flooring:

Timber

- BS EN 383:2007 – Timber structures. Tested by determining embedment strength and foundation values for dowel type fasteners.
- BS 5268-2:2002 – Structural use of timber with a code of practice for permissible stress design, materials and workmanship.

Concrete, aggregates and masonry

- BS EN 12350-1:2009 – Testing fresh concrete. A sample of concrete is tested.
- BS EN 1097-8:2009 – Tests for mechanical and physical properties of aggregates.
- BS EN 12390-3:2009 – Testing hardened concrete. A compressive strength test is made of specimens.
- BS EN 12390-5:2009 – Testing hardened concrete. A flexural strength test is made of specimens.
- BS EN 12390-7:2009 – Testing hardened concrete. The density of hardened concrete is tested.

Materials that have been stamped with the relevant BS number will have been tested to meet the required standards or a sample of the materials will have been tested.

Depth dimensions and heights

The depth dimensions and heights of materials used in flooring construction will be identified by the architect. They will then use the relevant BSI specification to decide which type, and size, of materials will be suitable for each job.

Schedules and specifications

Specifications

The specification or 'spec' is a document produced alongside the plans and drawings and is used to show information that

> **Remember**
>
> Diagrams and drawings include a great deal of information about the type and quality of materials used in their construction.

cannot be shown on the drawings. Specifications are almost always used, except in the case of very small contracts. A specification should contain:

- **site description** – a brief description of the site including the address
- **restrictions** – what restrictions apply such as working hours or limited access
- **services** – what services are available, what services need to be connected and what type of connection should be used
- **materials description** – including type, sizes, quality, moisture content, etc.
- **workmanship** – including methods of fixing, quality of work and finish.

The specification may also name subcontractors or suppliers, or give details such as how the site should be cleared, and so on.

> **Working life**
>
> You are working on a job and have received the site plans, which show the layout of the services. You start to dig out for the services but when you reach the site where the mains gas should be, you find it is not where the drawing shows.
>
> What could have caused this problem? You will need to look at the sources of information you have used to make your decisions, and check to see what could have caused the mistake. What other problems could arise from using faulty information?
>
> What effect could this have financially? You will also need to think about the impact not only on money but also the time that might be needed to carry out the project. What impact could this have on your company's reputation?

Functional skills

This exercise will allow you to practise **FM 2.3.1** Interpret and communicate solutions to multistage practical problems.

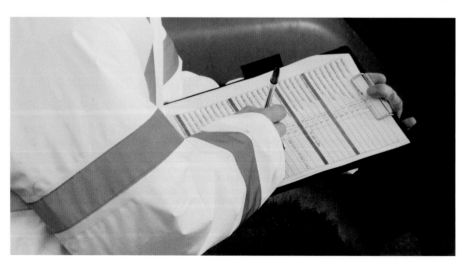

Figure 2.19 A good spec helps to avoid confusion when checking material deliveries

Schedules

A schedule is used to record repeated design information that applies to a range of components or fittings. Schedules are mainly used on bigger sites where there are multiples of several types of house (4-bedroom, 3-bedroom, 3-bedroom with dormers, etc.), each type having different components and fittings. The schedule avoids the wrong component or fitting being put in the wrong house. Schedules can also be used on smaller jobs such as a block of flats with 200 windows, where there are six different types of window.

The need for a specification depends on the complexity of the job and the number of repeated designs that there are. Schedules are mainly used to record repeated design information for:

- doors
- windows
- ironmongery
- joinery fitments
- sanitary components
- heating components and radiators
- lintels
- kitchens.

A schedule is usually used in conjunction with a range drawing and a floor plan.

Figures 2.20–2.22 are basic examples of these documents, using a window as an example:

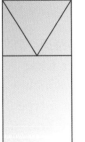 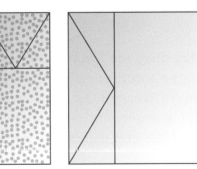 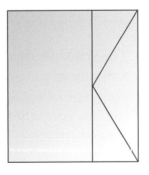 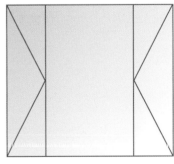

Window 1   Window 2   Window 3   Window 4   Window 5

Figure 2.20 Range drawing

Find out

Schedules are not always needed on contracts, particularly smaller ones. Think of a job/contract that would require a schedule and produce one for a certain part of that job: for example, doors or brick types.

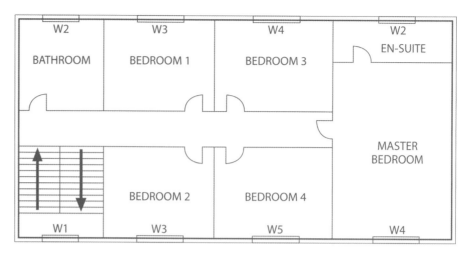

Figure 2.21 Floor plan

WINDOW	SIZE	EXTERIOR	INTERIOR	LOCATION	GLASS	FIXING
Window 1	600 x 1200 mm	Mahogany wood grain uPVC	White uPVC	Stairwell	22 mm thermal resistant double glazed units	Fixed with 100 mm frame fixing screws
Window 2	600 x 1200 mm	Mahogany wood grain uPVC	White uPVC	Bathroom En suite	22 mm thermal resistant double glazed units with maple leaf obscure pattern	Fixed with 100 mm frame fixing screws
Window 3	1100 x 1200 mm	Mahogany wood grain uPVC	White uPVC	Bedroom 1 Bedroom 2	22 mm thermal resistant double glazed units	Fixed with 100 mm frame fixing screws
Window 4	1100 x 1200 mm	Mahogany wood grain uPVC	White uPVC	Bedroom 3 Master bedroom	22 mm thermal resistant double glazed units	Fixed with 100 mm frame fixing screws
Window 5	1500 x 1200 mm	Mahogany wood grain uPVC	White uPVC	Bedroom 4	22 mm thermal resistant double glazed units	Fixed with 100 mm frame fixing screws

Figure 2.22 Schedule for windows

The schedule shows that there are five types of window, each differing in size and appearance; the range drawing shows what each type of window looks like; and the floor plan shows which window goes where. For example, the bathroom window is a type 2 window, which is 600 x 1200 mm with a top-opening sash and obscure glass.

Setting out drawings

Setting out drawings are as important as contract documents. You must be aware of how certain tasks are set out and what drawings can be created to aid in the setting out process.

Setting out drawings are most often needed on smaller jobs, where there is limited or no information from the architect in the form of contract document drawings. Setting out drawings can also be used on larger sites where there has been an alteration or an oversight by the architect.

Here is where the most common forms of setting out drawings are used:

- in carpentry, for cut roofing, where there may be no information on the true lengths of rafters
- in joinery, when setting out for stairs, where there may be no information on the individual rise, etc.
- in bricklaying, where you may come across setting out drawing for arch centres, such as segmental or gothic arches.

We will now look at a brief example of how roofing and brick arches are set out.

Finding the true length of a common rafter

Most drawings will tell you the **span** and **rise** of the roof. From these, you can create a drawing that will tell you the true length of the common rafter, and also what angle the ends of the rafter should be cut at.

This true length is the actual length that the rafter needs to be, and all the rafters can be cut to length from the setting out drawing. The setting out drawing for a roof is usually drawn on a sheet of plywood to a scale that fits the sheet.

Figure 2.23 Setting out drawings are crucial for creating arches like these

Key terms

Span – the distance measured in the direction of ceiling joists, from the outside of one wall plate to another, known as the overall (O/A) span

Rise – the distance from the top of the wall plate to the roof's peak

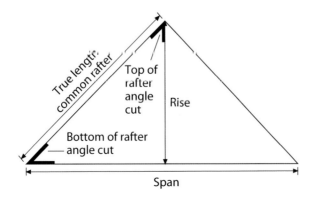

Figure 2.24 Finding common rafter true length

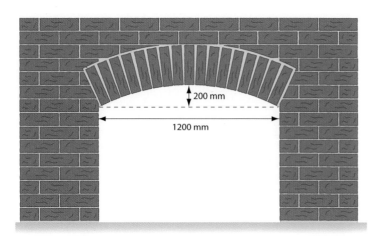

Figure 2.25 An example of a segmental arch

Unit 3002 Knowledge of information, quantities and communicating with others 3

Setting out a segmental brick arch

Most drawings will show you the opening span of the arch, but some may not tell you the radius. Without the radius, you cannot build the arch correctly.

We will now look at how setting out drawings can aid you in setting out this arch.

Find out

Using the Internet and other resources, find out what sort of scales are best to use for drawing up setting out drawings for these different components and builds.

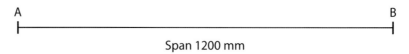

Figure 2.26 Establish the span (a length of 1200 mm has been used here, shown as A–B)

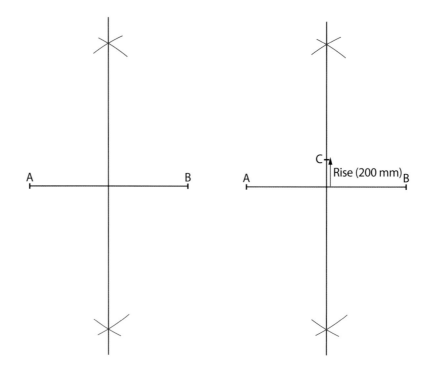

Figure 2.27 Bisect this line

Figure 2.28 Establish the rise (the distance from the springing line (A–B) to the highest point of the soffit shown as C). The rise is normally one sixth of the span so, in this case, the rise is shown as 200 mm

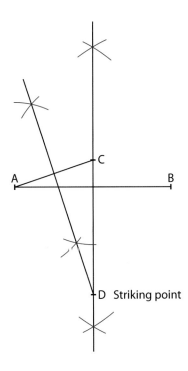

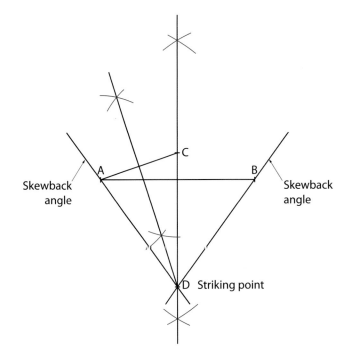

Figure 2.29 Draw a line from A to C and bisect this line. The point where this bisecting line crosses the bisecting line of the span will be the striking point for the arch (shown here as point D). From striking point D open out compass to point A and draw an arc across to point B. This will provide the **intrados** for the arch

Figure 2.30 Draw a line from D through A and a line from D through B. These lines will provide the angle for the **skewbacks**. From point A establish depth of arch ring (point E) above point A along A–D. Set compass from point D to point E and draw an arch. This will provide the **extrados**

Setting out for a segmental arch can also be drawn out on a sheet of plywood but, in this case, it can be drawn full size, with the drawing being cut out and used as a template for the arch centre.

Reasons for the use of elevations and projections

Building, engineering and similar drawings aim to give as much information as possible in a way that is easy to understand. They frequently combine several views on a single drawing. These may be of two kinds:

- **elevation** – the view we would see if we stood in front or to the side of the finished building
- **plan** – the view we would have if we were looking down on it.

The view we see depends on where we are looking from. There are then different ways of 'projecting' what we would see onto the drawings. The three main methods of projection, used on standard building drawings, are orthographic, isometric and oblique.

Key terms

Skewbacks – the angle at the springing point at which the arch rings will be laid

intrados – the interior curve of the arch ring

extrados – the outside line of the arch ring

Orthographic projection

Orthographic projection works as if parallel lines were drawn from every point on a model of the building on to a sheet of paper held up behind it (an elevation view), or laid out underneath it (plan view). There are then different ways that we can display the views on a drawing. The method most commonly used in the building industry, for detailed construction drawings, is called 'first angle projection'. In this the front elevation is roughly central. The plan view is drawn directly below the front elevation and all other elevations are drawn in line with the front elevation. An example is shown in Figure 2.31.

Front elevation

Side elevation

Figure 2.31 Orthographic projection

Find out

Research, using the Internet and other resources, how isometric projection is used to sketch components.

Isometric projection

In isometric views, the object is drawn at an angle where one corner of the object is closest to the viewer. Vertical lines remain vertical but horizontal lines are drawn at an angle of 30 degrees to the horizontal. This can be seen in Figure 2.32.

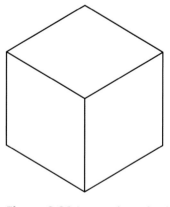

Figure 2.32 Isometric projection

Oblique projection

Oblique projection is similar to an isometric view, with the object drawn at an angle where one corner of the object is closest to the viewer. Vertical lines remain vertical but horizontal lines are drawn at an angle of 45 degrees to the horizontal. This can be seen in Figure 2.33.

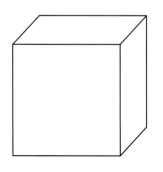

Figure 2.33 Oblique projection

Working life

You have been tasked with building a segmental brick arch, but there is minimal information on the drawing. You decide to just build the arch but soon run into problems with the radius.

What could have prevented the problems? You will need to think about the processes you could have followed to check information and who you could have consulted with about any problems. What should you do now? You will need to think about the impact any action could have not only on you but also anyone else you may be working with on site. What effect can this have on the building and on the profitability of the job?

Functional skills

This task will allow you to practise **FE 2.3.1–2.3.5** Write documents, including extended writing pieces, communicating information, ideas and opinions effectively and persuasively.

Use of hatchings and symbols

All plans and drawings contain symbols and abbreviations, which are used to show the maximum amount of information in a clear and legible way.

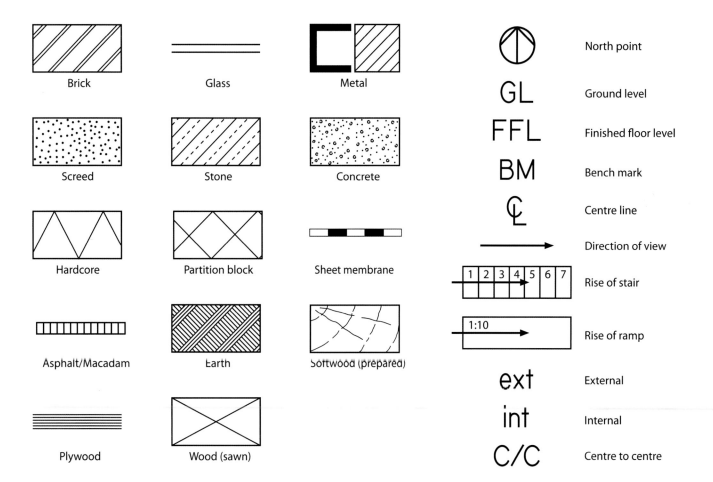

Figure 2.34 Symbols

Item	Abbreviation	Item	Abbreviation
Airbrick	AB	Hardcore	He
Asbestos	asb	Hardwood	Hwd
Bitumen	bit	Insulation	Insul
Boarding	bdg	Joist	Jst
Brickwork	bwk	Mild steel	MS
Building	bldg	Plasterboard	Pbd
Cast iron	CI	Polyvinyl acetate	PVA
Cement	ct	Polyvinyl chloride	PVC
Column	col	Reinforced concrete	RC
Concrete	conc	Satin chrome	SC
Cupboard	cpd	Satin anodised aluminium	SAA
Damp proof course	DPC	Softwood	Swd
Damp proof membrane	DPM	Stainless steel	SS
Drawing	dwg	Tongue and groove	T&G
Foundation	fnd	Wrought iron	WI
Hard board	hdbd		

Table 2.01 Abbreviations

Remember

A scale is merely a convenient way of reducing a drawing in size.

Why different scales are used

All building plans are drawn to scales by using symbols and abbreviations. To draw a building on a drawing sheet, its size must be reduced. This is called a scale drawing.

Using scales

The scales that are preferred for use in building drawings are shown in Table 2.02.

Type of drawing	Scales
Block plans	1:2500, 1:1250
Site plans	1:500, 1:200
General location drawings	1:200, 1:100, 1:50
Range drawings	1:100, 1:50, 1:20
Detail drawings	1:10, 1:5, 1:1
Assembly drawings	1:20, 1:10, 1:5

Table 2.02 Preferred scales for building drawings

These scales mean that, for example, on a block plan drawn to 1:2500, 1 mm on the plan would represent 2500 mm (or 2.5 m) on the actual building. Some other examples are:

- on a scale of 1:50, 10 mm represents 500 mm
- on a scale of 1:100, 10 mm represents 1000 mm (1.0 m)
- on a scale of 1:200, 30 mm represents 6000 mm (6.0 m).

Accuracy of drawings

Printing or copying of drawings introduces variations that affect the accuracy of drawings. Hence, although measurements can be read from drawings using a rule with common scales marked (Figure 2.35), you should work to written instructions and measurements wherever possible.

> **Find out**
>
> With a little practice, you will easily master the use of scales. Try the following:
>
> - On a scale of 1:50, 40 mm represents: _____
> - On a scale of 1:200, 70 mm represents: _____
> - On a scale of 1:500, 40 mm represents: _____

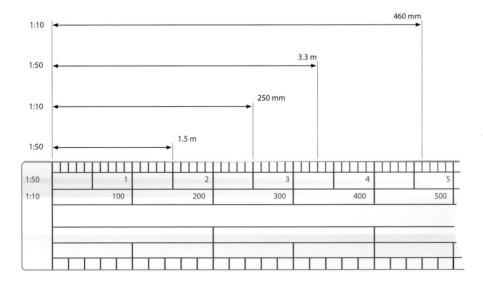

Figure 2.35 Rule with scales for maps and drawings

> **Remember**
>
> You can use a scale to:
>
> • work out the actual measurement from a plan
> • work out how long to draw a line on the plan to represent an actual measurement.

> **Key term**
>
> **Ratio** – one value divided by the other

Scale drawings

Building plans are drawn to scale. Each length on the plan is in proportion to the real length. On a drawing that has been drawn to a scale of 1:10, 1 mm represents 10 mm. On the same scale:

• a length of 50 mm represents an actual length of $5 \times 10 = 500$ mm
• a length of 120 mm represents an actual length of $12 \times 10 = 1200$ mm
• an actual length of 34 m is represented by a line $34 \div 10 = 3.4$ cm long.

Scales are often given as **ratios**. For example:

• a scale of 1:100 means that 1 cm on the drawing represents an actual length of 100 cm (or 1 m)
• a scale of 1:20 000 means that 1 cm on the drawing represents an actual length of 20 000 cm (or 20 m).

Table 2.03 shows some common scales used in the construction industry.

1:5	1 mm represents 5 mm	5 times smaller than actual size
1:10	1 mm represents 10 mm	10 times smaller than actual size
1:20	1 mm represents 20 mm	20 times smaller than actual size
1:50	1 mm represents 50 mm	50 times smaller than actual size
1:100	1 mm represents 100 mm	100 times smaller than actual size
1:1250	1 mm represents 1250 mm	1250 times smaller than actual size

Table 2.03 Common scales used in the construction industry

Now look at the following examples.

> **Example**
>
> A plan is drawn to a scale of 1:20. On the plan, a wall is 45 mm long. How long is the actual wall?
>
> 1 mm on the plan = actual length 20 mm
>
> So 45 mm on the plan = actual length $4.5 \times 20 = 900$ mm or 0.9 m.

> **Remember**
>
> To make scale drawings, architects use a scale rule. The different scales on the ruler give the equivalent actual length measurements for different lengths in cm, for each scale.

> **Example**
>
> A window is 3 m tall. How tall is it on the plan of 1:20?
>
> 3 m = 3000 mm
> an actual length of 20 mm is 1 mm on the plan
> actual length 3000 mm = 3000 ÷ 20
> = 150 mm
> Therefore, the window is 150 mm tall on the plan.

K2. Know how to estimate quantities and price work

For all construction projects it is necessary to calculate the amounts of materials and other resources that will be needed. As part of this you will also need to be able to make a calculation on the expected cost of these materials. This is called an estimate.

Estimates are used on all construction projects when setting a budget for the work. For many projects, a client will look for tenders from a range of contractors. This means the potential contractors put together their own estimates for the work, with the client selecting the estimate that best meets their needs – usually the estimate that presents the best value.

This section will look at the information used to create an estimate and plan a project.

The tender process

Tendering is a competitive process where the contractor works with a specification and drawings from the client and submits a cost estimate for the work (including materials, labour and equipment). Tenders are often invited for large contracts, such as government contracts, with strict fixed deadlines for the tenders to be received.

An estimator will calculate the total cost in the tender. Using the information in the specification the estimator calculates the amount of materials and labour needed to complete the work. The final tender is based on this estimation.

All the tenders for a contract will then present their case and costs to the client, who will then decide on one business to be offered the contract.

Working life

You have been invited to tender a bid for a large public contract. Business has been slow, and you really need it if you are to keep your business afloat and avoid redundancies.

Two of the other tenders concern you. One is priced so low that, if you match it, you may make a small loss. In the other, the contractor promises to recycle 45 per cent of materials, to use only sustainable materials and to employ 70 per cent of the workforce locally – matching this may mean you have to lay off some workers and may only make a small profit.

What should you do? What stipulations could you introduce to help improve your bid? What could the consequences be of not getting the contract – or, indeed, of getting it?

Functional skills

This exercise will allow you to practise **FM 2.3.1** Interpret and communicate solutions to multistage practical problems. If you give oral answers to questions from your tutor, you will be able to practise **FE 2.1.1–2.1.4** Make a range of contributions to discussions and make effective presentations in a wide range of contexts.

Quoting

A quote is basically part of the tender process but it will only contain pricing information on materials, labour, etc. The quote will state how much the job will cost without any additional information that may appear on a tender, such as making a percentage of the workforce local or recycling a certain amount of materials.

The quote is then used as part of the tender to give an idea of the potential cost of a job. Companies submitting tenders will look to make this quote as attractive as possible to the client.

Estimated pricing

Estimated pricing is used to create the quote. An estimator will look at what is required and provide an estimated price for it.

Tenders for jobs may take many months for the successful tender to be selected so an estimator who prices everything up exactly as it is now may be wrong in six months time as the price of labour or materials may have changed. This means they will instead give an estimated price, based on a calculation of how much the materials or labour may cost in the future.

The resources used for making an estimated price and a final price include:

- materials
- purchase orders and invoices
- time study sheets, labour schedules, job sheets and site diaries
- building supplier's price lists and equipment availability lead times.

Prime cost

This is the final total cost of all material costs, labour costs and expenses for the project. This sum will need to be agreed by all parties before work begins.

Provisional sums

A provisional sum describes work for which the exact scope and extent have yet to be defined. Neither party involved will attempt to create an accurate price for this work until a contract is agreed. The provisional sum is usually included in the contract price as an estimate. Many contracts include a clause allowing for the provisional sum to be omitted and replaced with the final figure.

Resources required for a construction task

The materials used for a job will usually depend on what the client wants. This is particularly the case for smaller jobs where the

Did you know?

On smaller jobs the client may wish to order the materials themselves as they may be able to get a better deal and save money.

client may want certain fixtures or fittings. Where any structural or large alterations will be needed to accommodate the client's plans, a client may want to consult an architect or local planning authority or even their contractor as to what materials they must have to meet regulations.

If a client insists on arranging and organising any material requirements then it is important to ensure that they are aware of exactly what type and size of materials are required and when they are required; otherwise not only can it hold up the job but may lead to a poor job being done with substandard materials, which can affect your reputation.

More problems can develop when clients order materials themselves as they may lack the technical knowledge needed for ordering materials. For example, they may think they are getting cheaper materials by ordering 3″ x 2″ timber studwork or cheaper common bricks. However 3″ x 2″ may not be strong enough and 4″ x 2″ should be used, or particular bricks, such as engineering bricks, may be needed.

Larger jobs will be led by the client's wishes, carried out through an architect. This will ensure the correct materials are stated on the building documentation. The larger companies will usually have contracts in place with suppliers which will allow them to purchase materials at cheap rates.

> **Remember**
>
> As well as ordering possibly the wrong size, other problems arising from the client dealing with the materials can be substandard materials and delays in materials delivery, all of which can cause delays in the job.

> **Working life**
>
> You are working on a renovation project when your boss calls you to ask what materials you need for the next few weeks. You are caught a bit off-guard, and you rush around – giving your boss a list of materials over the phone. When the materials are delivered, there are some discrepancies: it's not what you said, as far as you can remember. You phone your boss to tell him and he gets cross, blaming you for the mistakes.
>
> Who is to blame? What should have been done? You will need to think about the ideal process that should have been followed. What information could you have used? Where would you get this information? What would be the best way of getting this information to your boss?

Any specialist materials will be resourced by a buyer. They will look at which companies provide the materials, what the cost is and what attributes the company has, such as whether they work with fair trade etc.

Bill of quantities

The bill of quantities is produced by the quantity surveyor. It gives a complete description of everything that is required to do the job, including labour, materials and any items or components, drawing

> **Remember**
>
> Bills of quantities are used to help contractors provide a tender for a contract. A bill of quantities is put together for a task, including labour, materials etc.

Figure 2.36 Every item needed should be listed on the bill of quantities

on information from the drawings, specification and schedule. The same single bill of quantities is sent out to all prospective contractors so they can submit a tender based on the same information – this helps the client select the best contractor for the job.

All bills of quantities contain the following information:

- **preliminaries** – general information such as the names of the client and architect, details of the work and descriptions of the site
- **preambles** – similar to the specification, outlining the quality and description of materials and workmanship, etc.
- **measured quantities** – a description of how each task or material is measured with measurements in metres (linear and square), hours, litres, kilograms or simply the number of components required
- **provisional quantities** – approximate amounts where items or components cannot be measured accurately
- **cost** – the amount of money that will be charged per unit of quantity.

The bill of quantities may also contain:

- any costs that may result from using subcontractors or specialists
- a sum of money for work that has not been finally detailed
- a sum of money to cover contingencies for unforeseen work.

Figure 2.37 is an extract from a bill of quantities that might be sent to prospective contractors, who would then complete the cost section and return it as their tender.

Item ref No	Description	Quantity	Unit	Rate £	Cost £
A1	Treated 50 × 225 mm sawn carcass	200	M		
A2	Treated 75 × 225 mm sawn carcass	50	M		
B1	50 mm galvanised steel joist hangers	20	N/A		
B2	75 mm galvanised steel joist hangers	7	N/A		
C1	Supply and fit the above floor joists as described in the preambles				

Figure 2.37 Sample extract from a bill of quantities

To ensure that all contractors interpret and understand the bill of quantities consistently, the Royal Institution of Chartered Surveyors and the Building Employers' Confederation produce a document called the Standard Method of Measurement of Building Works (SMM). This provides a uniform basis for measuring building work, for example stating that carcassing timber is measured by the metre whereas plasterboard is measured in square metres.

Advantages and disadvantages of purchasing and hiring plant

Plant hire is an important aspect of a construction job to be taken into consideration – usually during the tender stage. The hiring of plant is not essential on all jobs but most jobs, and especially large ones, will require some plant to be hired in one way or another.

The type of plant that can be hired ranges from portable power tools to mobile tower scaffolding. It could also include cranes and diggers.

However, not all plant is hired and some items are bought outright by the company rather than hired. Most companies will have all the relevant trade-related power tools. For example, carpenters will have bought their own cordless drills or circular saws and bricklayers will have bought their own cement mixers.

If a certain item of plant is required and is not already owned, is it better to buy or hire? The final decision you make will depend on a variety of factors but will mainly come down to cost. If something large like a crane is required then obviously the cheapest option is to hire one rather than buy it. But for something small it may still often be better to hire. Similarly, if you only need to use an item for a small length of time for a specialist job, it would be much better to hire it rather than buy it.

> **Remember**
>
> If you are hiring plant such as cranes, you will also need to employ a qualified operator to use it.

There are exceptions to this. For example if a carpenter had ten kitchens to fit then it would be better to buy a worktop jig for a router at £80 rather than hire one on ten different occasions at £10 per hire.

Planning the sequence of material and labour requirements

We have already looked at how specifications and schedules are used to plan construction projects and establish the requirements of the project.

The main planning relating to the sequence of material and labour requirements will be taken into account when the programme of work is devised. This usually takes the form of a bar or progress chart which is covered in more detail below.

To plan sequences of material and labour requirements, you will also need to be familiar with some of the common methods of working used to ensure the smooth operation of materials and labour. This includes:

- work programmes and critical path analysis
- stock rotation systems
- lead times
- pricing systems.

Work programmes

Bar charts

> **Did you know?**
>
> The Gantt chart is named after the first man to publish it. This was Henry Gantt, an American engineer in 1910.

The bar or Gantt chart is the most popular work programme as it is simple to construct and easy to understand. Bar charts have tasks listed in a vertical column on the left and a horizontal timescale running along the top.

Time in days										
Activity	1	2	3	4	5	6	7	8	8	10
Dig for foundation and service routes										
Lay foundations										
Run cabling, piping, etc. to meet existing services										
Build up to DPC										
Lay concrete floor										

Figure 2.38 Basic bar chart

Each task is given a proposed time, which is shaded in along the horizontal timescale. Timescales often overlap as one task often overlaps another.

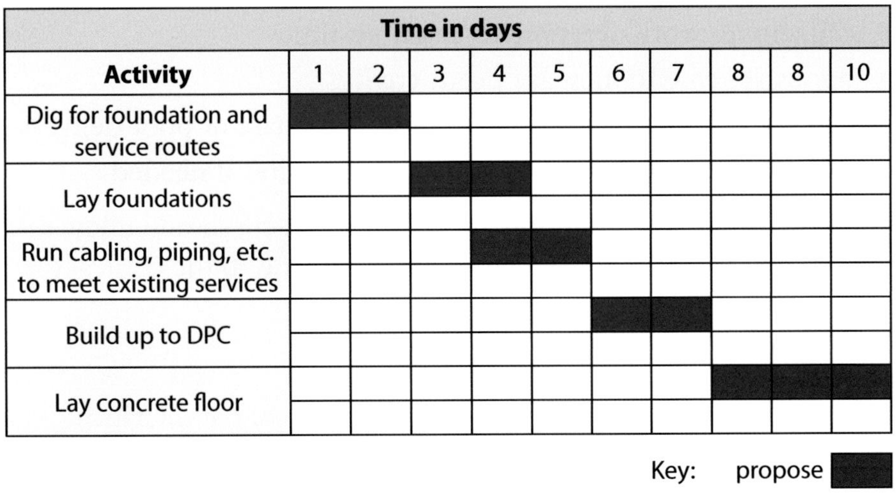

Time in days										
Activity	1	2	3	4	5	6	7	8	8	10
Dig for foundation and service routes	■	■								
Lay foundations			■	■						
Run cabling, piping, etc. to meet existing services				■	■					
Build up to DPC						■	■			
Lay concrete floor								■	■	

Key: propose ■

Figure 2.39 Bar chart showing proposed time for a contract

The bar chart can then be used to check progress. Often the actual time taken for a task is shaded in underneath the proposed time (in a different way or colour to avoid confusion). This shows how what has been done matches up to what should have been done.

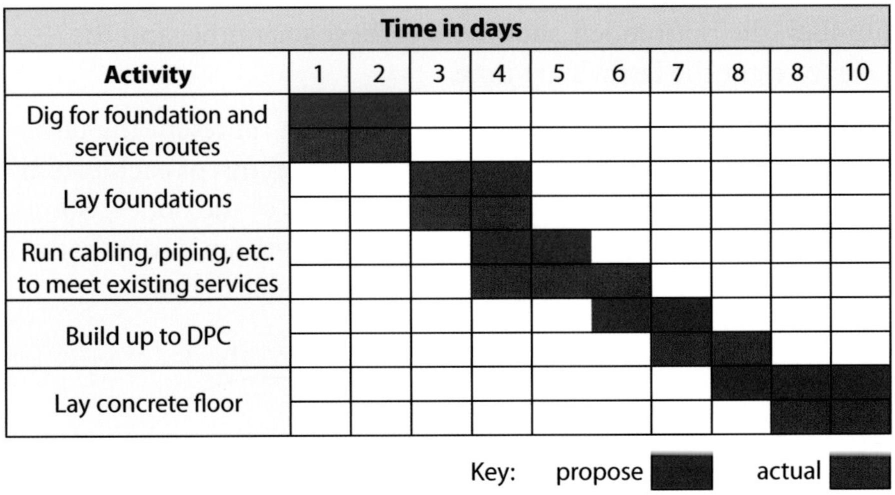

Time in days										
Activity	1	2	3	4	5	6	7	8	8	10
Dig for foundation and service routes	■	■								
Lay foundations			■	■						
Run cabling, piping, etc. to meet existing services				■	■					
Build up to DPC					■	■	■			
Lay concrete floor								■	■	

Key: propose ■   actual ■

Figure 2.40 Bar chart showing actual time half way through a contract

As you can see, a bar chart can help you plan when to order materials or plant, see what trade is due in and when, and so on. A bar chart can also tell you if you are behind on a job; if you have a penalty clause written into your contract, this information is vital.

Did you know?

Bar charts are used to identify areas that could cause problems. You will need to have an idea about the sort of things that can go wrong on a project and plan contingencies to deal with any problems.

Did you know?

Bad weather is the main external factor responsible for delays on building sites in the UK. A Met Office survey showed that the average UK construction company experiences problems caused by the weather 26 times a year.

When creating a bar chart, you should build in some extra time to allow for things such as bad weather, labour shortages, delivery problems or illness. It is also advisable to have contingency plans to help solve or avoid problems, such as:

- capacity to work overtime to catch up time
- bonus scheme to increase productivity
- penalty clause on suppliers to try to avoid late or poor deliveries
- source of extra labour (e.g. from another site) if needed.

Good planning, with contingency plans in place, should allow a job to run smoothly and finish on time, leading to the contractor making a profit.

Critical paths

Another form of work programme is the critical path. Critical paths are rarely used these days as they can be difficult to decipher. The final part of this chapter will give a brief overview of the basics of a critical path, in case you should come across one.

A critical path can be used in the same way as a bar chart to show what needs to be done and in what sequence. It also shows a timescale but in a different way from a bar chart: each timescale shows both the minimum and the maximum amount of time a task might take.

The critical path is shown as a series of circles called event nodes. Each node is split into three: the top third shows the event number, the bottom left shows the earliest start time, and the bottom right the latest start time.

The nodes are joined together by lines, which represent the tasks being carried out between those nodes. The length of each task is shown by the times written in the lower parts of the nodes. Some critical paths have information on each task written underneath the lines that join the nodes, making them easier to read.

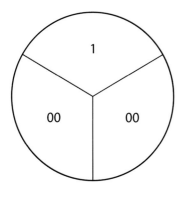

Figure 2.41 Single event node

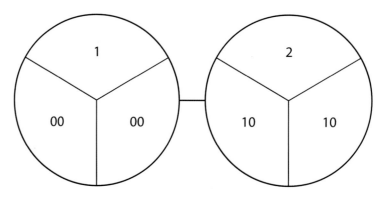

Figure 2.42 Nodes joined together

On a job, many tasks can be worked on at the same time, e.g. the electricians may be wiring at the same time as the plumber is putting in the pipes. To show this on a critical path, the path can be split.

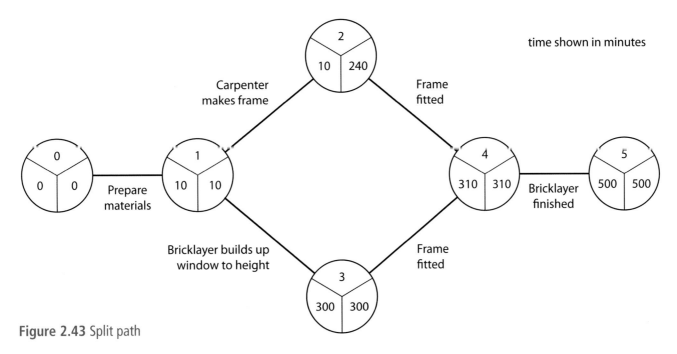

time shown in minutes

Figure 2.43 Split path

The example in Figure 2.43 shows how a critical path can be used for planning building in a window opening, with a carpenter creating a dummy frame.

The event nodes work as follows:

- **Node 0** – This is the starting point.
- **Node 1** – This is the first task, where the materials are prepared.
- **Node 2** – This is where the carpenter makes the dummy frame for the opening. Notice that the earliest start time is 10 minutes and the last start time is 240 minutes. This means that the carpenter can start building the frame at any time between 10 minutes and 240 minutes into the project. This is because the frame will not be needed until 300 minutes, but the job will only take 60 minutes. If the carpenter starts after 240 minutes, there is a possibility that the job may run behind.
- **Node 3** – This is where the bricklayer must be at the site, ready for the frame to be fitted at 300 minutes, or the job will run behind.
- **Node 4** – With the frame fitted, the bricklayer starts at 310 minutes and has until node 5 (500 minutes) to finish.
- **Node 5** – The job should be completed.

When working with a split path it is vital to remember that certain tasks have to be completed before others can begin. If this is not taken into account on the critical path, the job will run over (which may prove costly, both through penalty clauses and also in terms of the contractor's reputation).

On a large job, it can be easy to misread a critical path as there may be several splits, which could lead to confusion.

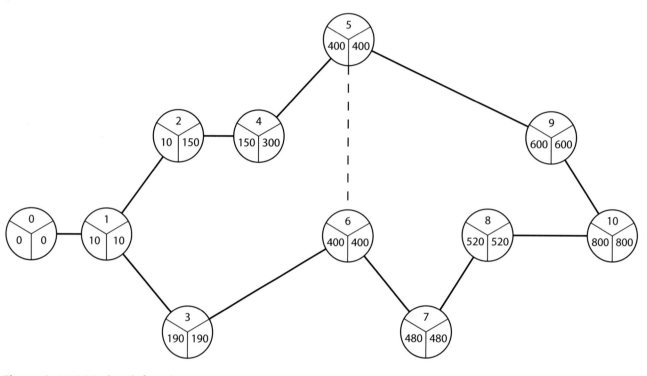

Figure 2.44 Critical path for a large job

Stock systems

Stock systems are mainly used with larger companies, suppliers and larger sites. A good stock system will ensure that all the materials required on site are available when needed and that no materials are damaged either through overstocking, which can lead to storage problems, or by materials such as plaster going off.

When taking delivery of materials, the newest materials are placed at the back in storage. This will ensure that the older materials are used first, while they are still in date.

Lead times

Lead times are how long you should expect to wait for a new delivery of materials. Certain materials are not always readily available in a supplier's stock and even suppliers may have to order certain things. For example oversized timbers would need to be ordered in or steel beams which required specially machining or manufacturing would need to be created to order. Where items like these are required, time is built into the planning stage to contact the suppliers and ask for the lead times for these items to ensure that they are available when they are required.

Pricing systems

Pricing systems are also thought through at the tender and the planning stage to ensure that the price paid for labour during price work is not too much. Price work, which is covered in more detail in the next section, is set to ensure that all labour tasks are given a price and that the price for the tasks is set in a way which will get the job done on time. Pricing tasks too high can see the job taking longer.

> **Remember**
>
> Materials such as plaster or cement have a use-by date on them; generally, such materials will set or go off about this date. To prevent this, it is vital that the materials are used before this happens.

> **Example**
>
> If hanging a door is priced at £40 per door then a tradesman may only do five doors in a day then finish as he feels he has earned enough for the day, whereas if the doors are priced at £30 or even £20 then the worker will try to do more so that they have earned a good daily wage.

The reverse of this is pricing the jobs too low – which may see the company struggling to get anyone to do the work for a low price.

Calculating hours

The way that labour is paid for can be split into two different methods.

Day work/Hourly rate

This rate is used when the tradesperson will be paid a specific amount for every hour that they work. The amount will depend on where the work is being carried out, as the cost of living is different in each area.

Places where the cost of living is low may receive £10–£20 per hour. In areas with a high cost of living (such as London) the rate may be £20–£30 per hour or more. The experience of a worker will also affect the day work rate. Newly qualified Level 2 apprentices will not be paid the same as someone with 30 years of experience.

Price work

This rate is used when the tradesperson will be paid for the work they carry out. Examples of this include a carpenter who receives £20 for every door they hang or a painter who gets £300 for every flat they decorate. This method is often preferred, although it can mean that you may have to work harder. However, the more work you do the more you will earn. Again, the prices for these will vary not only from area to area but even within trades.

> **Did you know?**
>
> When estimating the labour costs for a job it is easier to use the day work rate method as you can calculate how many hours the job will take.

> **Example**
>
> A carpenter may get paid £2000 to fit a truss roof but only £250 to fit a small kitchen in a flat. A painter may get paid £15 to paint the inside of a window compared with £20 to paint the outside. These differences in price are worked out prior to the job starting and take into account things such as weather or hazards. The roof may look like the best job at £2000, but if it is raining heavily for a week, or alterations to the scaffold are required, then you may not get much work done. However, you may be able to fit seven kitchens in a week no matter what the weather.

The price work method is calculated by working out how many hours it will take to complete the task and then giving a certain price to that task, based on the day work rate.

> **Remember**
>
> The £2000 price is for the whole roof. If four people work on it they will get paid £500 each, not the full £2000.

For example, the day work rate may be £20 per hour and a roof should take 100 hours. This means a price of £2000 will be put forward.

Range of added costs for estimating which affect profitability

When estimating prices, there is a range of added costs that need to be considered. You will need to factor in these costs before you begin pricing a job.

> **Remember**
>
> Other factors that can affect profitability include delays caused by weather, worker strike action and other external elements over which you may have no control.

These added costs can also affect the final profitability of a project.

Types of insurance

All companies that carry out work must be insured through public liability and if they employ others then they will also need employer's liability insurance.

- **Public liability insurance** – this will cover you if someone is accidentally injured by you or your business operation. It will also cover you if you damage third party property while on any work-related business. The cover should include any legal fees and expenses which can result from any claim by a third party. You should aim to have a level of insurance which covers you for at least £1,000,000. This may seem a lot but you could have several cases directed at you at any one time. **Premiums** for public liability can start from around £100 per year. Failure to have public liability insurance can see your company go bankrupt if a claim is made and you are not covered.

- **Employer's liability insurance** – this is also required by law if you employ other people. If an employee should be injured at work, or become ill as a result of the work that you ask them to carry out, then employer's liability insurance gives you a minimum level of cover if you are sued. Cover for this should start at £5,000,000. Again this may seem a lot but the premium can again be as little as £100. Failure to have employer's liability insurance can lead to a fine of up to £2,500 for any day you operate without this insurance. Insurance policy certificates must be retained for 40 years, as illness that can occur may appear at a later stage and you need evidence of cover.

You will need to make National Insurance contributions. These are paid to build up your entitlement to certain social security benefits, including state pensions. The amount of money you pay will depend upon your employment status (employed or self-employed). Employers will also be expected to make a contribution to each employee's National Insurance, again with the amount depending on how much they earn.

Stage payments

Stage payments are often used in contracts of any size but more so in large contracts and they usually mean that a percentage of the total price for the job will be paid upon the construction reaching a certain stage. This can be beneficial to both parties, as some small contractors will like a small percentage paid up-front so that they can organise the delivery of materials or pay for other costs that have arisen during the job. If the job is half done, then 50 per cent of the payment can be made. Usually, with a stage payment, a small percentage is held back at the end of the job for a short period of time to allow for any faults or blemishes that appear to be fixed.

> **Key term**
>
> **Premium** – the amount you pay in order to be covered by an insurance company. The premium will be based on a quote given to you by the company and will be paid in one lump sum or, as is more common, in instalments over a year

> **Did you know?**
>
> Combined policies for both of these types of insurance are usually the best way to operate and premiums can start from around £180.

VAT

VAT or Value Added Tax is a form of tax that is charged on most goods and services that VAT registered businesses provide in the UK. The current rate of VAT in the UK is 20% (since January 2011) but it can fluctuate. This happened after the financial crisis in 2009 when it was lowered to 15%. The VAT amount means that services or goods have an extra percentage added to them as a tax. For example a power tool may cost £100 but with the current rate of VAT added you will have to pay £120.00 for it.

PAYE

PAYE or Pay As You Earn is a method of paying income tax and National Insurance contributions. Your employer will deduct these amounts from your wages before you are paid. For example you may earn £300 per week but, after deductions, this could fall to just over £200. With regard to PAYE, every employed person is given a tax code which relates to the amount of tax you pay. A tax code could be 117L which means that you could earn up to £6,475 per year (c. 2010–11) before you pay tax but any money you earn over this amount will be taxed.

Self-employed workers will not follow the PAYE system but will be paid the full amount. However, they are expected to keep a note of their earnings and expenses and once a year will file a tax return in which they will pay all the year's taxes in one lump sum (usually in January, six months in arrears and for the six months ahead, with another sum payable in July). Employers will also pay tax on each employee

Travel expenses

Travel expenses are occurred when travelling to and from a job and although they usually consist of fuel expenses it is also important to consider other things such as bridge tolls or congestion charges. It may not seem like much at the time but a job that lasts 20 or 30 days and which includes a £10 charge for these can easily see the profits start to fall so it is worth considering this when pricing up a job.

Profit and loss

It is important that profit and loss balance sheets are kept by a company, as these will show how the company is performing over a period of time. The simplest form of profit and loss will show how much money a company has taken and deduct from it the amount spent. For example, a job may be priced at £10,000 which has taken four weeks to complete – during which £8,000

Find out

Using the Internet and other sources, find out the current rate of tax and show the impact it would have on earnings.

Functional skills

This task will allow you to practise **FE 2.3.1–2.3.5** Write documents, including extended writing pieces, communicating information, ideas and opinions effectively and persuasively.

has been spent on materials, wages, taxes etc.; this means that the profit for this period is £2,000.

Suppliers' terms and conditions

All suppliers will have some form of terms and conditions which will outline what restrictions are in place for the use of goods and services. These are used as a form of insurance by the company and will include things such as payments, the customer's responsibilities and the company's liability.

Wastage

Wastage can have a massive effect on profitability as the more waste there is, with regard to materials and other ancillaries, the more money is lost out of your profits. A simple way to keep a tab on wastage is to monitor what is ordered against what is needed. For example if 2.5 m lengths of timber are required then you should only order the next size up, which would be 2.7 m, as ordering 3.0m lengths would create waste and expense.

Building up a price

As has been shown previously, building up a price is not simply about calculating what materials, equipment and labour are required but also involves other factors such as insurances, taxes, expenses and so on. If you do not take these things into account, you can quickly see your profits evaporate.

K3. Know how to ensure good working relationships

Good working relationships are absolutely vital when working on site. It is important to have good relationships not only with those who you are working with directly, but also with other trades and professionals you come into contact with. In addition, you need to have a good relationship with the client, who is the overall 'boss' of the entire project!

There are number of methods that can be used to achieve good working relationships on site. These include the following.

- **Good planning** – it has been mentioned time and again that good planning is vital on a site but never more so than when ensuring that good working relationships are maintained. Planning that the correct trades are in when needed will avoid problems between them, as having the wrong trades in or having them arrive in the wrong order can lead to work having to be re-done, which will cause conflict.

- **Regular site meetings** – these can be vital in preventing conflict as each trade should be represented and they can give updates on progress or possible conflicts.
- **Ensuring that competent tradespeople are employed** – working with or after workers who have not done a good job will lead to conflicts as the work they do may have to be re-done. This will cause problems for the people who have to put the work right and can lead to delays which will create conflict with the trades who are waiting to get on with their work.
- **Leaving your work area clean and clear** – this may sound simple but leaving a mess for the following tradespeople will upset them as they will either have to clean up themselves or wait until it is clean. This will delay their work and if on price work will cost them money.
- **Working safely** – again a simple point but this is crucial as not working safely will lead to hazards and possible injuries which can cause conflicts.

Maintaining trust and confidence in colleagues

One of the main components of a continued good working relationship is trust. Just as in everyday life, having trust and confidence in a colleague or friend can help with the relationship in the same way that having no trust or confidence can break it. By doing simple things such as arriving when you say, doing what you say and by being open and honest you can start to bring trust into the relationship. Being professional, helpful and working to the best of your ability will instil confidence in your colleagues. This is important as having no confidence in work colleagues can create problems and conflict.

Explain the need for accurate communication throughout the stages of construction

Accurate communication is vital for efficient relations between everyone who may be involved in a business, from the employer and employees through to clients and suppliers.

Most of the crucial moments when you will need to use good, clear and effective communication relate to decisions that will have a wider effect on the business and those working around you. Some examples of these include the following.

- **Alterations to drawings** – it is important to communicate any changes to these to everyone involved, as all the planning, estimating, material orders and work programmes will be based in part on these drawings. Not communicating changes could lead to mistakes in all these areas.

- **Variations to contracts** – the contract with the client is the crucial document that dictates all decisions that are made on a worksite. Changes to this document must be made known throughout a business.
- **Risk assessments** – the results of these assessments have a direct impact on the safety of workers on site, and should be made known to all.
- **Work restrictions** – these should be communicated to everyone as a restriction is put in place for a specific reason. The restrictions may be put in place for safety reasons. This would mean the area is unsafe so everyone who may be affected needs to be told.

Functional skills

In answering the Check it out and Check your knowledge questions, you will be practising **FE 2.2.1** Select and use different types of texts to obtain relevant information, **FE 2.2.2** Read and summarise succinctly information/ideas from different sources and **FE 2.2.3** Identify the purposes of texts and comment on how effectively meaning is conveyed.

You will also cover and **FM 2.3.1** Interpret and communicate solutions to multistage practical problems and **FM 2.3.2** Draw conclusions and provide mathematical justifications.

FAQ

How do I know what scale the drawing is at?

The scale should be written on the title panel (the box included on a plan or drawing giving basic information such as who drew it, how to contact them, the date and the scale).

How do I know if I need a schedule?

Schedules are only really used in large jobs where there is a lot of repeated design information. If your job has a lot of doors, windows, etc., it is a good idea to use one.

Which type of programme should I use: bar chart or critical path?

It is up to the individual which programme they use – both have their good points – but a bar chart is the easiest to set up and work from.

What if it rains for the entire 20-day duration of the job?

The job would be seriously behind schedule. You can't plan for the weather in this country, but it would be unwise to start an outside job during a rainy season. There are companies that can provide scaffolding with a fitted canopy to protect the work area, which would be ideal for a job in this situation. Larger jobs have longer programmes, and when they are drawn up they are made more flexible to allow for a lot of rainy days.

Check it out

1. Describe the main advantages of using a CAD system and use it to create a 3-D wireframe and dumb solids program.
2. Produce a component drawing for an item that you are familiar with.
3. Produce a detailed drawing of a component you are familiar with.
4. Using a suitable scale, create a setting out drawing for a segmental brick arch with an opening span of 1.8 m, so that the rise and radius can be identified.
5. Using a suitable scale, create a setting out drawing for a rafter with a span of 3.5 m and a rise of 1.4 m, so that the true length of the rafter and angles of cuts can be identified.
6. Explain in detail the process followed in the client/architect consultation on projects.
7. Describe the purpose of a bill of quantities and then put together your own example using a job you are familiar with.
8. Draw up a flow chart explaining the different steps involved in the tender process, both for the client and for those companies who are submitting tenders.
9. Put together your own schedule for the work on one of the jobs you have carried out. Put together two versions of this schedule: a bar chart and a critical path, using event nodes.
10. Take a task that you are familiar with as part of your work. Think about all the possible costs and implications that are connected with this job. Try to work out a price for it, including all the ancillaries discussed above, such as taxes.
11. Draw up a method statement that describes the best working practices for communicating with other trades on site. Make a clear note of the important information that you will need to make sure is conveyed from one person to another while working.

Getting ready for assessment

The information contained in this unit, as well as continued practical assignments that you will carry out in your college or training centre, will help you with preparing for both your end-of-unit test and the diploma multiple choice test. It will also aid you in preparing for the work that is required for the synoptic practical assignments.

Working with contract documents such as drawings, specifications and schedules is something that you will be required to do within your apprenticeship and even more so after you have qualified. Similarly, when working professionally you will need to be able to build up a price accurately and correctly.

You will need to be familiar with:

- producing drawing information
- determining quantities of material and price estimates
- a knowledge of good working relationships.

A particular focus of this unit has been the estimating of quantities and materials needed to build up a price. Learning outcome two has shown you how to analyse the resources required for a construction task, as well as the advantages and disadvantages that exist in hiring or purchasing equipment. You will need to be able to assess and evaluate the material needs of a project and then complete a plan for the sequence of labour and materials. You will also need to be able to identify the added costs that can contribute to the final price you build for a project.

To get all the information you need you will need to build on the maths and arithmetic skills that you learned at school. These skills will give you the understanding and knowledge you will need to complete many of the practical assignments, which will require you to carry out calculations and measurements including estimations of price for tasks to be completed.

You will also need to use your English and reading skills. These skills will be particularly important, as you will need to make sure that you are following all the details of any instructions you receive. This will be the same for the instructions you receive for the synoptic test, as it will for any specifications you might use in your professional life.

Communication skills have also been a focus of this unit, and of learning outcome three. This unit has shown the importance not only of communicating clearly and consistently with everyone on site, but also of building up relationships that are built on trust and confidence.

Teamwork is a very important part of all construction work and can help work to run smoothly and ensure people's safety. Relationships are a vital part of all teamwork and you will need to be able to demonstrate how the key personnel should communicate effectively within this team. The communication skills that are explained within the unit are also vital in all tasks that you will undertake throughout your training and in life.

Good luck!

Check your knowledge

1 What scale are block plans are usually drawn at?

a) 1:1250
b) 1:500
c) 1:200
d) 1:10

2 What stage is CAD normally used in a project?

a) final planning
b) drafting
c) pricing
d) on-site plans

3 What is the British standard code number for structural timber?

a) BS EN 12390-3:2009
b) BS 5268-2:2002
c) BS EN 1097-8:2009
d) BS EN 12350-1:2009

4 What information will a specification contain?

a) site description
b) services
c) workmanship
d) all of the above

5 What does a line drawn 45 mm long at a scale of 1:20 represent?

a) 90 mm
b) 900 mm
c) 9000 mm
d) 45 mm

6 A line drawn 25 mm long at a scale of 1:250 represents what?

a) 6000 mm
b) 6250 mm
c) 6500 mm
d) 6750 mm

7 When is employer's liability insurance required?

a) if you are employed
b) if you employ others
c) if you do any work
d) if you have public liability insurance

8 What must an employee pay?

a) VAT
b) PAYE
c) public liability insurance
d) all of the above

9 When might a stage payment be used?

a) when a small contractor may need some payment up front
b) when a job is to be completed in stages
c) when a contractor does not have all the money ready
d) for all large contracts

10 Which of these is the most important for building good working relationships?

a) good planning
b) working safely
c) regular communication
d) all of the above

UNIT 3003

Knowledge of building methods and construction technology 3

Many of us are aware of the growing concerns around global warming and the current focus on minimising our 'carbon footprint'. This unit deals with some of the factors that may be contributing to climate change, and the way in which modern construction methods and design can help to tackle it by creating a more sustainable environment – one that provides for the needs of the present without compromising the needs of future generations.

As such it is important that, when looking at building methods and construction technology, the use of sustainable building methods and materials is considered for the basic elements of a building.

This unit contains material that supports NVQ Units QCF 209 Confirm work activities and resources for the work and QCF 211 Confirm the occupation method for work.

This unit also contains material that supports TAP Unit 2 Set out for masonry structures, Unit 3 Erect masonry structures and Unit 5 Carry out masonry cladding to timber-framed structures. The unit also contains material that supports the generic units.

This unit will cover the following learning outcomes:

- Know about new technology and methods used in construction
- Know about energy efficiency in new construction buildings
- Know about sustainable methods and materials in construction work.

K1. Know about new technology and methods used in construction

One of the most controversial issues affecting new technologies and methods used in construction is climate change. Climate change is a very controversial issue that has been at the centre of a number of disagreements between experts.

However, it is hard to ignore the changes in weather patterns that we have witnessed in recent years – not just in the UK but also around the world. In the UK, these changes have resulted in extensive flooding, with winter months becoming warmer and summer months becoming wetter. Around the world, the ice caps are melting at worrying speeds, sea levels are rising and adverse weather systems have resulted in more frequent tornados and tropical storms.

The changing climate will certainly have an impact on the way we design buildings in order to cope with some of the possible effects, which include:

- rising temperatures
- rising sea levels
- rising levels of rainfall
- higher humidity levels.

Figure 3.01 Area of land under flood

Although not fully proved, a number of factors are thought to contribute to global warming. The main causes are considered to be burning fossil fuels and the high levels of CO_2 being emitted into the air. CO_2 is emitted in many different ways including through car emissions, aerosol gases and burning untreated waste products.

Many practices have been introduced in an attempt to reduce the carbon footprint, and many more initiatives are being planned, including:

- recycling of packaging such as plastics, paper, cardboard, metals and glass
- use of alternative fuels to power cars and industrial machinery
- use of natural resources such as wind to supply electricity
- transport sharing to reduce the number of cars on the road, thus reducing CO_2 emissions.

Energy efficiency and the reduction of waste are now goals for every building project, and must be considered carefully from the design stage right through the building process.

New legislation has been introduced to make sure that the industry works towards the design of energy-efficient buildings, but at the same time the construction industry is becoming more conscious of the need to address climate change itself, by introducing its own initiatives and practices to minimise its carbon footprint.

- The construction industry is putting greater emphasis on reducing building waste, and is being proactive in recycling many materials that would once have been disposed of to the detriment of the environment.
- There have been significant changes in the design of both domestic and industrial buildings.
- More natural resources are being used in the construction of buildings which, when the building is demolished, can be reused on a new development.
- Buildings now have improved insulation properties, thus reducing fuel usage for heating.
- There are alternative methods of providing energy for a building, including the use of solar panels to provide natural heat.

There are many, many ways of making buildings eco-friendly and we will look at some of these later in this unit.

Key term

Carbon footprint – total amount of CO_2 emissions produced by individuals and industry

Find out

Identify other initiatives and practices currently being used or developed in an attempt to reduce people's carbon footprint.

Different structures used in commercial and domestic dwellings

There are several different construction methods that can be used both commercially and domestically. The table below shows the types of construction that are used in these different structures for the key elements of the building.

We will cover the different structures in greater detail later in this unit.

Find out

What is a steel portal frame used for in commercial building insulation?

Element	Domestic	Commercial
Foundations	• Traditional strip footings and stepped foundations • Raft foundations on poor load-bearing ground • Mass-fill trench foundations	• Piled foundations with pile caps • Ground beams • Raft foundations with edge beam • Pad foundations • Reinforced wide strip
Structural frame	• Traditional cavity wall • Timber-framed construction • Load-bearing insulated formwork	• Steel portal frame • Steel columns and beams • Composite construction • Concrete frameworks
Cladding	• Facing brickwork • Rendering • Timber cladding • Clay tiles	• Insulated composite cladding panels • Steel powder-coated panels • Brickwork facing skin dwarf walls • Timber cladding
Flooring	• Solid concrete floors • Beam and block • Traditional timber flooring joists	• Solid reinforced concrete floors, power-floated with edge beams
Roofing	• Roof trusses with interlocking roof tiles • Traditional roof timbering with clay/concrete roof tiles	• Insulated cladding panels

Table 3.01 Comparison between domestic and commercial construction techniques

Good environmental design

The design of a building or structure should now take on elements that make it environmentally friendly, both in its construction and in the way the occupants use it. The design should also take into account the needs of the local community, in terms of the infrastructure that will be needed to support its eventual construction and use.

Environmental considerations may include some or all of these elements.

- **The design brief** – This should aim to create a design that lowers pollutants to the atmosphere, reduces waste in its construction, reduces noise pollution, and gives the local community something that it can enjoy.

- **Recycling materials** – The design should specify the inclusion of recycled materials into the structure and aesthetics of the building project: for example, the use of crushed hardcore from demolition on site, or the reuse of slate roofing materials.

- **Energy efficiency** – The amount of **embedded** and used energy must be carefully considered for each element of the design, from boiler management systems to highly engineered aerated concrete thermal blocks.

- **Sustainability** – The design must contain elements that will meet the needs of future generations. A long, maintenance-free lifespan for the building is essential. Spending more at the initial cost stage can pay dividends in the future by reducing the cost of energy use and maintenance later on.

- **Green materials** – The use of green materials is a vital environmentally friendly way of ensuring minimum impact on the local and global environment. For example, cedar timber boarding is a sustainable timber product that does not require chemical treatment or painting.

> **Key term**
>
> **Embedded energy** – the amount of energy that has been used to create and manufacture the material and transport it to site for inclusion in the structure

> **Did you know?**
>
> In a good environmental design, you can include a rainwater harvesting system that collects the rainwater from guttering and uses it to flush toilets and to wash down. This is known as 'grey water'.

K2. Know about energy efficiency in new construction buildings

Whatever type of building you may be involved in constructing, there are certain elements that must be included and certain principles that must be followed. For example, a block of flats and a warehouse will both have foundations, a roof, and so on.

At Level 2, you learned about the basic elements of a building. In this learning outcome, you will look in greater depth at the main elements and principles of building work and the materials used.

Accurate setting out of foundations

Any building work will start with the foundations. The design of any foundation will depend on a number of factors including ground conditions, soil type, the location of drains and trees in relation to the building, and any loads that may be generated, either by the structure or naturally.

Dead load – the weight of the structure

Imposed load – the additional weight/loading that may be placed on the structure itself

Figure 3.02 A building damaged through subsidence

Key term

Load-bearing capacity of subsoil – the load that can be safely carried by the soil without any adverse settlement

The purpose of foundations

The foundations of a building ensure that all **dead** and **imposed loads** are safely absorbed and transmitted through to the natural foundation or subsoils on which the building is constructed. Failure to adequately absorb and transmit these loads will result in the stability of the building being compromised, and will undoubtedly cause structural damage.

Foundations must also be able to allow for ground movement brought about by the soil shrinking as it dries out and expanding as it becomes wet. The severity of shrinkage or expansion depends on the type of soil you are building on.

Frost may also affect ground movement, particularly in soils that hold water for long periods. When this retained water freezes, it can make the subsoil expand.

Tree roots and future excavations can also cause movement that affects the subsoil.

Types of soil

As you can imagine there are many different types of soils. For foundation design purposes, these have been categorised as follows:

* rock
* gravel
* clay
* sand
* silt.

Each of these categories of subsoil can be broken down even further; for example:

* clay which is sandy and very soft in its composition
* clay which is sandy but very stiff in its composition.

This information will be of most interest to the architect, but nonetheless is of the utmost importance when designing the foundation.

A number of calculations are used to determine the size and make-up of the foundation. These calculations take into account the **load-bearing capacity of the subsoil**. Calculations for some of the more common types of foundations can be found in the current Building Regulations. However, these published calculations cannot possibly cover all situations. Ultimately it will be down to the expertise of the building design teams to accurately calculate the bearing capacity of soils and the make-up of the foundation.

In the early stages of the design process, before any construction work begins, a site investigation will be carried out to ascertain any conditions, situations or surrounding sites which may affect the proposed construction work. A great deal of data will need to be established during site investigations, including:

- position of boundary fences and hedges
- location and depth of services, including gas, electricity, water, telephone cables, drains and sewers
- existing buildings which need to be demolished or protected
- position, height, girth and spread of trees
- types of soil and the depths of these various soils.

The local authorities will normally provide information relating to the location of services, existing buildings, planning restrictions, preservation orders and boundary demarcation. However, all of these will still need to be identified and confirmed through the site investigation. In particular, hidden services will need to be located with the use of modern electronic surveying equipment.

Soil investigations are critical. Samples of the soil are taken from various points around the site and tested for their composition and for any contamination. Some soils contain chemicals that can seriously damage the foundation concrete. These chemicals include sodium and magnesium sulphates. The effects of these chemicals on the concrete can be counteracted with the use of sulphate-resistant cements.

Many different tests can be carried out on soil. Some are carried out on site; others need to be carried out in laboratories. Tests on soil include:

- **penetration tests** – to establish density of soil
- **compression tests** – to establish **shear strength** of the soil or its load-bearing capacity
- **various laboratory tests** – to establish particle size, moisture content, humus content and chemical content.

Once all site investigations have been completed and all necessary information and data has been established in relation to the proposed building project, site clearance can take place.

Find out

Look at the different methods and equipment used to locate and identify various hidden services.

Find out

How are different soil tests carried out?

Key term

Shear strength – the ability of the soil to resist shear stress, which occurs when one object slips or slides over another

Working life

You have been tasked with building a garage. You decide not to have a soil survey as this is an extra expense, and you just put in a standard strip foundation.

What could go wrong? You will need to think about the implications of not finding out as much as you can about the type of soil you are building on.

What could the cost implications be? You may have saved money avoiding the soil survey, but what impact could this have on your future spending? What effect could this have on your business?

What other implications could there be? Consider how not only the finances, but the stability and long-term life of the building could be affected in a number of ways.

Did you know?

Site investigations or surveys will also establish the contours of the site. This will identify where certain areas of the site will need to be reduced or increased in height. An area of the site may need to be built up in order to mask surrounding features outside the boundaries of the proposed building project.

Find out

How can plant growth affect some structures?

Site clearance

The main purpose of site clearance is to remove existing buildings, waste, vegetation and, most importantly, the surface layer of soil referred to as topsoil. It is necessary to remove this layer of soil, as it is unsuitable to build on. This surface layer of soil is difficult to compact down due to the high content of vegetable matter, which makes the composition of the soil soft and loose. The topsoil also contains various chemicals that encourage plant growth, which may adversely affect some structures over time.

The process of removing the topsoil can be very costly, in terms of both labour and transportation. The site investigations will determine the volume of topsoil that needs to be removed.

In some instances, the excavated topsoil may not be transported off site. Where building projects include garden plots, the topsoil may just need to be stored on site, thus reducing excessive labour and transportation costs. However, where this is the case, the topsoil must be stored well away from areas where buildings are to be erected or materials are to be stored, to prevent contamination of soils or materials.

Once the site clearance is complete, excavations for the foundations can start.

Figure 3.03 Removing soil from a site

Trench excavation

In most modern-day construction projects, trenches are excavated by mechanical means. Although this is an expensive method, it reduces labour time and the costs and risks associated with manual excavation work. Even with the use of machines to carry out excavations, an element of manual labour will still be needed to clean up the excavation work: loose soil from both the base and sides of the trench will have to be removed, and the sides of the trench will have to be finished vertically.

Manual labour is still required for excavating trenches on some projects where machine access is limited and where only small strip foundations of minimum depths are required.

Trenches to be excavated are identified by lines attached to and stretched between profiles. This is the most accurate method of ensuring trenches are dug to the exact widths.

Excavation work must be carefully planned as workers are killed or seriously injured every year while working in and around trenches. Thorough risk assessments need to be carried out and method statements produced before any excavation work is started.

Potential hazards are numerous and include: possible collapse of the sides of the trench, hitting hidden services, plant machinery falling into the trench and people falling into the trench.

One main cause of trench collapse is the poor placement of materials near to sides of the trench. Not only can materials cause trench collapse, but they may also fall into the trench onto workers. Materials should not be stored near to trenches. Where there is a need to place materials close to the trench for use in the trench itself, always ensure these are kept to a minimum, stacked correctly and used quickly and, most importantly, ensure the trench sides are supported.

Trench support

The type and extent of support required in an excavated trench will depend predominantly on the depth of the trench and the stability of the subsoil.

Traditionally, trench support was provided just by using varying lengths and sizes of timber, which can easily be cut to required lengths. However, timber can become unreliable under certain loadings, pressures and weather conditions and can fail in its purpose.

> **Did you know?**
>
> The Health and Safety Executive (HSE) has produced detailed documents that deal exclusively with safety in excavations. These documents can be downloaded from the HSE website or obtained directly from the HSE upon request.
>
> Regulations relating to safety in excavations are set out in the Building Regulations and these must be strictly adhered to during the work.

Figure 3.04 Trenches are often excavated by mechanical means

More modern types of materials have been introduced as less costly and time-consuming methods of providing the required support. These materials include steel sheeting, rails and props. Trench support can be provided with a mixture of both timber and steel components.

Here you can see the methods of providing support in trenches with differing materials and a combination of these materials.

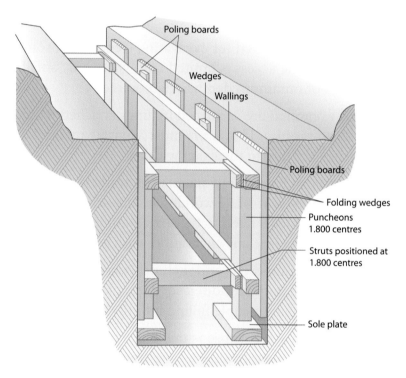

Figure 3.05 Timber used in trench support

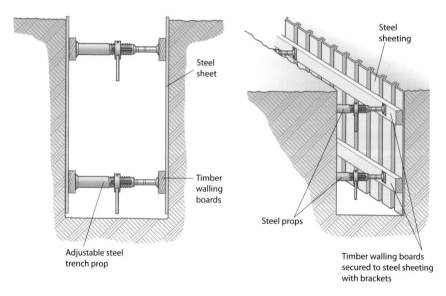

Figure 3.06 Combination of timber and steel used in trench support

The amount of timber or other materials required to provide adequate temporary support will be determined by the characteristics of the soil and the soil's ability to remain stable during the time over which the work is carried out. The atmospheric conditions will also affect the soil's ability to remain stable. The longer the soil is exposed to the natural elements, the greater chance of the soil shrinking or expanding.

Without support, soil will have a natural angle of repose: in other words, the angle at which the soil will rest without collapsing or moving. Again, this will be affected by the natural elements to which the soil is exposed. It is virtually impossible to accurately establish the exact angle at which a type of soil will settle, so it is always advisable to provide more support than is actually required.

Site engineers will carry out calculations in relation to the support requirements for trenches.

Temporary barriers or fences should also be provided around the perimeters of all trenches, to prevent people falling into the trenches and also to prevent materials from being knocked into them. Good trench support methods will incorporate extended trench side supports, which provide a barrier – similar to a toe board on a scaffold – to prevent materials being kicked or knocked into the trench. Where barriers or fences are impractical, then trenches should be covered with suitable sheet materials.

In addition to the supports already mentioned, any services which run through the excavated trenches (in particular drains and gas pipes) need to be supported, especially where the ground has to be excavated underneath them.

Where trenches have to be excavated close to existing buildings, it may be necessary to provide support to the elevation adjacent to the excavation. This is due to the fact that, as ground is taken away from around the existing foundations, the loads will not be adequately and evenly distributed and absorbed into the natural or sub-foundation, possibly causing the structure to collapse. This support is known as shoring.

One other factor that can affect the safety of workers in excavations and the stability of the soil is surface water. Surface water can be found at varying levels within the soil and, depending on the depth, trenches can easily cause flooding. Where this occurs, water pumps will need to be used to keep the trench clear. Failure to keep the trench free of water during construction will not only make operations difficult, but may also weaken and loosen the support systems due to soil displacement.

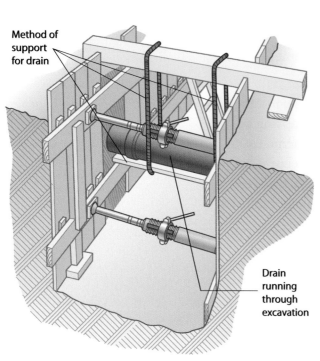

Figure 3.07 Support for drains running through an excavation

Labels on Figure 3.07:
- Method of support for drain
- Drain running through excavation

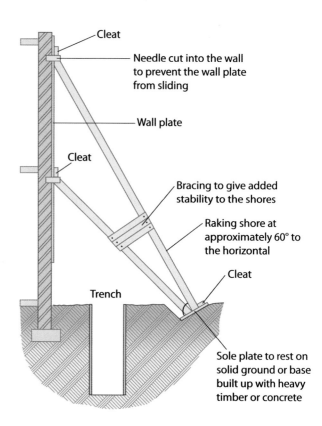

Figure 3.08 Raking shores used to support an existing building

Labels on Figure 3.08:
- Cleat
- Needle cut into the wall to prevent the wall plate from sliding
- Wall plate
- Cleat
- Bracing to give added stability to the shores
- Raking shore at approximately 60° to the horizontal
- Cleat
- Trench
- Sole plate to rest on solid ground or base built up with heavy timber or concrete

---

Functional skills

This exercise will allow you to practise **FM 2.3.1** Interpret and communicate solutions to multistage practical problems and **FM 2.3.2** Draw conclusions and provide mathematical justifications.

Working life

You have been asked by your boss to enter an excavation to clean out some loose soil. The excavation is 1.5 m deep, and has been excavated for a foundation. There are no supports on the excavation sides and overnight there has been a considerable amount of rainfall. Your boss shouts at you to get on with it as the concrete for the foundation will be here in 10 minutes.

What should you do? What could the implications be if you do it? What could the implications be if you don't?

Types of foundation

As previously stated, the design of a foundation will be down to the architect and structural design team. The final decision on the suitability and depth of the foundation, and on the thickness of the concrete, will rest with the local authority's building control department.

Strip foundations

The most commonly used strip foundation is the 'narrow strip' foundation, which is used for small domestic dwellings and low-rise structures. Once the trench has been excavated, it is filled with concrete to within 4–5 courses of the ground level DPC. The level of the concrete fill can be reduced in height, but this makes it difficult for the bricklayer due to the confined area in which to lay bricks or blocks.

The depth of this type of foundation must be such that the subsoil acting as the natural foundation cannot be affected by the weather. This depth would normally not be less than 1 m.

The narrow strip foundation is not suitable for buildings with heavy structural loading or where the subsoil is weak in terms of supporting the combined loads imposed on it. Where this is the case, a wide strip foundation is needed.

Wide strip foundations

Wide strip foundations consist of steel reinforcement placed within the concrete base of the foundation. This removes the need to increase the depth considerably in order to spread the heavier loads adequately.

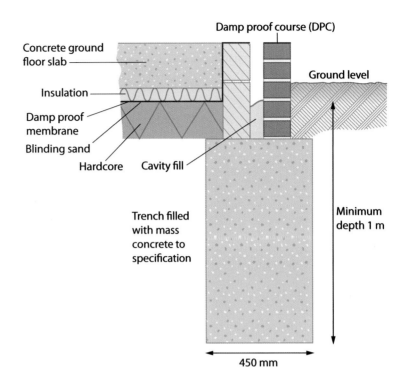

Figure 3.09 Narrow strip foundation

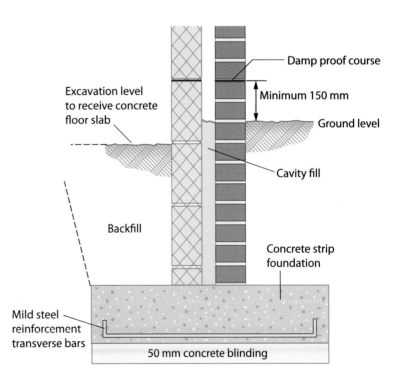

Figure 3.10 Wide strip foundation

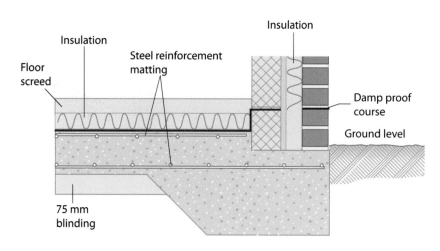

Insulation

Floor screed

Insulation

Steel reinforcement matting

Damp proof course

Ground level

75 mm blinding

Figure 3.11 Raft foundation

Raft foundations

These types of foundation are used where the soil has poor bearing capacity, making the soil prone to settlement. A raft foundation consists of a slab of reinforced concrete covering the entire base of the structure. The depth of the concrete is greater around the edges of the raft in order to protect the load-bearing soil directly beneath the raft from further effects of moisture taken in from the surrounding area.

Pad foundations

Pad foundations are used where the main loads of a structure are imposed at certain points. An example would be where brick or steel columns support the weight of floors or roof members, and walls between the columns are of non-load-bearing cladding panels. The simplest form of pad foundation is where individual concrete pads are placed at various points around the base of the structure, and concrete ground beams span across them. The individual concrete pads will absorb the main imposed loads, while the beams will help support the walls.

The depth of a pad foundation will depend on the load being imposed on it; in some instances, it may be necessary to use steel reinforcement to prevent excessive depths of concrete. This type of pad foundation can reduce the amount of excavation work required, as trenches do not need to be dug out around the entire base of the proposed structure.

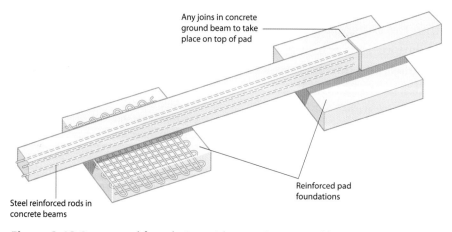

Any joins in concrete ground beam to take place on top of pad

Steel reinforced rods in concrete beams

Reinforced pad foundations

Figure 3.12 Square pad foundation with spanning ground beams

Piled foundations

There are a large number of different types of piled foundations, each with an individual purpose in relation to the type of structure and ground conditions.

Short bored piled foundations are the most common piled foundations. They are predominantly used for domestic buildings where the soil is prone to movement, particularly at depths below 1 m.

A series of holes are bored, by mechanical means, around the perimeter of the base of the proposed building. The diameter of the bored holes will normally be between 250 and 350 mm and can extend to depths of up to 4 m. Once the holes have been bored, shuttering is constructed to form lightweight reinforced concrete beams, which span across the bored piles. The bored holes are then filled with concrete, with reinforcement projecting from the top of the pile concrete, so it can be incorporated into the concrete beams that span the piles.

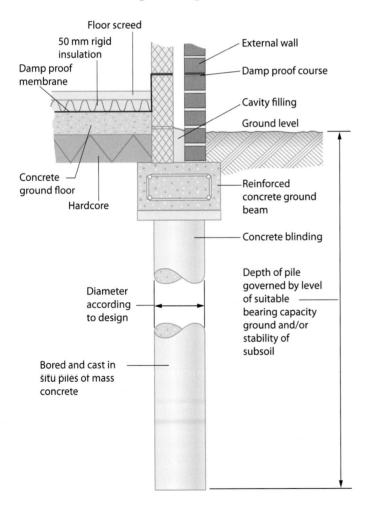

Figure 3.13 Typical short bored piled foundation

As with the pad foundation, short bored piled foundations can significantly reduce the amount of excavated soil, because there is no need to excavate deep trenches around the perimeter of the proposed structure.

Stepped foundations

A stepped foundation is used on sloping ground. The height of each step should not be greater than the thickness of the concrete, and should not be greater than 450 mm. Where possible, the height of the step should coincide with brick course height in order to avoid oversized mortar bed joints and eliminate the need for split brick courses. The overlap of the concrete to that below should not be less than 300 mm or less than the thickness of the concrete.

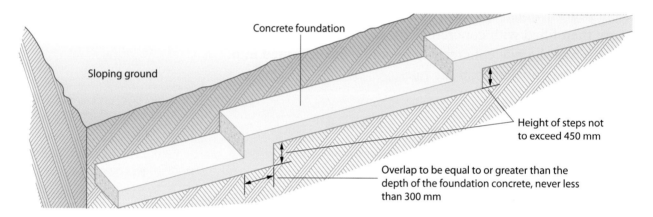

Figure 3.14 Typical stepped foundation

Key terms

R-value – the standard way of describing how effective an insulation is. The higher the R-value, the more effective the insulation will be

U-value – a measure of thermal transmittance through a building component, usually a roof, wall, window, door or floor

Remember

The R-value is the inverse of the **U-value** (see page 108).

Different methods used to insulate against heat loss and gain

The term 'building insulation' refers broadly to any object in a building used as insulation for any purposes – the term applies to acoustic insulation and fire insulation as well as thermal insulation. Often an insulation material will be chosen for its ability to perform several of these functions at once.

Insulating buildings is vital: maintaining acceptable temperature in buildings (by heating or cooling) uses a large proportion of a building's total energy consumption, and the insulation can help to reduce this energy use.

The effectiveness of insulation is commonly related to its **R-value**. However, the R-value does not take into account the quality of construction or local environmental factors for each building. Construction quality issues include poor vapour barrier and problems with draught-proofing. Local environmental factors are simply about where the building is located. With cold climates, the main aim is to reduce heat flow from the building; with hot climates, the main aim is to reduce the heat from entering the building, usually through solar radiation, which can enter a building through the windows.

Materials used in insulating homes

There are essentially two types of building insulation: bulk insulation and reflective insulation.

- **Bulk insulation** – this blocks conductive heat transfer and convective flow, either into or out of a building. The denser the material is, the better it will conduct heat. As air has such a low density, it is a very poor conductor – and therefore a good insulator. This is why air trapped between two materials is often used as an insulator, as in cavity walling.
- **Reflective insulation** – this works by creating a radiant heat barrier in conjunction with an air space, to reduce the heat transfer across the air space. Reflective insulation reflects heat rather than absorbing it or letting it pass through. It is often seen in the form of reflective pads placed behind radiators to reflect the heat from the rear of the radiator back into the room.

Forms of insulation

There are various forms of insulation, but the most common are:

- **mineral wool/rock wool** – these products are made from molten rock spun on a high-spinning machine at a temperature of about 1600°C, similar to the process of making candy floss, with the product being a mass of fine, intertwined fibres
- **fibreglass** – made in a similar way to rock wool, but using molten glass.

Mineral wool usually comes in sheets that are cut to fit between the rafters or studs. Fibreglass is similar, although it can come in rolls that can be cut to fit. Both materials are available in a variety of thicknesses to suit where they are going to be laid.

Other forms of insulation include:

- **polystyrene sheets** – polystyrene is a thermoplastic substance that comes in sheets which can be cut to size, again available in different thicknesses
- **loose-fill insulation** – this is particularly used where there is no insulation in the cavity walls: holes are drilled in the exterior wall and glass wool insulation is blown into the holes until the cavity is full.

Where to insulate

Where insulation should be used depends on the climate and the particular living needs, but generally insulation should be placed:

- in the roof space, between rafters or trusses and between joists
- on all exterior walls
- between the joists at every floor level, including ground floor
- in solid ground floor construction
- in partition walls
- around any ducts and pipes.

Over the next few pages you will see how insulation is used and applied in the different elements of the structure that you will be working with.

Types of floor construction and components

Floors have a number of standard components, including the following:

- **DPC** – This is the damp proof course that is inserted into both skins of the external cavity wall construction. It should be a proprietary product that is tested and has a long life expectancy.
- **DPM** – This is the damp proof membrane, which is placed in large sheets within the floor structure so it can resist the passage of moisture and rising damp. This keeps the floors dry. The DPM should be taken up vertically and tucked into the DPC to form a complete seal. All DPM should be lapped by at least 300 mm, with any joints taped.
- **Screeds** – Floor screeds are considered in the solid concrete floor section (see page 89). They provide a finish to the concrete surface, cover up services and provide a level for floor finishes to be applied to. They also provide falls to floors: for example, in a wet room for the shower waste.
- **Wall plate** – The wall plate is on top of the sleeper wall that supports the floor joists. It has a DPC underneath it to prevent damp penetrating the timber. Wall plates should be treated.

The most common types of flooring used are:

- suspended timber floors
- solid concrete floors
- pre-cast beam floors
- floating floors.

Suspended timber floors

Suspended timber floors can be fitted at any level, from top floor to ground floor. In the next few pages, you will look at:

* basic structure
* joists
* construction methods
* floor coverings.

Basic structure

Suspended timber floors are constructed with timbers known as joists, which are spaced parallel to each other spanning the distance of the building. Suspended timber floors are similar to traditional roofs in that they can be single or double, a single floor being supported at the two ends only and a double floor supported at the two ends and in the middle by way of a honeycombed sleeper/dwarf wall, steel beam or load-bearing partition.

All floors must be constructed to comply with the Building Regulations, in particular Part C, which is concerned with damp. The bricklayer must insert a damp proof course (DPC) between the brick or block work when building the walls, situated no less than 150 mm above ground level. This prevents moisture moving from the ground to the upper side of the floor. No timbers are allowed below the DPC. Air bricks, which are built into the external walls of the building, allow air to circulate round the underfloor area, keeping the moisture content below the dry rot limit of 20 per cent, thus preventing dry rot.

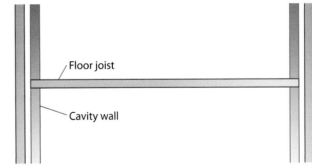

Figure 3.15 Single floor

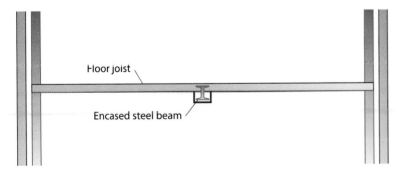

Figure 3.16 Double floor

Joists

In domestic dwellings, suspended upper floors are usually single floors, with the joist supported at each end by the structural walls but, if support is required, a load-bearing partition is used. The joists that span from one side of the building to the other are called bridging joists, but any joists that are affected by an opening in the floor such as a stairwell or chimney are called trimmer, trimming and trimmed joists.

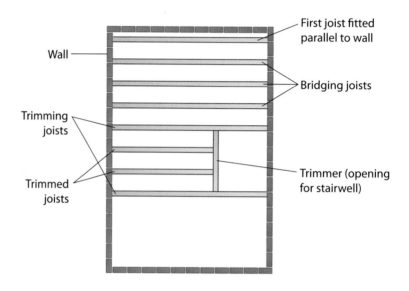

Figure 3.17 Joists and trimmers

Types of joist

As well as the traditional method of using solid timber joists, there are now alternatives available. These are the most common.

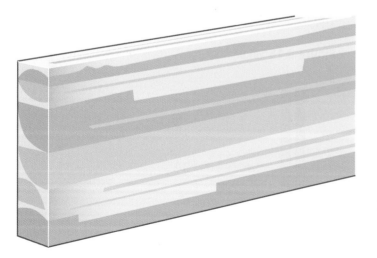

Figure 3.18 Laminated joists

Laminated joists

These were originally used for spanning large distances, as a laminated beam could be made to any size, but now they are more commonly used as an environmental alternative to solid timber – recycled timber can be used in the laminating process. They are more expensive than solid timber, as the joists have to be manufactured.

I type joists

These are now some of the most commonly used joists in the construction industry: they are particularly popular in new build and are the only joists used in timber kit house construction. I type beam joists are lighter and more environmentally friendly as they use a composite panel in the centre, usually made from oriented strand board, which can be made from recycled timber.

The following construction method shows how to fit solid timber joists but, whichever joists you use, the methods are the same.

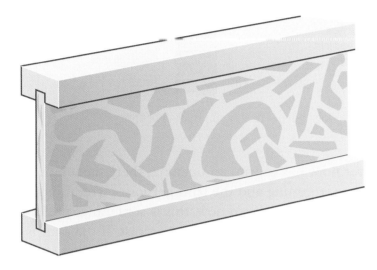

Figure 3.19 I Type joist

Construction methods

A suspended timber floor must be supported at either end. The figures below show ways of doing this.

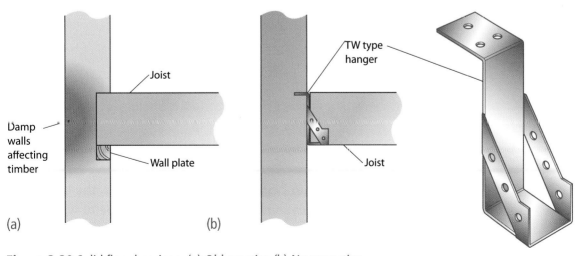

Figure 3.20 Solid floor bearings: (a) Old practice (b) New practice

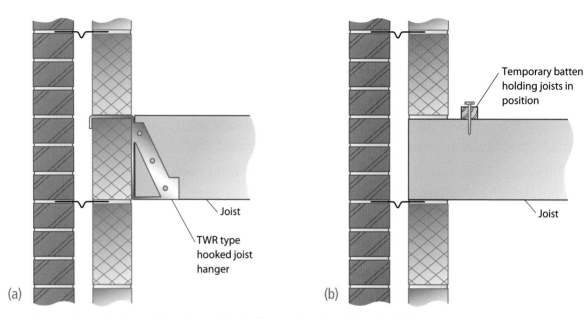

Figure 3.21 Cavity wall bearings: (a) Joist hanger bearing (b) Built-in bearing

Key term

Tusk tenon joint – a kind of mortise and tenon joint that uses a wedge-shaped key to hold the joint together

If a timber floor has to trim an opening, there must be a joint between the trimming and the trimmer joists. Traditionally, a **tusk tenon joint** was used (even now, this is sometimes preferred) between the trimming and the trimmer joist. If the joint is formed correctly a tusk tenon is extremely strong, but making one is time-consuming. A more modern method is to use a metal framing anchor or timber-to-timber joist hanger.

Figure 3.22 Traditional tusk tenon joint

Figure 3.23 Joist hanger

Fitting floor joists

Before the carpenter can begin constructing the floor, the bricklayer needs to build the honeycomb sleeper walls. This type of walling has gaps in each course to allow the free flow of air through the underfloor area. It is on these sleeper walls that the carpenter lays the timber wall plate, which will provide a fixing for the floor joists.

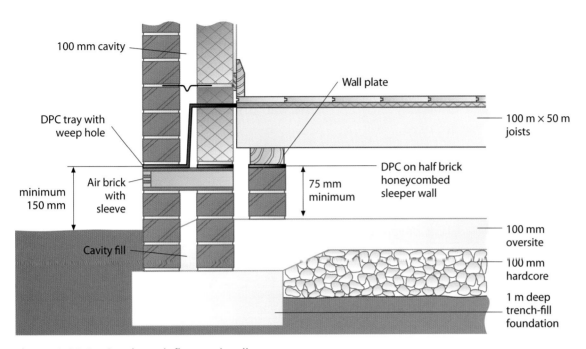

Figure 3.24 Section through floor and wall

Labels in figure:
- 100 mm cavity
- Wall plate
- DPC tray with weep hole
- 100 m × 50 m joists
- Air brick with sleeve
- minimum 150 mm
- 75 mm minimum
- DPC on half brick honeycombed sleeper wall
- Cavity fill
- 100 mm oversite
- 100 mm hardcore
- 1 m deep trench-fill foundation

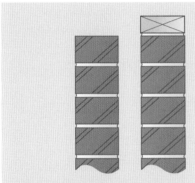

Step 1 Bed in the wall plate

Step 1 Bed and level the wall plate onto the sleeper wall with the DPC under it.

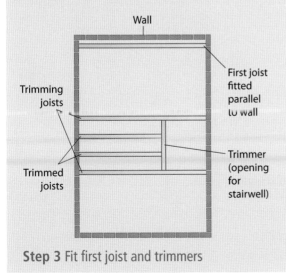

Step 3 Fit first joist and trimmers

Labels: Wall, Trimming joists, Trimmed joists, First joist fitted parallel to wall, Trimmer (opening for stairwell)

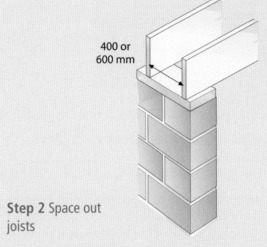

400 or 600 mm

Step 2 Space out joists

Step 2 Cut joists to length and seal the ends with a coloured preservative. Mark out the wall plate with the required centres, space the joists out and fix temporary battens near each end to hold the joists in position. Ends should be kept away from walls by approximately 12 mm. It is important to ensure that the camber is turned upwards.

Step 3 Fix the first joist parallel to the wall with a gap of 50 mm. Fix trimming and trimmer joists next to maintain the accuracy of the opening.

Step 4 Fix subsequent joists at the required spacing as far as the opposite wall. Spacing will depend on the size of joist and/or floor covering, but usually 400 mm to 600 mm centres are used.

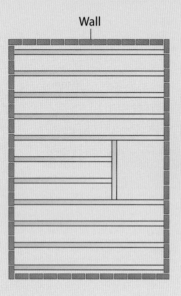

Step 4 Fit remaining joists

Step 5 Fit folding wedges to keep the end joists parallel to the wall. Overtightening is to be avoided in case the wall is strained.

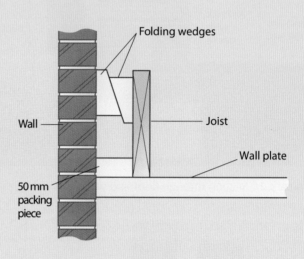

Step 5 Fit folding wedges

Step 6 Check that the joists are level with a straight edge or line and, if necessary, pack with slate or DPC.

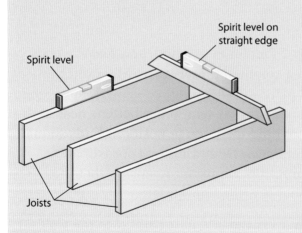

Step 6 Ensure joists are level

Step 7 Fit restraining straps and, if the joists span more than 3.5 m, fit strutting and bridging, described in more detail next.

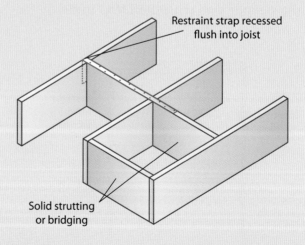

Step 7 Fix restraining straps, struts and bridges

Strutting and bridging

When joists span more than 3.5 m, a row of struts must be fixed midway between each joist. Strutting or bridging stiffens the floor in the same way that noggins stiffen timber stud partitions, preventing movement and twisting, which is useful when fitting flooring and ceiling covering. A number of methods are used, but the main ones are solid bridging, herringbone strutting and steel strutting.

Solid bridging

For solid bridging, timber struts the same depth as the joists are cut to fit tightly between each joist and **skew-nailed** in place. A disadvantage of solid bridging is that it tends to loosen when the joists shrink.

Herringbone strutting

Here timber battens (usually 50 x 25 mm) are cut to fit diagonally between the joists. A small saw cut is put into the ends of the battens before nailing to avoid the battens splitting. This will remain tight even after joist shrinkage. The following steps describe the fitting of timber herringbone strutting.

> **Remember**
>
> It is very important to clean the underfloor area before fitting the flooring in, as timber cuttings or shavings are likely to attract moisture.

> **Key term**
>
> **Skew-nailed** – nailed with the nails at an angle

Figure 3.25 Solid bridging

Step 1 Nail a temporary batten near the line of strutting to keep the joists spaced at the correct centres.

Step 2 Mark the depth of a joist across the edge of the two joists, then measure 12 mm inside one of the lines and remark the joists. The 12 mm less than the depth of the joist ensures that the struts will finish just below the floor and ceiling level (as shown in Step 5).

Step 1 Space joists

Step 2 Mark joist depths

Step 3 Lay the strut across two joists at a diagonal to the lines drawn in Step 2.

Step 3 Lay struts across two joists at a diagonal

Step 4 Draw a pencil line underneath as shown in Step 3 and cut to the mark. This will provide the correct angle for nailing.

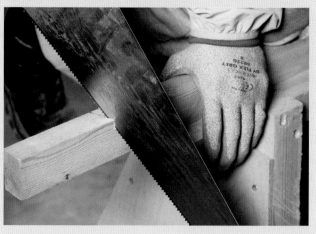

Step 4 Cut to the mark

Step 5 Fix the strut

Step 5 Fix the strut between the two joists. The struts should finish just below the floor and ceiling level. This prevents the struts from interfering with the floor and ceiling if movement occurs.

Steel strutting

There are two types of galvanised steel herringbone struts available.

The first has angled lugs for fixing with the minimum 38 mm round head wire nails.

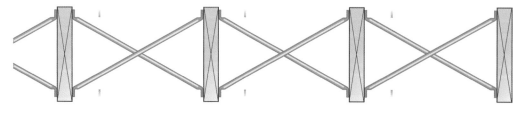

Figure 3.26 Catric® steel joist struts

The second has pointed ends, which bed themselves into joists when forced in at the bottom and pulled down at the top. Unlike other types of strutting, this type is best fixed from below.

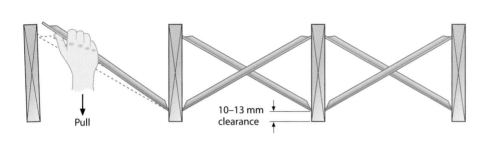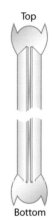

Figure 3.27 Batjam® steel joist struts

The disadvantage of steel strutting is that it only comes in set sizes, to fit centres of 400, 450 and 600 mm. This is a disadvantage as there will always be a space in the construction of a floor that is smaller than the required centres.

Restraint straps

Anchoring straps, normally referred to as restraint straps, are needed to restrict any possible movement of the floor and walls due to wind pressure. They are made from galvanised steel, 5 mm thick for horizontal restraints and 2.5 mm for vertical restraints, 30 mm wide and up to 1.2 m in length. Holes are punched along the length to provide fixing points.

When the joists run parallel to the walls, the straps will need to be housed into the joist to allow the strap to sit flush with the top of the joist, keeping the floor even. The anchors should be fixed at a maximum of 2 m centre to centre. More information can be found in schedule 7 of the Building Regulations.

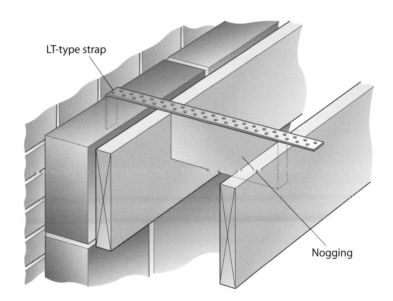

Figure 3.28 Restraint straps for joists parallel or at right angles to the wall

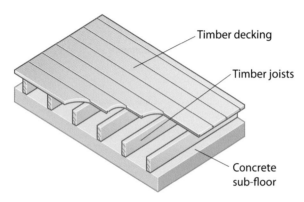

Figure 3.29 Floating floor

Timber decking

Timber joists

Concrete sub-floor

Floating floors

These are basic timber floor constructions that are laid on a solid concrete floor. The timbers are laid in a similar way to joists, although they are usually 50 mm thick maximum as there is no need for support. The timbers are laid on the floor at predetermined centres, and are not fixed to the concrete base (hence floating floor); the decking is then fixed on the timbers. Insulation or underfloor heating can be placed between the timbers to enhance the thermal and acoustic properties.

This type of floor 'floats' on a cushion of insulation. Floating floors are normally manufactured from chipboard – either standard or moisture-resistant – for use in bathrooms. This type of floor is ideal for refurbishment work and where insulation upgrading is required.

Beam and block floors

Construction of these floors is generally quite simple.

Depending on site conditions, beam and block floors can be installed in most types of weather and by using a variety of methods including mobile cranes or other site lifting plant or by hand.

Standard beam and block floors consist of 150 mm and 225 mm beams with standard 100 mm deep concrete building blocks inserted between the beams.

The beams are pre-cast away from the site environment and are pre-stressed with high tensile steel wires suited to the environment and purpose for which they are to be used.

Once the blocks have been placed in position, the floor should be grouted with sand and cement grout consisting of four parts sand to one part cement. The grout should be brushed into the joints between the beams and the blocks in order to stabilise the floor.

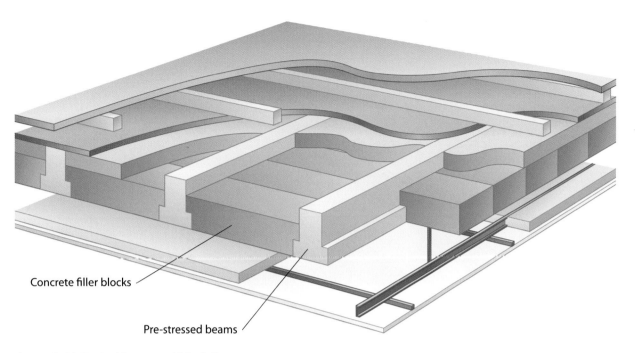

Concrete filler blocks

Pre-stressed beams

Figure 3.30 Typical beam and block floor

Insulation can be slung underneath the beams or over the blocks where it is to be covered with a suitable finish.

Figure 3.30 shows a typical beam and block floor construction.

Solid concrete floors

Solid concrete floors are more durable than suspended timber floors. They are constructed on a sub-base incorporating hardcore, damp proof membranes and insulation.

In the next few pages, you will look at:

* formwork for concrete floors
* reinforcement
* compacting of concrete
* surface finishes
* curing.

Any concreting job has to be supported at the sides to prevent the concrete just running off and this support comes in the way of formwork.

Floors for buildings such as factories and warehouses etc. have large areas and would be difficult to lay in one slab. Floors of this type are usually laid in alternative strips up to 4.5 m wide, running the full length of the building (see Figure 3.31). The actual formwork would be similar to that used for paths.

> **Remember**
>
> The depth of the hardcore and concrete will depend on the nature of the building, and will be set by the Building Regulations and the local authority.

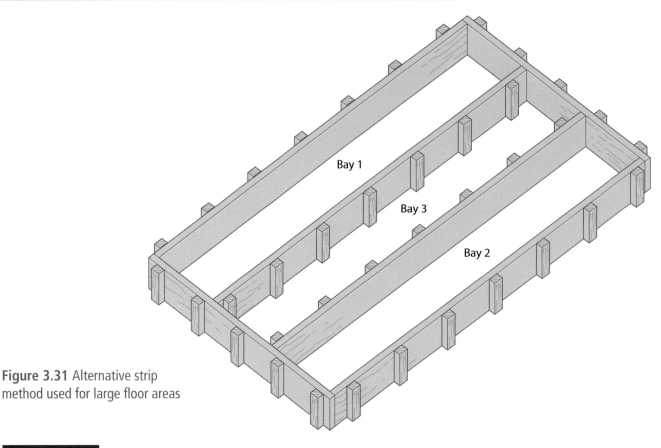

Figure 3.31 Alternative strip method used for large floor areas

Key terms

Compression – being squeezed or squashed together

Tension – being stretched

Reinforcement

Concrete is strong in **compression** but weak in **tension** so, to prevent concrete from being 'pulled' apart when under pressure, steel reinforcement is provided. The type and position of the reinforcement will be specified by the structural engineer.

The reinforcement must always have a suitable thickness of concrete cover to prevent the steel from rusting if exposed to moisture or air. The amount of cover required depends upon the location of the site with respect to exposure conditions, and ranges from 20 mm in mild exposure to 60 mm for very severe exposure to water.

To prevent the reinforcement from touching the formwork, spacers made from concrete, fibre cement or plastic are used. They are available in several shapes and various sizes to give the correct cover.

Figure 3.32 Steel reinforcement of concrete

Compacting

When concrete has been placed, it contains trapped air in the form of voids. To get rid of these voids we must compact the concrete. The more workable the concrete the easier it would be to compact, but also if the concrete is too wet, the excess water will reduce the strength of the concrete.

Failure to compact concrete results in:

* reduction in the strength of the concrete
* water entering the concrete, which could damage the reinforcement
* visual defects, such as honeycombing on the surface.

The method of compaction depends on the thickness and the purpose of the concrete. For oversite concrete, floors and pathways up to 100 mm thick, manual compaction with a tamper board may be sufficient. This requires slightly overfilling the formwork and tamping down with the tamper board.

For slabs up to 150 mm thick, a vibrating beam tamper should be used. This is simply a tamper board with a petrol-driven vibrating unit bolted on. The beam is laid on the concrete with its motor running and is pulled along the slab.

For deeper structures, such as retaining walls for example, a poker vibrator would be required. The poker vibrator is a vibrating tube at the end of a flexible drive connected to a petrol motor. The pokers are available in various diameters from 25 mm to 75 mm.

The concrete should be laid in layers of 600 mm with the poker in vertically and penetrating the layer below by 100 mm. The concrete is vibrated until the air bubbles stop and the poker is then lifted slowly and placed 150 to 1000 mm from this incision, depending on the diameter of the vibrator.

> **Did you know?**
>
> For larger spans the tamper board may be fitted with handles.

Figure 3.33 Tamper board with handles

Figure 3.34 Vibrating beam tamper

Figure 3.35 Vibrating poker in use

Key term

Screeding – levelling off concrete by adding a final layer

Remember

Make sure you always clean all tampers and tools after use.

Surface finishes

Surface finishes for slabs may include the following.

- **Tamped finish.** Simply using a straight edge or tamper board when compacting the concrete will leave a rough finish to the floor, ideal for a path or drive surface, giving grip to vehicles and pedestrians. This finish may also be used if a further layer is to be applied to give a good bond.

- **Float and brush finish.** After **screeding** off the concrete with a straight edge, the surface is floated off using a steel or wooden float and then brushed lightly with a soft brush (see Figure 3.36). Again, this would be suitable for pathways and drives.

- **Steel float finish.** After screeding off using a straight edge, a steel float is applied to the surface. This finish attracts particles of cement to the surface, causing the concrete to become impermeable to water but also very slippery when wet. This is not very suitable for outside but ideal for use indoors for floors, etc.

- **Power trowelling/float.** Three hours after laying, a power float is applied to the surface of the concrete. After a further delay to allow surface water to evaporate, a power trowel is then used. A power float has a rotating circular disc or four large flat blades powered by a petrol engine. The edges of the blades are turned up to prevent them digging into the concrete slab. This finish would most likely be used in factories where a large floor area would be needed.

- **Power grinding.** This is a technique used to provide a durable wearing surface without further treatment. The concrete is laid, compacted and trowel finished. After 1 to 7 days the floor is ground, removing the top 1–2 mm, leaving a polished concrete surface.

Figure 3.36 Brushed concrete finish

Figure 3.37 Power float

Surface treatment for other surfaces may include the following.

- **Plain smooth surfaces.** After the formwork has been struck, the concrete may be polished with a carborundum stone, giving a polished water-resistant finish.

- **Textured and profiled finish.** A simple textured finish may be made by using rough sawn boards to make the formwork. When struck, the concrete takes on the texture of these boards. A profiled finish can be made by using a lining inside the formwork. The linings may be made from polystyrene or flexible rubber-like plastics, and gives a pattern to the finished concrete.

- **Ribbed finish.** Made by fixing timber battens to the formwork.

- **Exposed aggregate finish.** The coarse aggregate is exposed by removing the sand and cement from the finished concrete with a sand blaster. Another method of producing this finish is by applying a chemical retarder to the formwork, which prevents the cement in contact with it from hardening. When the formwork is removed, the mortar is brushed away to uncover the aggregate in the hardened concrete.

Figure 3.38 Ribbed concrete finish

> **Remember**
>
> If the water is allowed to evaporate from the mix shortly after the concrete is placed, there is less time for the cement to 'go off'.

> **Remember**
>
> In hot weather the concrete must be placed quickly and not left standing for too long.

> **Safety tip**
>
> Take precautions in hot weather against the effect of the sun on your skin, for example wear sun block and a T-shirt.

Curing

When concrete is mixed, the quantity of water is accurately added to allow for hydration to take place. The longer we can keep this chemical reaction going, the stronger the concrete will become.

To allow the concrete to achieve its maximum strength, the chemical reaction must be allowed to keep going for as long as possible. To do this we must 'cure' the concrete. This is done by keeping the concrete damp and preventing it from drying out too quickly.

Curing can be done by:

1. Spraying the concrete with a chemical sealer which dries to leave a film of resin to seal the surface and reduces the loss of moisture.

2. Spraying the concrete with water which replaces any lost water and keeps the concrete damp. This can also be done by placing sand or hessian cloth or other similar material on the concrete and dampening.

3. Covering the concrete with a plastic sheet or building paper, preventing wind and sun from evaporating the water into the air. Any evaporated moisture due to the heat will condense on the polythene and drip back on to the concrete surface.

Concreting in hot weather

When concreting in temperatures over 20°C, there is a reduction in workability due to the water being lost through evaporation. The cement also tends to react more quickly with water, causing the concrete to set rapidly.

To remedy the problem of the concrete setting quickly, a 'retarding mixture' may be used. This slows down the initial reaction between the cement and water, allowing the concrete to remain workable for longer.

Extra water may be added at the time of mixing so that the workability is correct at the time of placing.

Water must not be added during the placing of the concrete, to make it more workable, after the initial set has taken place in the concrete.

Concreting in cold weather

Water expands when freezing. This can cause permanent damage if the concrete is allowed to freeze when freshly laid or in hardened concrete that has not reached enough strength ($5 N/mm^2$, which takes 48 hours).

Concreting should not take place when the temperature is 2°C or less. If the temperature is only slightly above 2°C, mixing water should be heated.

After being laid, the concrete should be kept warm by covering with insulating quilts, which allows the cement to continue its reaction with the water and prevents it from freezing.

Working life

You are working for a construction company and have been asked to complete a quote for the building of a garage. The client is unsure what type of floor to have and they ask your opinion.

What type of information would you need to know in order to make a decision? What type of floor do you think you are likely to pick? You will need to think about what the floor is likely to be used for. Why would you select that type of floor?

Floor coverings

Softwood flooring

Softwood flooring can be used at either ground or upper floor levels. It usually consists of 25 x 150 mm tongued and grooved (T&G) boards. The tongue is slightly off centre to provide extra wear on the surface that will be walked upon.

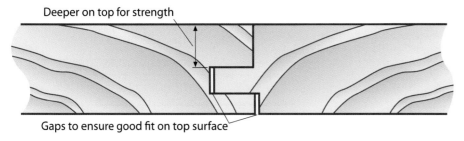

Deeper on top for strength

Gaps to ensure good fit on top surface

Figure 3.39 Section through softwood covering

When boards are joined together, the joints should be staggered evenly throughout the floor to give it strength. They should never be placed next to each other, as this prevents the joists from being tied together properly.

The boards are either fixed with floor brads nailed through the surface and punched below flush, or secret nailed with lost head nails through the tongue. The nails used should be $2\frac{1}{2}$ times the thickness of the floorboard.

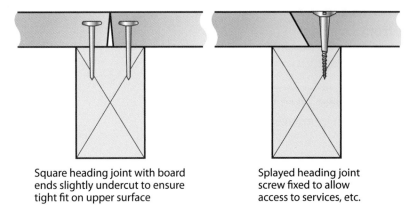

Square heading joint with board ends slightly undercut to ensure tight fit on upper surface

Splayed heading joint screw fixed to allow access to services, etc.

Figure 3.40 Square and splayed heading

The first board is nailed down about 10–12 mm from the wall. The remaining boards can be fixed four to six boards at a time, leaving a 10–12 mm gap around the perimeter to allow for expansion. This gap will eventually be covered by the skirting board.

There are two methods of clamping the boards before fixing.

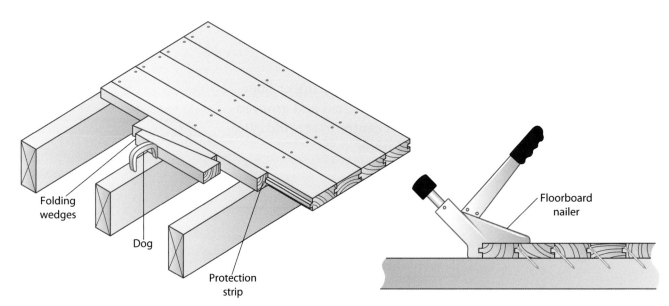

Folding wedges

Dog

Protection strip

Floorboard nailer

Figure 3.41 Clamping methods

Chipboard flooring

Flooring-grade chipboard is increasingly being used for domestic floors. It is available in sheet sizes of 2440 x 600 x 18 mm and can be square edged or tongued and grooved on all edges, the latter being preferred. If square-edged chipboard is used it must be supported along every joint.

Tongued and grooved boards are laid end to end, at right angles to the joists. Cross-joints should be staggered and, as with softwood flooring, expansion gaps of 10–12 mm left around the perimeter. The ends must be supported.

When setting out the floor joists, the spacing should be set to avoid any unnecessary wastage. The boards should be glued along all joints and fixed using either 50–65 mm annular ring shank nails or 50–65 mm screws. Access traps must be created in the flooring to allow access to services such as gas and water.

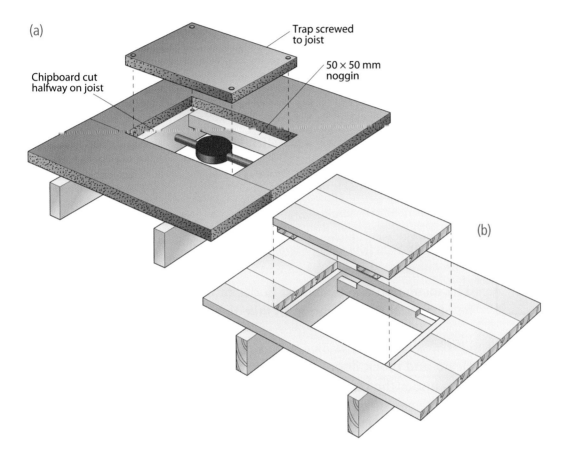

(a)

Trap screwed to joist

Chipboard cut halfway on joist

50 × 50 mm noggin

(b)

Figure 3.42 Access traps: (a) Chipboard floor (b) Tongued and grooved board

Insulation in flooring

Flooring insulation in timber flooring usually takes the form of a quilted insulation such as mineral or rock wool, or solid insulation such as polystyrene sheeting or insulation boards. Insulation in solid concrete flooring or slabs will usually take the form of insulation boards (which need to be a minimum of 50 mm thick to ensure the target U-value is reached). These should be staggered to avoid movement and can be placed under the slab or between the slab and floor screed with a damp-proof membrane being placed under the insulation to prevent any punctures in the boarding.

Solid floors

The construction of concrete floors is shown in Figure 3.43.

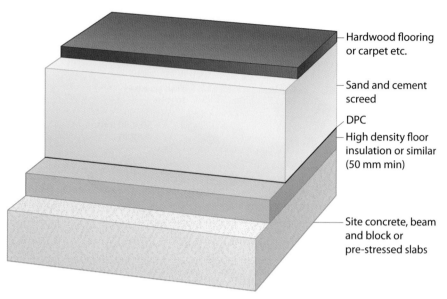

- Hardwood flooring or carpet etc.
- Sand and cement screed
- DPC
- High density floor insulation or similar (50 mm min)
- Site concrete, beam and block or pre-stressed slabs

Figure 3.43 Solid floor construction

> **Remember**
>
> The insulation manufacturer will be able to help you with typical installation details for placing the thermal insulation into a design.

The insulation can be placed under or over the concrete, and must be of the right specification to take the loadings from the floor.

Hollow floors

Beam and block floors require specialist thermal insulation that clips under the beams, below the level of the blocks.

Roofing components

Roofs are made up of a number of different parts called 'elements'. These in turn are made up of 'members' or 'components'.

Elements

The main elements are defined below.

- **gable** – the triangular part of the end wall of a building that has a pitched roof
- **hip** – where two external sloping surfaces meet
- **valley** – where two internal sloping surfaces meet
- **verge** – where the roof overhangs at the gable
- **eaves** – the lowest part of the roof surface where it meets the outside walls.

Members or components

The main members or components are defined below and shown in Figure 3.44. They include:

- **ridge board** – a horizontal board at the apex acting as a spine, against which most of the rafters are fixed
- **wall plate** – a length of timber placed on top of the brickwork to spread the load of the roof through the outside walls and give a fixing point for the bottom of the rafters
- **rafter** – a piece of timber that forms the roof, of which there are several types
- **common rafters** – the main load-bearing timbers of the roof
- **hip rafters** – used where two sloping surfaces meet at an external angle, this provides a fixing for the jack rafters and transfers their load to the wall

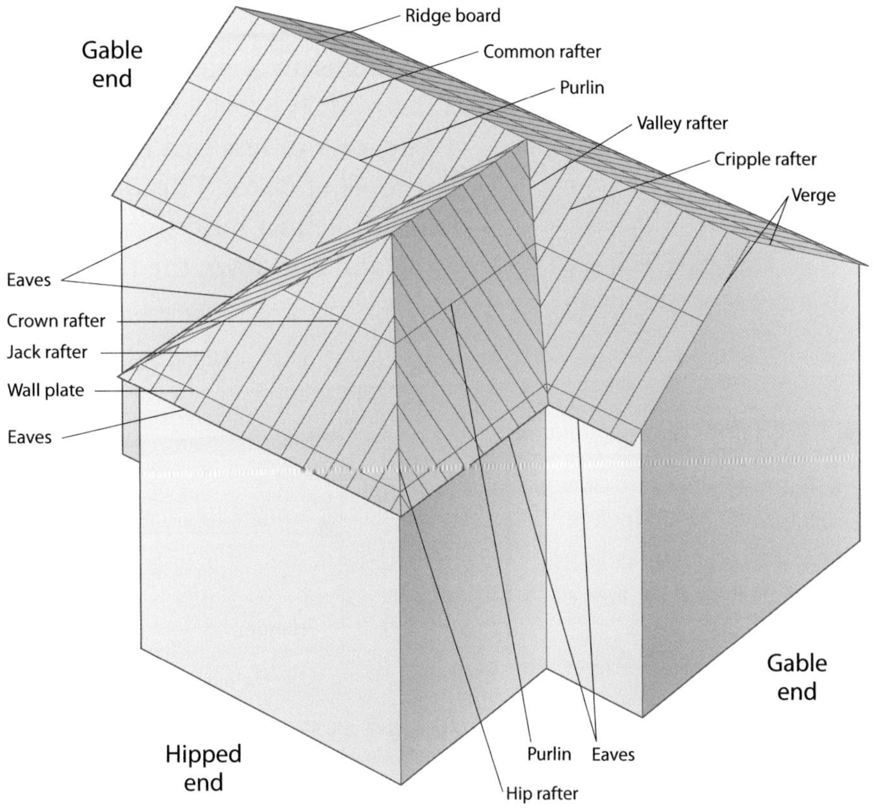

Figure 3.44 Roofing terminology

- **crown rafter** – the centre rafter in a hip end that transfers the load to the wall
- **jack rafters** – these span from the wall plate to the hip rafter, enclosing the gaps between common and hip rafters, and crown and hip rafters
- **valley rafters** – like hip rafters but forming an internal angle, acting as a spine for fixing cripple rafters
- **cripple rafters** – similar to a jack rafter, these enclose the gap between the common and valley rafters
- **purlins** – horizontal beams that support the rafters midway between the ridge and wall plate.
- **bracing** – lengths of timber attached along the trusses to hold them in place.

These components combine to form three main types of roofs:

- flat roofs
- pitched roofs
- hipped roofs.

Find out

Roofs are often covered with slate or tile. Using the Internet and manufacturers' catalogues find out more about these different types of roof covering and prepare a short report.

Firrings

A firring is an angled piece of wood, laid on top of the joints on a flat roof. It provides a fall. This supplies a pitch of around 10 degrees or less to a roof. This pitch will allow the draining of flat roofs of water. This drainage is vital. The edge – where the fall leads to – must have suitable guttering to allow rain water to run away and not down the face of the wall.

Did you know?

A flat roof without drainage will have a lot of strain on it when rain water collects there. This could lead the roof to collapse.

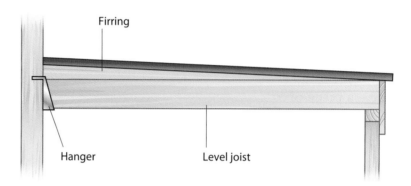

Figure 3.45 Firrings

Figure 3.46 Battens on a roof

Battens

Battens are wood strips that are used to provide a fixing point for roof sheet or roof tiles. The spacing between the battens depends on the type of roof and they can be placed at right angles to the trusses or rafters.

Some roofs use a grid pattern in both directions. This is known as a counter-batten system.

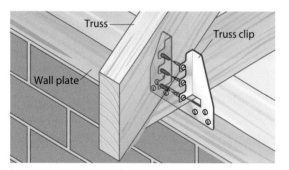

Figure 3.47 Truss clips

Hangers and clips

Hangers, or clips, are galvanised metal clips that are used to fix trusses or joists in place on wall plates. This anchors them to the wall. This makes the roof stable and helps it withstand wind pressure.

Felt

Felt is rolled over the top of the joists to provide a waterproof barrier. It is then fastened down to provide a permanent barrier. Overlapping the felt strips when placing them will help make this barrier even more effective, as will making sure that there are no air bubbles in the felt.

Figure 3.48 Roofing felt

Flashings

Flashings are made from aluminium or lead. They are used to provide water resistance around openings in a roof, such as chimneys or roof windows or when a roof butts up to an existing wall. The joints can be sealed evenly by applying a mastic finish.

Metal flashing can be purchased in rolls or in sections specifically designed for certain roles – such as around a chimney.

Main types of roof

Flat roofs

A flat roof is any roof which has its upper surface inclined at an angle (also known as the fall, slope or pitch) not exceeding 10 degrees.

A flat roof has a fall to allow rainwater to run off, preventing puddles forming as they can put extra weight on the roof and cause leaks. Flat roofs will eventually leak, so most are guaranteed for only 10 years (every 10 years or so the roof will have to be stripped back and re-covered). Today **fibreglass** flat roofs are available that last much longer, so some companies will give a 25-year guarantee on their roof. Installing a fibreglass roof is a job for specialist roofers.

Flat roofs use bitumen to provide a waterproof seal. This is a black, sticky substance, a type of pitch or tar that turns into a liquid when it is heated. It is then used on flat roofs to provide a waterproof seal. It is a flexible DPC.

The amount of fall should be sufficient to clear water away to the outlet pipe(s) or guttering as quickly as possible across the whole roof surface. This may involve a single direction of fall or several directional changes of fall such as:

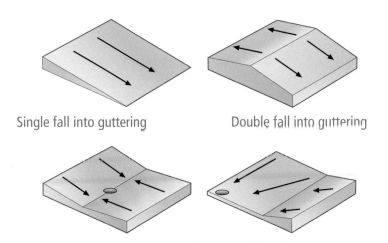

Single fall into guttering   Double fall into guttering

Double fall to internal funnel outlet   Double fall to corner funnel outlet

Figure 3.51 Falls on a flat roof and direction of fall

Figure 3.49 Roof flashing

Remember

A roof with an angle of *more* than 10 degrees is classified as a pitched roof.

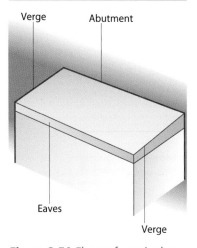

Figure 3.50 Flat roof terminology

Key term

Fibreglass – a material made from glass fibres and a resin that starts in liquid form and then hardens to be very strong

Did you know?

If a puddle forms on a roof and is not cleared away quickly, over a period of years the water will eventually work its way through.

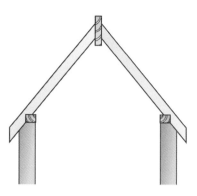

Figure 3.52 Single roof

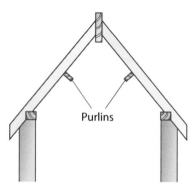

Purlins

Figure 3.53 Double roof

Pitched roofs

There are several different types of **pitched roof** but most are constructed in one of two ways.

- **Trussed roof** – A prefabricated pitched roof, specially manufactured prior to delivery on site, saving timber as well as making the process easier and quicker. Trussed roofs can also span greater distances without the need for support from intermediate walls.
- **Traditional roof** – A roof entirely constructed on site from loose timber sections using simple jointing methods.

Pitched roof types

A pitched roof can be constructed either as a single roof, where the rafters do not require any intermediate support, or a double roof where the rafters are supported. Single roofs are used over a short span such as a garage; double roofs are used to span a longer distance such as a house or factory.

There are many different types of pitched roof including:

- **mono pitch** with a single pitch
- **lean-to** with a single pitch, which butts up to an existing building
- **duo pitch** with **gable ends**

Safety tip

Roofing requires working at height so always use the appropriate access equipment (i.e. a scaffold, properly secured ladders, trestles or a temporary working platform).

Figure 3.54 Mono pitch roof

Figure 3.55 Lean-to roof

Figure 3.56 Duo pitch roof with gable ends

Figure 3.57 Hipped roof

Figure 3.58 Over hip roof

Figure 3.59 Gambrel roof

Figure 3.60 Mansard roof

- **hipped roof** with hip ends incorporating crown, hip and jack rafters
- **over hip** with gable ends, hips and valleys incorporating valley and cripple rafters
- **mansard** with gable ends and two different pitches used mainly when the roof space is to be used as a room
- **gable hip** or **gambrel** – double-pitched roof with a small gable (gablet) at the ridge and the lower part a half-hip
- **jerkin-head** or **barn hip** – double-pitched roof hipped from the ridge part-way to the eaves, with the remainder gabled.

Figure 3.61 Jerkin-head roof

The type of roof to be used will be selected by the client and architect.

Trussed rafters

Most roofing on domestic dwellings now comprises factory-made trussed rafters. These are made of stress graded, **PAR** timber to a wide variety of designs, depending on requirements. All joints are butt jointed and held together with fixing plates, face fixed on either side. These plates are usually made of galvanised steel and either nailed or factory pressed. They may also be **gang-nailed** gusset plates made of 12 mm resin bonded plywood.

One of the main advantages of this type of roof is the clear span achieved, as there is no need for intermediate, load-bearing partition walls. Standard trusses are strong enough to resist the eventual load of the roofing materials. However, they are not able to withstand pressures applied by lateral bending. Hence, damage is most likely to occur during delivery, movement across site, site storage or lifting into position.

Key terms

PAR – a term used for timber that has been 'planed all around'

Gang-nailed – galvanised plate with spikes used to secure butt joints

Knowledge of building methods and construction technology 3 **Unit 3003**

103

Remember

Never alter a trussed rafter without the structural designer's approval.

Wall plates are bedded as described above. Following this, the positions of the trusses can be marked at a maximum of 600 mm between centres along each wall plate. The sequence of operations then varies between gable and hipped roofs.

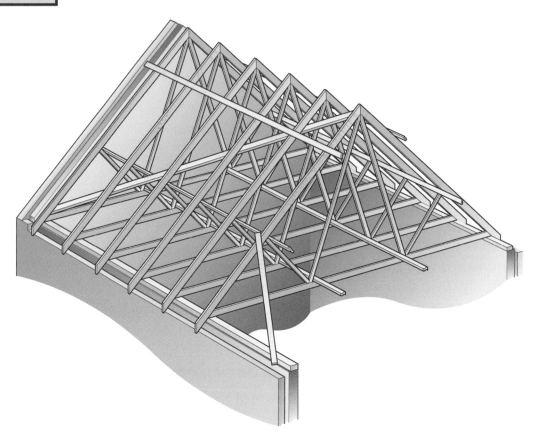

Figure 3.62 Erection of common trussed rafters

Hipped roofs

In a fully hipped roof there are no gables and the eaves run around the perimeter, so there is no roof ladder or bargeboard.

Marking out for a hipped roof

All bevels or angles cut on a hipped roof are based on the right-angled triangle and the roof members can be set out using the following two methods:

- **roofing ready reckoner** – a book that lists in table form all the angles and lengths of the various rafters for any span or rise of roof
- **geometry** – working with scale drawings and basic mathematic principles to give you the lengths and angles of all rafters.

The ready reckoner will be looked at later in this chapter, so for now we will concentrate on geometry.

Pythagoras' theorem

When setting out a hipped roof, you need to know Pythagoras' theorem. Pythagoras stated that 'the square on the hypotenuse of a right-angled triangle is equal to the sum of the squares on the other two sides'. For the carpenter, the 'hypotenuse' is the rafter length, while the 'other two sides' are the run and the rise.

From Pythagoras' theorem, we get this calculation:

$A = \sqrt{B^2 + C^2}$ ($\sqrt{}$ means the square root and ^{2} means squared)

If we again look at our right-angled triangle we can break it down to:

A (the rafter length – the distance we want to know)
B^2 (the rise, multiplied by itself)
C^2 (the run, multiplied by itself).

Therefore, we have all we need to find out the length of our rafter (A):

$A = \sqrt{4^2 + 3^2}$
$A = \sqrt{4 \times 4 + 3 \times 3}$
$A = \sqrt{16 + 9}$
$A = \sqrt{25}$
$A = 5$

So our rafter would be 5 m long.

Finishing a roof at the gable and eaves

There are two types of finish for a gable end:

- **a flush finish**, where the bargeboard is fixed directly onto the gable wall
- **a roof ladder** – a frame built to give an overhang and to which the bargeboard and soffit are fixed.

The most common way is to use a roof ladder which, when creating an overhang, stops rainwater running down the face of the gable wall.

The continuation of the fascia board around the verge of the roof is called the bargeboard. Usually the bargeboard is fixed to the roof ladder and has a built-up section at the bottom to encase the wall plate.

The simplest way of marking out the bargeboard is to temporarily fix it in place and use a level to mark the plumb and seat cut.

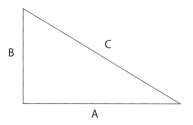

Did you know?

The three angles in a triangle always add up to 180 degrees.

Functional skills

While working through this section, you will be covering **FM 2.2.1–2**, which relate to applying a range of mathematics skills to find solutions, using appropriate checking procedures and evaluating their effectiveness at each stage.

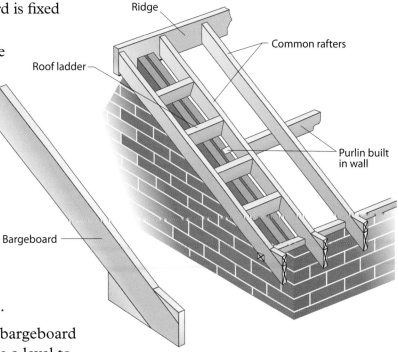

Figure 3.63 Roof ladder with bargeboard fixed

Eaves details

The eaves are where the lower part of the roof is finished where it meets the wall, and they incorporate fascia and soffit. The fascia is the vertical board fixed to the ends of the rafters. It is used to close the eaves and allow fixing for rainwater pipes.

The soffit is the horizontal board fixed to the bottom of the rafters and the wall. It is used to close the roof space to prevent birds or insects from nesting there, and usually incorporates ventilation to help prevent rot.

There are various ways of finishing a roof at the eaves. The following are the four most common.

Flush eaves

Here the eaves are finished as close to the wall as possible. There is no soffit, but a small gap is left for ventilation.

Open eaves

Open eaves are where the bottom of the rafter feet are planed as they are exposed. The rafter feet project beyond the outer wall and eaves boards are fitted to the top of the rafters to hide the underside of the roof cladding. The rainwater pipes are fitted via brackets fixed to the rafter ends.

Closed eaves

Closed eaves are completely closed or boxed in. The ends of the rafters are cut to allow the fascia and soffit to be fitted. The roof is ventilated either by ventilation strips incorporated into the soffit or by holes drilled into the soffit with insect-proof netting over them. If closed eaves are to be re-clad due to rot you must ensure that the ventilation areas are not covered up.

Sprocketed eaves

Sprocketed eaves are used where the roof has a sharp pitch. The **sprocket** reduces the pitch at the eaves, slowing down the flow of rainwater and stopping it overshooting the guttering. Sprockets can either be fixed to the top edge of the rafter or bolted onto the side.

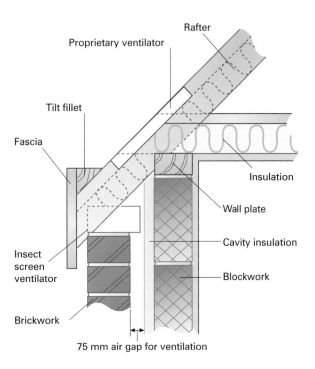

Figure 3.64 Flush eaves

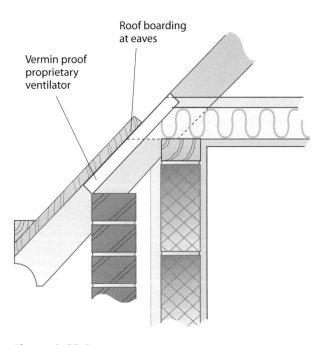

Figure 3.65 Open eaves

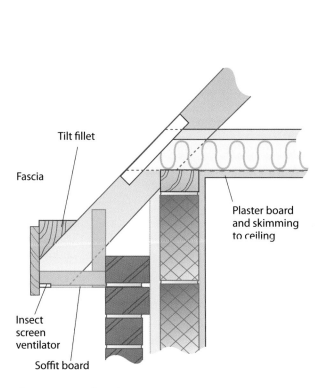

Figure 3.66 Closed eaves

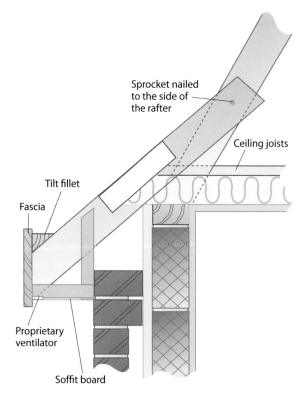

Figure 3.67 Sprocketed eaves

Roof coverings

Once all the rafters are on the roof, the final thing is to cover it. There are two main methods of covering a roof, each using different components. Factors affecting the choice of roof covering include what the local weather is like and what load the roof will have to take.

Method 1

This method is usually used in the north of the country where the roof may be expected to take additional weight from snow.

1. Clad the roof surface with a man-made board such as OSB or exterior grade plywood.

2. Cover the roof with roofing felt starting at the bottom and ensuring the felt is overlapped to stop water getting in.

3. Fit the felt battens (battens fixed vertically and placed to keep the felt down while allowing ventilation) and the tile battens (battens fixed horizontally and accurately spaced to allow the tiles to be fitted with the correct overlap).

4. Finally, fit the tiles and cement on the ridge.

Key term

Sprocket – a piece of timber bolted to the side of the rafter to reduce the pitch at eaves

Did you know?

Where you live may have an effect on your choice of roof: in areas more prone to bad weather, the roof will need to be stronger.

Method 2

This is the most common way of covering a roof.

1. Fit felt directly onto the rafters.

2. Fit the tile battens at the correct spacing.

3. Fit the tiles and cement on the ridge.

Another way to cover a roof involves using slate instead of tiles. Slate-covered roofing is a specialised job as the slates often have to be cut to fit, so roofers usually carry this out.

Working life

You have been asked to quote for building a garage. The client is unsure about what type of roof to have. They ask your opinion.

What type of roof would you select? Just as with the other components of the garage, you will need to think about the likely use of the roof, the shape and design that will fit the client's requirements and the conditions it will probably be experiencing. Why would you select that type of roof? What could influence your selection?

Energy conservation in roofing

A roof serves several functions: it protects the building from the elements, directs water into gutters and makes the building look aesthetically pleasing. A roof must also meet the requirements of Part L of the Building Regulations, which detail the levels of insulation that must be included to achieve the required U-value.

Waterproofing, ventilation and insulation are crucial in making a roof efficient and long lasting, and contribute to the energy efficiency and sustainability of the whole structure.

A pitched roof is made from the following.

- Softwood rafters span from the ridge to the eaves and are fixed to a wall plate, which is strapped to the internal skin of the wall.

- The rafters are then covered with a felt or a breathable membrane, which stops moisture entering the building if the roof tiles are weakened.

- The felt or membrane is held in place with tile battens manufactured from treated softwood, which are fixed to the rafters using galvanised nails.

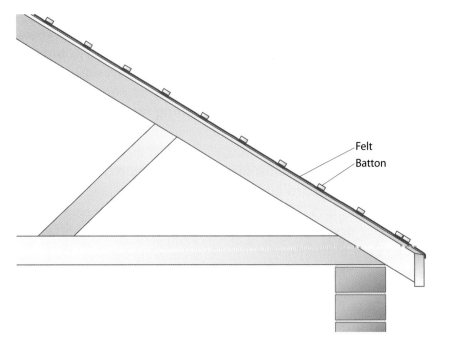

Figure 3.68 Cross section of a pitched roof showing positioning of felt and battens

Felt
Batton

Insulation

The insulation can be placed in two locations:

- between and over ceiling joists – up to 300 mm of mineral wool insulation (manufactured from glass or rock) is laid, 150 mm between the joists and 150 mm at 90 degrees to this, to form the full thickness
- between or over rafters – form insulation boards are cut and fitted between roof timbers or, with a loft conversion, are laid over the joists before the tile battens and tiling are fitted.

Waterproofing, damp-proofing and ventilation

The ridge is where the two rafters meet at the top of the roof. A fascia and soffit complete the eaves detail of the roof and make it waterproof. Ventilation is provided to prevent the air stagnating, which could lead to the roof timbers rotting. Ventilation may be provided to the roof by placing vents into the soffit or on top of the fascia. In this case, insulation is placed in two layers: one between the ceiling joists, and the other perpendicular to the first layer.

Valleys are formed where two roofs meet within an internal corner. Here a valley board is formed using plywood, which is covered with a flashing to stop water entering. All roof abutments, such as chimneys, must have flashings placed around them to make sure that water cannot get in, causing problems with damp and rot.

Roof tiles

Roof tiles tend to be chosen to fit in with the local environment, and are often made of local materials: for example, slate in Wales. Most modern roof tiles are manufactured from concrete and have an interlocking system to stop water getting into the roof space.

Guttering

> **Did you know?**
>
> In the past, guttering used to be manufactured from timber or cast iron.

With both pitched and flat roofs (see below), guttering must be fixed to the fascia board laid to falls, so that rainwater can be directed to fall pipes. The fall pipes connect the guttering to the surface water drainage system. Modern guttering is manufactured from uPVC or aluminum.

Flat roofs

Flat roofs have notoriously short lifespans due to the low pitch and the continual heating and cooling cycle of the environment.

* Normally felt, manufactured with bitumen, is used to cover a plywood decking and is laid in three layers, each bonded with bitumen.
* Falls are produced by nailing timber firrings to the roof joists.
* Finally, the roof is covered with a layer of white spar chippings, which reflect the sunlight and prevent solar heat gain from damaging the roof.

With flat roofs, the insulation is set between the joists within the ceiling void or as cut-to-falls insulation, which is laid over the plywood decking and covered with roofing felt. Both methods need a vapour barrier to be fitted, to resist the passage of moisture.

Asphalt can be heated up to melting point it can be laid in a single layer onto the prepared roof, forming a single, impenetrable barrier. However, it is poisonous so is not often used in buildings today.

Materials used in external walling

External walls come in a variety of types, but the most common is cavity walling. Cavity walling is simply two masonry walls built parallel to each other, with a gap between acting as the cavity. The cavity wall acts as a barrier to weather, with the outer leaf preventing rain and wind penetrating the inner leaf. The cavity is usually filled with insulation to prevent heat loss.

Cavity walls

Cavity walls mainly consist of a brick outer skin and a blockwork inner skin. There are instances where the outer skin may be made of block and then rendered or covered by tile hanging. The minimum cavity size allowed is 75 mm but the cavity size is normally governed by the type and thickness of insulation to be used and whether the cavity is to be fully filled or partially filled with insulation.

The thickness of blocks used will also govern the overall size of the cavity wall. On older properties, the internal blocks were always of 100 mm thickness. Nowadays, due to the emphasis on energy conservation and efficiency, blocks are more likely to be 125 mm or more.

In all cases, the cavity size will be set out to the drawing with overall measurements specified by the architect and to local authority requirements.

Once the **foundations** have been concreted the **sub-structural walling** can be constructed, usually by using blocks for both walls (see Figure 3.69).

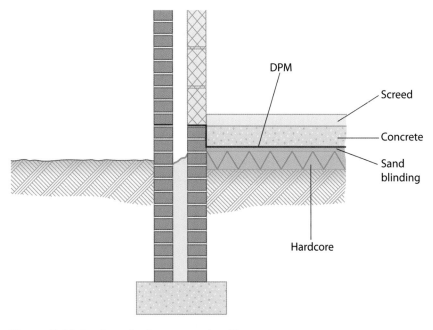

Figure 3.69 Section of sub-structural walling

In some situations trench blocks may be used below ground level and then traditional cavity work constructed up to the damp proof course (DPC). A horizontal DPC must be inserted at a minimum height of 150 mm above ground level to both walls. This is to prevent damp rising, below ground, up through the block and brickwork to penetrate to the inside. The cavity must also be filled with weak concrete to ground level to help the sub-structural walling resist lateral pressure.

Key terms

Foundations – concrete bases supporting walls

Sub-structural walling – brickwork between the foundation concrete and the horizontal damp proof course (DPC)

Remember

The correct size must be used for the internal wall, with the cavity size to suit.

> ### Key terms
>
> **Wall ties** – stainless steel or plastic fixings to tie cavity walls together
>
> **Bridge** – where moisture can be transferred from the outer wall to the inner leaf by material touching both walls
>
> **Window head** – top of a window

Cavity walls above DPC

The older traditional way to build a cavity wall is to build the brickwork first and then the blockwork. Now, due to the introduction of insulation into the cavity, the blockwork is generally built first, especially when the cavity is partially filled with insulation. This is because the insulation requires holding in place against the internal block wall, by means of special clips that are attached to the **wall ties**. In most cases the clips are made of plastic as they do not rust or rot. The reason for clipping the insulation is to stop it from moving away from the blocks, which would cause the loss of warmth to the interior of the building, as well as causing a possible **bridge** of the cavity, which could cause a damp problem.

The brick courses should be gauged at 75 mm per course but sometimes course sizes may change slightly to accommodate window or door heights. In most instances these positions and measurements are designed to work to the standard gauge size. This will also allow the blockwork to run level at every third course of brick, although the main reason will be explained in the wall tie section below.

On most large sites, patent types of corner profile are used rather than building traditional corners (see Figure 3.70). These allow the brickwork to be built faster and, if set up correctly, more accurately. But they must also be marked for the gauge accurately and it makes sense to mark window cill heights or **window heads** and door heights, so they do not get missed, which would result in brickwork being taken down.

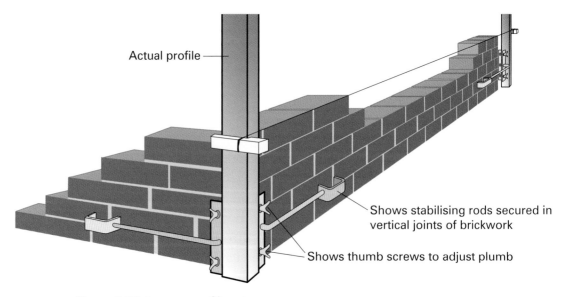

Actual profile

Shows stabilising rods secured in vertical joints of brickwork

Shows thumb screws to adjust plumb

Figure 3.70 A corner profile set-up

Wall ties

Wall ties are a very important part of a cavity wall as they tie the internal and external walls together, resulting in a stronger job. If we built cavity walls to any great height without connecting them together, the walls would be very unstable and could possibly collapse.

A wall tie should be:

- rust-proof
- rot-proof
- of sufficient strength
- able to resist moisture.

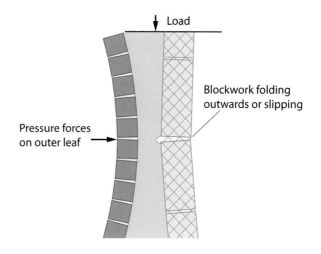

Figure 3.71 Section of wall without wall ties

There are many designs of wall tie currently on the market, with a wide selection suitable for all types of construction methods. One of the most common types used when tying together brick and block leaves is the masonry general purpose tie. These ties are made from very strong stainless steel, and incorporate a twist in the steel at the midpoint of the length. This twist forms a drip system, which prevents the passage of water from the outer to the inner leaf of the structure.

Figure 3.72 General purpose wall tie

You must take care to keep the wall ties clean when they are placed in the wall: if bridging occurs, it may result in moisture penetrating the internal wall.

The positioning and density of wall ties

In cavity walling where both the outer and inner leaves are 90 mm or thicker, you should use ties at not less than 2.5 per square metre, with 900 mm maximum horizontal distance by a maximum 450 mm vertical distance and staggered.

At positions such as vertical edges of an opening, unreturned or unbonded edges and vertical expansion joints, you need to use additional ties at a maximum of 300 mm in height (usually 225 mm to suit block course height) and located not more than 225 mm from the edge. Wall ties should be bedded into each skin of the cavity wall to a minimum distance of 50 mm.

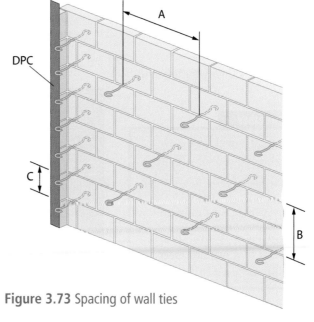

Figure 3.73 Spacing of wall ties

A 900 mm maximum horizontal distance
B 450 mm maximum vertical distance
C Additional ties, 300 mm maximum vertical distance

Unit 3003 Knowledge of building methods and construction technology 3

Keeping a cavity wall clean

It is important to keep the cavity clean to prevent dampness. If mortar is allowed to fall to the bottom of the cavity it can build up and allow the damp to cross and enter the building. Mortar can also become lodged on the wall ties and create a bridge for moisture to cross. We can prevent this by the use of **cavity battens**, pieces of timber the thickness of the cavity laid on to the wall ties and attached by wires or string (to prevent dropping down the cavity) to the wall and lifted alternately as the wall progresses.

The bottom of the wall can be kept clean by either leaving bricks out or bedding bricks with sand so they can be taken out to clean the cavity. These are called core holes and are situated every fourth brick along the wall to make it easy to clean out each day. Once the wall is completed the bricks are bedded into place.

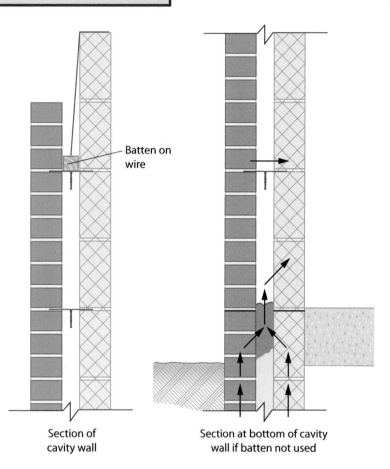

Batten on wire

Section of cavity wall

Section at bottom of cavity wall if batten not used

Figure 3.74 Cavity batten in use

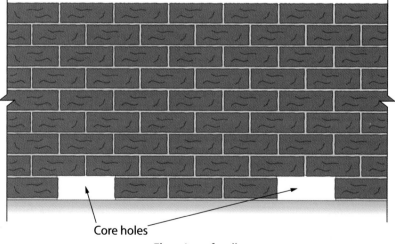

Core holes

Elevation of wall

Figure 3.75 Core holes

Steps to take to prevent damp penetration

- Set out openings carefully to avoid awkward bonds.
- Care is needed in construction to make sure dampness or water does not enter the building.
- DPCs and wall ties should be carefully positioned.
- Steel cavity lintels should have minimum 150 mm bearings solidly bedded in the correct position.
- **Weep holes** should be put in at 450 mm centres immediately above the lintel in the outer leaf.

No insulation has been shown in the drawings because they only show one situation. In most cavity wall construction, insulation of one kind or another will have to be incorporated to satisfy current Building Regulations.

Fire spread

In addition to the prevention of damp penetration and cold bridging, there is a requirement under the Building Regulations that cavities and concealed spaces in a structure or fabric of a building are sealed by using cavity barriers or fire stopping. This cuts down the hidden spread of smoke or flames in the event of fire breaking out in a building.

Closing at eaves level

The cavity walls have to be 'closed off' at roof level for two main reasons:

1. to prevent heat loss and the spread of fire
2. to prevent birds or vermin entering and nesting.

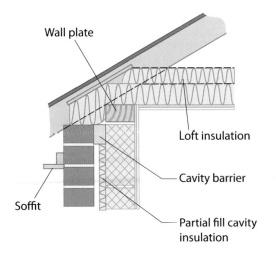
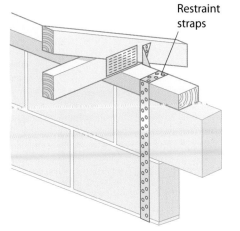

Figure 3.76 Roof section

This area of the wall is where the roof is connected, by means of a timber wall plate bedded on to the inner leaf. The plate is then secured by means of restraint straps that are galvanised ' shaped straps screwed to the top of the wall plate and down the blockwork. This holds the roof structure firmly in place and also prevents the roof from spreading under the weight of the tiles, etc. The minimum distance that the straps should be apart is 1.2 m. In some instances they may be connected directly from the roof truss to the wall.

If a gable wall is required, restraint straps should be used to secure the roof to the end wall (see Figure 3.76).

The external wall can be built to the height of the top of the truss so as not to leave gaps, or 'closed off' by building blocks laid flat to cover the cavity above the external soffit line from inside, avoiding damp penetration. In some instances the cavity may be left open with the cavity insulation used as the seal.

Insulation properties of cavity walls

Cavity walls are insulated mainly to prevent heat loss and therefore save energy. The Building Regulations tell us how much insulation is required in various situations, and in most cases this would be stipulated in the specification for the relevant project to obtain planning permission from the local council.

Cavity insulation can be either rock wool or polystyrene beads.

There are three main ways to insulate the cavity:

1. total or full fill
2. partial fill
3. injection (after construction).

Total or full fill

Figure 3.77 shows a section of a total fill cavity wall. The cavity is completely filled with insulation 'batts' as the work proceeds. The batts are 450 mm x 1200 mm, are made of mineral fibres, and placed between the horizontal wall ties.

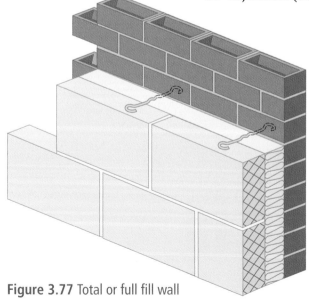

Figure 3.77 Total or full fill wall

Partial fill

Figure 3.90 shows a partial filled cavity, where the cavity insulation batts are positioned against the inner leaf and held in place by a plastic clip. More wall ties than usual are used to secure the insulation in place.

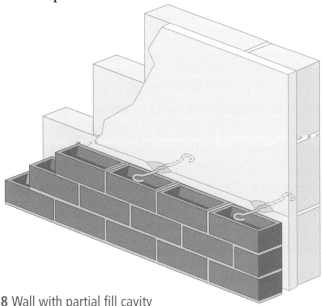

Figure 3.78 Wall with partial fill cavity

Injection

This is where the insulation is injected into the cavity after the main structure of the building is complete. Holes are drilled into the inner walls at about 1 m centres and the insulation is pumped into the cavity. The two main materials used are rock wool fibreglass or polystyrene granules. The holes are then filled with mortar. If an older property were injected, then the holes would be drilled into the external mortar joints.

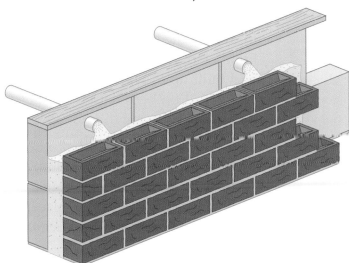

Figure 3.79 Wall being injected

> **Remember**
>
> When injecting insulation, great care must be taken not to drill the bricks as they will be difficult and costly to replace.

There are three key points regarding insulating cavity walls.

1. Handle and store insulation material carefully to avoid damage or puncturing.

2. Cavities should be clean.

3. Read drawing specifications and follow manufacturers' instructions carefully.

Timber-framed construction

This type of timber-framed construction is a recent method of construction, and is highly efficient at preventing heat loss. The timber frame is the main means of structural support. In timber-framed construction, the traditional internal skin of block work has been replaced by timber-framed panels, which support the load of the structure. The breather membrane allows the passage of vapour in one direction so that the timber can 'breathe', but moisture is not allowed back in – the internal vapour barrier does not allow moisture to pass into the plasterboard.

The insulation within timber-framed construction is kept 'warm' by being placed within the warm side of the construction. It is protected by the vapour barrier and breather membrane.

The outside skin of a timber-framed building can be clad in several different materials, from a traditional brick skin of facing brickwork to rendered blockwork, which is painted.

Timber-kit houses are becoming more and more popular as they can be erected wind-tight and watertight within a few days.

Constructing timber-kit houses

Timber-kit house construction starts off in exactly the same way as any house build, with the foundations and the cavity wall built up to DPC level. Then the preformed timber sections can be erected. These can be made to most specific designs from an architect.

The timber panels are lifted into place (usually by crane) and are bolted together. Once the wall panels are in place, the exterior face brickwork can begin.

> **Find out**
>
> Find a breather membrane supplier and have a close look at the specification for this material.

> **Remember**
>
> There must be a way for any trapped moisture to be 'breathed out' or the timbers could deteriorate.

Figure 3.80 Timber-framed construction

There are also other types of exterior walling, such as solid stone or log cabin style. Industrial buildings may have steel walls clad in sheet metal.

Using timber-framed construction

Using timber-framed construction delivers a range of advantages. It is quick to erect thus saving labour costs, there is no significant difference in price between block or timber frame and there are fewer delays due to bad weather.

Timber-framed systems are suited to brownfield sites with poor soil conditions as construction is lighter than traditional brick and block builds and the modular components are easy to transport to site. Timber frame complies to the codes of sustainability and environmental requirements to timber including responsible sourcing, waste reduction in materials, airtightness and sound insulation. As well as wood being a carbon neutral material timber frame has the lowest CO_2 cost of any commercially available building material as timber is an organic, non-toxic and naturally renewable building material.

Solid walls

Occasionally, during refurbishment work, you may come upon an existing wall that is of solid construction. This tends to be in older houses from the 1890s, where solid brick walls were laid in English bond, with alternate courses of headers and stretchers. This method of construction did not contain a cavity or any insulation, and as such is not thermally efficient.

Walls for modern-day uninhabited rooms – for example, an outbuilding – can be solid-block walls that are rendered externally to prevent water getting in.

Find out

Find out the cost of a standard timber-kit panel, then compare the price to building an area the same size in traditional cavity walling.

Remember

Solid walls have to have high-quality brickwork and bonding with full mortar joints in order to prevent moisture getting in.

Working life

You are working on the first phase of a new housing complex. The construction type will be timber framed, with a brick outer skin. You have started the first course above DPC and the general foreman has told you to place the insulation between the breather membrane and the brick skin. You are not happy about this.

What might happen if you do what the foreman says? You will need to think about all the implications of what could happen during the construction, as well as the qualities of the materials that are to be used. What should you do?

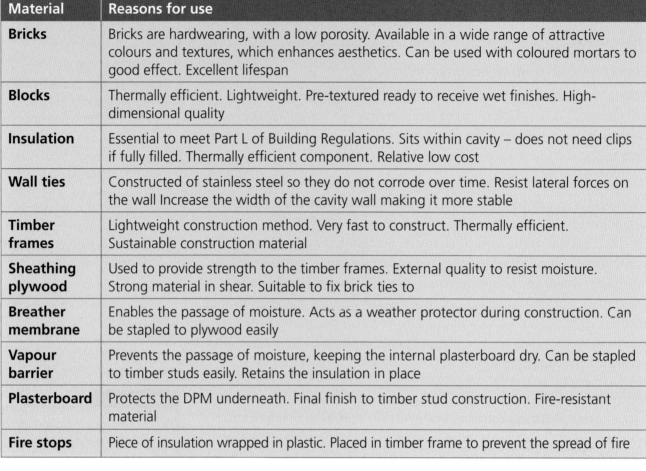

Material	Reasons for use
Bricks	Bricks are hardwearing, with a low porosity. Available in a wide range of attractive colours and textures, which enhances aesthetics. Can be used with coloured mortars to good effect. Excellent lifespan
Blocks	Thermally efficient. Lightweight. Pre-textured ready to receive wet finishes. High-dimensional quality
Insulation	Essential to meet Part L of Building Regulations. Sits within cavity – does not need clips if fully filled. Thermally efficient component. Relative low cost
Wall ties	Constructed of stainless steel so they do not corrode over time. Resist lateral forces on the wall Increase the width of the cavity wall making it more stable
Timber frames	Lightweight construction method. Very fast to construct. Thermally efficient. Sustainable construction material
Sheathing plywood	Used to provide strength to the timber frames. External quality to resist moisture. Strong material in shear. Suitable to fix brick ties to
Breather membrane	Enables the passage of moisture. Acts as a weather protector during construction. Can be stapled to plywood easily
Vapour barrier	Prevents the passage of moisture, keeping the internal plasterboard dry. Can be stapled to timber studs easily. Retains the insulation in place
Plasterboard	Protects the DPM underneath. Final finish to timber stud construction. Fire-resistant material
Fire stops	Piece of insulation wrapped in plastic. Placed in timber frame to prevent the spread of fire

Table 3.02 Reasons for using different materials in external walling

> **Remember**
> Cost is just one of the factors that will affect the choice of material.

> **Remember**
> Any insulation that is retrofitted is normally put in by a specialist contractor after a building survey.

Comparison of insulation properties between cavity and timber-framed constructions

Existing cavity wall

A house that is over 50 years old will have been built with the level of insulation that was required at that time under legislation – which may mean none at all within the cavity wall. The insulation properties of the existing wall can be upgraded in three ways.

- The first is to use a foaming insulation, which is pumped in from the outside. You must take care with any gases that the insulation may give off.
- The second method is to use a blown glass fibre insulation, which is 'blown' under pressure through holes formed in the external brickwork to fill the cavity.
- The final method is to clad the internal walls with either insulation-backed plasterboard attached by dot and dab or timber battens clad in plasterboard. This method does reduce the internal dimensions of the room.

New cavity construction

This construction is much more thermally efficient, as you can look at reducing heat loss through the structure as a whole. Highly efficient internal blocks are used to form the internal skin, with a 100 mm cavity, which is fully filled using a mineral wool insulation material. The traditional brickwork skin is the same as for the older type of construction – this has not changed over the years.

Modern sheet insulation materials can also be used within cavity construction. Manufactured from high-performance rigid urethane, these materials use space age technology to resist the passage of heat, but may require clipping within a cavity to the wall ties. Therefore, the cavity is said to be partially filled, rather than fully filled.

Timber-framed construction

This is the most thermally efficient system. It uses insulation (usually quilted) fixed within the timber studs.

Again, rigid insulation products can be used to fill between the timber studs. You can increase the level of insulation by making the timber studs deeper in a mineral wall, or doubling up on rigid insulation boards.

Rigid insulation is normally covered with a foil surface that resists the passage of vapour and slows down the resistance of heat, reflecting it back towards the warm side of the construction.

Internal walling

Internal walls are either **load bearing** – meaning they support any upper floors or roof –- or are non-load bearing, used to divide the floor space into rooms.

Internal walls also come in a variety of styles. Here is a list of the most common types.

- **Solid block walls** – simple blockwork, either covered with plasterboard or plastered over to give a smooth finish, to which wallpaper or paint is applied. Solid block walls offer low thermal and sound insulation qualities, but advances in technology and materials mean that blocks manufactured from a lightweight aggregate can give better sound and heat insulation.
- **Solid brick walling** – usually made with face brickwork as a decorative finish. It is unusual for all walls within a house to be made from brickwork.

> **Find out**
>
> Find a rigid insulation manufacturer's details for a wall insulation board, and have a look at the fixing details.

> **Find out**
>
> Research the visual differences between cavity and timber-framed construction by using the Internet to research sketch drawings of a cross section through a wall, looking for sketches that clearly show the positioning of the insulation within the construction, for either rigid or quilt insulation materials.

> **Key term**
>
> **Load bearing** – walls that carry a load from floors, walls and roofs (dead load) and occupancy (live load)

> **Find out**
>
> Using the Internet and other sources of information, find out the thermal properties of both a timber stud wall and an internal solid block wall.

- **Timber stud walling** – more common in timber-kit houses and newer buildings. Timber stud walling is also preferred when dividing an existing room, as it is quicker to erect. Clad in plasterboard and plastered to a smooth finish, timber stud partitions can be made more fire resistant and sound/thermal qualities can be improved with the addition of insulation or different types of plasterboard. Another benefit of timber stud walling is that timber noggins can be placed within the stud to give additional fixings for components such as radiators or wall units. Timber stud walling can also be load bearing, in which case thicker timbers are used.

- **Metal stud walling** – similar to timber stud, except metal studs are used and the plasterboard is screwed to the studding.

- **Grounds lats** – timber battens that are fixed to a concrete or stone wall to provide a flat surface, to which plasterboard is attached and a plaster finish applied.

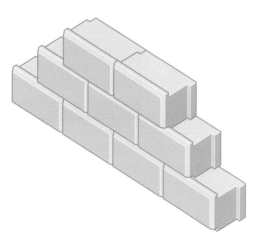

Figure 3.81 Solid block wall

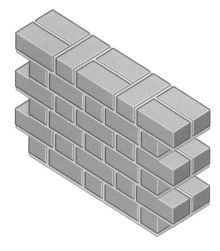

Figure 3.82 Solid brick wall

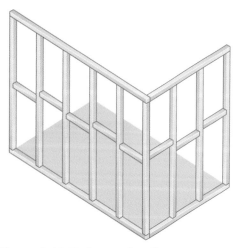

Figure 3.83 Timber stud wall

Figure 3.84 Metal stud wall

Working life

You have been tasked with creating an opening in an internal blockwork wall.

What can you do to check if the wall is load bearing? What should be done if the wall is load bearing? What could the consequences be if the wall is load bearing and you create the opening without shoring?

Energy saving materials in internal walls

Internal walls can either be load bearing or non-load bearing. If they are load bearing, they must be made of materials that can resist the load. In this section, you will investigate the sustainability and energy efficiency of the internal walls and linings most often used in modern construction.

Fair-faced blockwork

This is economical in terms of the energy used to produce the desired finish: the blockwork produces the completed finish itself, and no secondary wet or dry finishes (plastering or plasterboard) are applied. If the wall is not to be painted, a good-quality block must be chosen; if it is to be painted, paint-grade blocks are needed. You must consider the joints between blocks carefully when looking at the type of pointing required. This must be neat and applied to both sides of the wall.

Fair-faced concrete blockwork is an ideal solution for heavily trafficked areas, sports halls and other walls that need a hardwearing surface. However, it may take several coats of paint to produce an acceptable finish on the blockwork surfaces.

Timber stud walls

These are constructed using regulated timber studs of equal widths. These are attached to head and sole plates, at the top and floor level respectively. Noggins are added to aid stability and fixing of finishes.

Timber studs are a sustainable timber product. Putting up a timber stud wall is an efficient process, as the walls do not have to dry out and no scaffolding is needed. The studs are normally clad with a plasterboard skin on each side, which can be dry lined or skim plastered. With this type of wall, it is also quick and easy to distribute services around a building.

Safety tip

Load-bearing walls must not be altered without first providing temporary supports to carry the load until the work has been completed.

Figure 3.85 A traditional timber stud wall construction

Metal stud walls

In this system, timber studs are replaced by preformed metal channels. These are fixed together by crimping (using a special tool) or screwing. Metal studs are made with recycled steel, but do have to go through a galvanising process. However, their strength-to-weight ratio is better than timber. Plasterboard finishes are normally screwed into the studs using dry wall screws and a hand-held drill.

Both timber studs and steel channels can be recycled after final use.

> **Example**
>
> The architect is unsure which of the three systems to incorporate into the ground floor internal layout design. You have been asked to discuss the fixing side of the three methods.
>
> Prepare a few notes so that you can discuss these issues with your tutor, who will act as the architect.

Dry lining

This is the process that lines a surface – normally blockwork – with a plasterboard finish.

'Dot and dab' is a dry lining process. Plasterboard adhesive is applied in dabs to the surface of the wall, and plasterboard is pressed onto the adhesive dabs, then knocked until vertical and aligned with the wall, using a straight edge. A temporary fixing is often used to hold the board in place, and then removed once set. The joints of the plasterboard are bevelled so that a jointing finish tape and filler can be applied to complete the wall.

This process leaves an air gap behind the board, which makes the wall more energy-efficient in terms of heat loss. This dry lining process is useful in refurbishment work, where untidy walls can be easily covered up and upgraded to a quality finish, saving the need to replace whole walls.

Plastered blockwork

This is the least energy-efficient process because the finish has to dry out, using dehumidifiers and a heat source if necessary (for example, in winter). Wet plaster cannot be painted. A plaster coat is normally applied in two layers, the second being a trowelled and polished final finish that produces a smooth wall. There are various types of plasters to suit the surface the plaster is being applied to and the level of wear the wall will be subjected to.

> **Find out**
>
> British Gypsum and Knauf are the UK's leading plaster suppliers. Have a look at their websites and investigate the different types of plaster they manufacture. Can you find any information about sustainability on their websites?

Material	Reasons for use
Fair-faced blockwork	• Economical single process • Can be left as a self-finish • High-quality block available • Saves on secondary resources and energy • Greater sound resistance
Timber stud walls	• No wet construction • No drying-out time • Renewable resource • Lightweight construction • Traps air within void that can be insulated • Easy hiding of services
Metal stud walls	• Can incorporate recycled steel into manufacture • Good weight-to-strength ratio • Screwed physical fixing of linings • Internal void can be insulated
Dry lining	• Covers up untidy backgrounds • Forms air void behind • Can be used with insulation bonded to plasterboard • Quick, easy method of providing a smooth finish • Does not use wet trades • No drying out period
Plastered blockwork	• Traditional finish • Hardwearing • Easy to repair

Table 3.03 Reasons for using energy-saving materials in internal wall construction

K3. Know about sustainable methods and materials in construction work

As you work in the construction industry, you will come across a vast range of materials. But which of these are the most sustainable? This section gives an overview of the most common building materials, looking at how they are made and any issues to do with their use and disposal.

Remember

Many factors will affect the choice of a material; fashion is just one.

Remember

Sustainability means meeting the needs of future generations, without depleting **finite** resources.

Key term

Finite – a resource that can never be replaced once used

Sustainable materials used in construction

Materials	Sustainability
Polystyrene	• Petroleum-based product • Can be recycled • Pollution caused through manufacture • Often used as packaging for equipment • High insulation properties
Polyurethane	• Made from volatile organic compounds that damage the environment • Often turned into foams • Gives off harmful chemicals if burned • Disposal issues: If the foam catches fire, it causes pollution and produces carcinogenic gases
Softwood	• Can be recycled into other products • A managed resource that can be grown over and over again • Provides a pollution filter, takes in carbon dioxide gives out oxygen • A natural 'green' product • Requires treatment to prevent rot
Hardwood	• Forms part of the tropical rainforest • Intensively felled • Takes a longer time to re-grow than softwood • Expensive resource
Concrete	• Cement production causes CO_2 emissions • Disposal issues – can only be crushed and used as hardcore • Hardwearing with a long lifespan • Relies on a lot of formwork and falsework
Common brick	• Manufacture involves clay extraction, which has environmental issues • Waste areas form ponds • Uses finite gas energy to fire bricks
Facing brick	• Secondary process to produce the patterns and colours • Useful life of up to 100 years • Uses natural products
Engineering brick	• Hardwearing, with a long lifespan • Water resistant • Heavy to transport to site, so fuel costs increase
Aggregates	• Extracted from gravel pits, causing environmental damage • After extraction, water fills pits to produce another habitat

Materials	Sustainability
Glass fibre quilt	• Can use recycled glass in manufacture • High insulation value and long lifespan • High thermal insulation-to-weight ratio • Economical transport from factory to site
Mineral wool	• Manufactured from glass or rock • Provides a lightweight, high insulation product • Can be used in walls and roof spaces • Can use recycled glass
Plasterboard and plaster	• Disposal issues, creating landfill with high sulphate content • High wastage with cutting to size • Manufacture uses gypsum, a waste by-product • Recycling skip agreements in place with manufacturers
Concrete block	• Uses cement • Can incorporate waste products from power stations • Sustainable manufacturing process • Take-back recycling schemes for waste blocks
Thermal block	• High thermal efficiency • Low weight-to-strength ratio • Uses cement in manufacture additives to produce a block full of air bubbles
Metals	• Can use recycled scrap steel in manufacture • Requires secondary treatment to prevent rust • Non-ferrous metals have a long lifespan
Glass	• Can be completely recycled • Waste from cutting can be recycled • Issues with recycling: toughened glass has been heat treated as a secondary process, so needs special recycling techniques

Table 3.04 Sustainability of common materials

Using sustainable materials

The following materials are the most sustainable of those listed in Table 3.04. You will now take a closer look at their use in domestic and commercial dwellings.

Find out

Use the Internet to find out more about these different types of material and their common uses in constructing domestic and commercial buildings.

Figure 3.86 Using softwood to clad the outside of this building is an attractive and sustainable method that requires no treatment

Find out

Find a local ready-mixed concrete supplier and establish what concrete products they can supply.

Find out

Visit a brick manufacturer's website and find out about their sustainable practices.

Did you know?

You can use sheep's wool as a modern insulation product. It is a fantastic insulator and can 'breathe out' moisture.

Softwood

This naturally occurring timber product is grown more in Scandinavian countries, where growth is slower, producing a more structured wood grain. It must be processed then transported to the UK for further manufacture into timber products. Softwood should be purchased locally to save on transport costs. Timber can be used in the following areas of a building: the roof, floor joists and flooring, second fix joinery products, stud walls, windows and doors. Timber can be completely recycled into a further product, such as chipboard.

Concrete

This is only sustainable in that the finished product has a very long life. Cement production is costly to the environment in terms of energy used and emissions released to the atmosphere. Concrete can be recycled into a crushed hardcore but no recycled materials can be used in its manufacture. Concrete is used in foundations, lintels, floors and some roof structures.

Common bricks

Common bricks are of lower quality and are used in areas where strength is required but facing bricks are not needed. They would be used as coursing bricks in internal skins of external walls and as levelling courses under floor joists.

Facing bricks

These are used where you can see the external brickwork as they look more attractive, but they are more expensive to make. They are mainly used for the external skin of a cavity wall or for garden walls where these have to match the house.

Engineering bricks

These are hard wearing, high-strength bricks that are water-resistant. They are used below DPC level as they are not affected by rising damp. They are an excellent brick to use within drainage manhole construction.

Aggregates

These are used for several purposes. Primarily they are constituents of concrete mixes, where a blend of coarse and fine aggregate plus cement and water is mixed to form concrete. A more modern application of aggregates is in external landscaping, where they are used to provide attractive areas that resist water run-off into the main drainage system, thereby adding to sustainable drainage for surface water.

Glass fibre quilt and mineral wool

These are used to insulate houses and commercial properties. They are used within ceiling voids above and between the joists. External walls use pre-cut 'batts' of mineral wool, which are built at full thickness into the cavity. Internal walls can also use mineral wool, but it must be of a heavier density, so as to resist the passage of sound. This type of insulation is very thermally efficient and will reduce heat loss from a building.

Metals

Using stainless steel in many building materials (such as wall ties) helps overcome corrosion problems. Mild-steel products require a secondary process, which could be galvanising, powder-coating or just a layer of paint. Metal is used in other products such as lintels, joist hangers and roof truss fixings, and in aluminum windows. Non-ferrous metals are used in water pipes and fittings.

Glass

Glass is a versatile material, used mainly in windows. In certain areas, only safety glass can be used. Glass can be manufactured from up to 80 per cent recycled product. It is transported in standard sheets from the factory to the supplier, who then cuts it to size locally. Any waste can be fully recycled, either locally or via the manufacturer.

Using different sustainable materials

Modern construction methods have been developed in response to the new legislation on sustainability.

Cavity walling

Thirty years ago, it was quite acceptable to build a cavity 75 to 85 mm wide that had very little insulation included in its construction. Modern methods of cavity wall construction now allow for a cavity that is 100 mm wide and is fully filled with glass fibre cavity wall batt insulation, with an engineered lightweight internal skin of blockwork. On page 116 you saw how spaced stainless steel wall ties are used to provide structural integrity to the completed wall, and how the insulation is not clipped.

In commercial buildings, cavity walls tend to be used in the bottom storey, while portal-framed construction with insulated cladding is usually used for the upper half of the unit.

Figure 3.87 Example of glass fibre quilt

Figure 3.88 Solar panels on a domestic dwelling

Knowledge of building methods and construction technology 3 **Unit 3003**

Timber-framed construction

Timber-framed construction is a fast, easy and efficient method of producing domestic buildings, and is sustainable in its approach as it uses timber from managed forests.

With timber-framed construction, the insulation is placed internally between the studs and covered with a vapour barrier and plasterboard. A traditional skin of brickwork clads the exterior, and a cavity can be formed by covering the plywood panels with a breathable membrane. Stainless steel ties are screwed to the plywood to provide support for the brickwork.

The floors and roof are traditionally constructed, but the timber-framed panels can be prefabricated off site, which can have its own implications for energy efficiency.

Alternative construction methods

A number of other energy-efficient construction methods are growing in popularity.

Insulated concrete formwork

This is the 'Lego brick' construction method where hollow, moulded polystyrene forms are literally snapped together to form a wall, with the help of locating **castellations** on each form. Reinforcing rods are added where required and concrete is poured into the moulds and allowed to set. A solid wall is formed that can be rendered externally and plastered internally. Traditional brick cladding can be used externally to clad the structure.

Insulated concrete formwork is faster and more energy-efficient than more traditional construction methods as it uses less concrete, saves on site resources (for example, no bricklayers are needed), and the insulation is included as part of the formwork. Once constructed, the formwork can simply be rendered and plastered.

Insulated panel construction

This is a system that uses insulation bonded to the plywood panels that form a structural wall. Traditional cladding – both external and internal – can then be used to cover the insulated panel frames, using the same process as with the timber-framed construction.

Find out

Locate a local timber frame manufacturer and research their methods of construction, to see what external cladding materials can be used to cover the frame.

Key term

Castellation – having turrets like a castle

Did you know?

Castellation comes from the word for castle – castellations have the staggered profile you often see at the top of castle walls.

Remember

Pouring concrete requires protection by using appropriate PPE.

Figure 3.89 Energy-efficient insulated framework

This construction method uses pre-formed factory panels that can be readily assembled on site, saving time and resources, and finishing trades can come in earlier than usual, while the outer skin is being completed. The insulated panels are also highly thermally efficient.

Thin joint masonry

This is a system that uses high-quality dimensioned blocks that are up to three times the size of normal blocks. A cement-based adhesive is used to bond the locks together using 1 mm tight joints. The starting base course of brickwork has to be very accurate in its setting out and level. Traditional cavities are formed using helix type wall ties that are just driven into the thin joint masonry using a hammer.

This uses lightweight, thermally efficient blocks with no mortar, so it is faster and cheaper to construct, there is less waste, and the end product is very energy efficient.

The impact of sustainability on the different elements of a structure

The substructure

Foundations need to be accurately set out to prevent wastage of materials: for example, the concrete in the foundations.

Cement manufacture is one of the processes that uses a high amount of energy and produces high carbon emissions. For example, by making a foundation larger than you require – perhaps because of an overdig by the excavator – you are using more material than you need to. As well as costing the client more, this will waste energy.

Sustainable excavation involves not removing the excavated material from the site. Removing excavated material incurs tip charges, which are part of the landfill tax. Dumping of waste into the land is now not a cheap option. By forming landscaped mounds on site, which can be planted and made into attractive green areas, you can increase the environmentally friendly impact of the excavation and save valuable resources in several ways, including reduced fuel charges, transport costs, air pollution and taxation.

The depth to which foundations have to be taken is governed by Building Control inspection. However, optical and levelling equipment such as profile boards and a **traveller** must be used to make sure the foundation depth is set out accurately, which will reduce wastage and hence energy use.

Unit 3003

Knowledge of building methods and construction technology 3

Generally, the deeper the foundation, the more expensive and more energy-consuming it is to produce. Deep strip and wide strip are expensive, and it could be better to use piled/ground beam foundations and raft foundations. These foundation types do not require deep, wasteful excavations on site. The soil report and site conditions will need careful consideration at the design stage to produce an energy-efficient design that supports the building's loads safely.

Functional skills

This exercise will allow you to practise **FM 2.3.1** Interpret and communicate solutions to multistage practical problems.

Working life

Your client is adamant that all excavated materials are to be removed from site. There is a large, open space at the rear of the development.

How would you convince the client of the benefits of leaving and landscaping the excavated material on site? You will need to think about the possible implications to the land and the project.

Cavity walls

Cavity walls rely on the external brick skin to keep the impact of the weather elements from crossing the cavity. The inner leaf of blockwork is now thermally engineered to trap as much air into its structure as possible, making it lightweight and easy to handle. Openings in cavity walls must be fitted into the construction properly to maximise their energy efficiency.

Figure 3.90 Blockwork, brick and insulation used in cavity wall construction

Insulating timber partitions/floors/roofs

Insulating between timbers – whether joists or studs – is simply a matter of placing either glass/rock wool or polystyrene between the timbers, with thicker insulation placed between joist roof spaces.

Insulating water pipes

All water pipes in a loft space or on exterior walls must be insulated to protect them from freezing, which may cause them to crack. There are two methods used when insulating pipes: mineral wool matting or pre-formed moulded insulation.

Figure 3.91 Insulation being fitted between timber

- **Mineral wool mat** – a small mat is wrapped around the pipes with a bandage and secured with tape or string. The pipes must be completely covered with no gaps, and taps and stopcocks must also be covered.

- **Preformed moulded insulation** – this is available to suit different sizes of pipe, and specially formed sections are available for taps and stopcocks. The mouldings can be cut at any angle to fit around bends and when installed the sections of insulation should be taped together to ensure that they are fully enclosed around the pipes and are tightly butted up to one another.

Insulating water tanks

Any water tanks in the loft space should be insulated around the sides and on the top. The insulation around the sides must extend down to the insulation on the floor of the loft. Insulation jackets are available to fit most sizes and styles of tank.

Figure 3.92 Insulating pipework using mineral wool

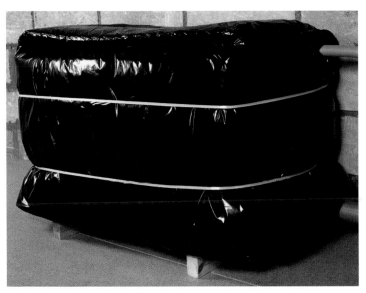

Figure 3.93 Insulation jacket used to protect water tanks against freezing

Figure 3.94 Use of preformed mouldings to insulate pipework

Key term

FENSA – Fenestration Self-Assessment scheme, under which window installers agree to install to certain standards

Find out

Use the Internet and other sources to find out the thermal value of a same-sized piece of polystyrene and mineral wool, then compare.

Preventing heat loss in windows and doors

A specialist **FENSA** installer should be used to supply and fit new uPVC windows and doors. These will meet the agreed insulation standard set by the Building Regulations. The cavity should be closed using a thermal bridging product that insulates across the cavity and acts as a DPM, if required.

Selecting appropriate materials for sustainability

When choosing materials, you should consider a number of factors that impact on energy efficiency and sustainability. These include the following.

- **Is it recyclable?** Ideally the material selected should be recyclable, at least at the end of its life, as should any wastage generated during its use or installation.

- **Is it local?** If the material is available locally, this reduces the cost of transporting it from the supplier to the construction site.

- **What are the transport implications?** The weight of the product will have an effect on the cost of its transport and the amount of fuels expended in getting it to the site.

- **How much waste is there?** A product that produces no wastage is valuable in terms of not having to throw away valuable resources and the energy that they have used in manufacture.

- **Is it a natural product?** A product that is produced naturally, for example growing timber, can be replenished time and time again.

- **Is it environmentally friendly?** A material that does not damage the environment in its manufacture and use is a sustainable product that is often referred to as a 'green product'.

- **What is its lifespan?** A longer lifespan, with as little maintenance as possible, means that less energy and resources will have to be put into the product in the future, which saves valuable future resources.

- **Is it worth spending more now?** A material that does not need, for example, painting every five years will save on energy time and costs. Spending a bit more money now will save future expenditure.

Effects of water, frost, chemicals and heat on materials

Many of the materials used in a building project can have their lifespan reduced by the effects of damp, water, frost and chemicals. Treating problems like this early – or, better still, preventing them from happening in the first place – is part and parcel of good environmentally aware building practice.

Effect of water

Masonry

Efflorescence is one cause of the effects of moisture migrating within a new brick structure. Water moves through the mortar into the brickwork causing salts to move to the outside of the newly constructed wall, this process is known as primary efflorescence. The water evaporates leaving a white deposit on the surface of the brick. It can be brushed off and the action of weathering will eventually remove the effect.

Concrete

The effect of water on concrete is to discolour its initial fresh new look from the airborne pollution that is present in the atmosphere and which is picked up within rainfall. Water staining on concrete where the designer has not detailed for the run-off from the building is another obvious effect. Water action within less porous concrete can result in the leaching of alkaline particles ('lime leaching') through the concrete that form deposits very much like those within caves.

Timber – wet and dry rot

This is caused by two different elements. Wet rot is caused by excessive exposure to moisture, which eventually causes the breakdown of the timber cells so that they rot and deteriorate. Dry rot is caused by a fungus that sends out long threads, which attack and eat away at the cells of the timber, causing structural damage.

Metal

Rust is caused by the oxidation of a ferrous metal. For the reaction to occur, three things must be present: metal, water and oxygen. Rust forms as an orange deposit on the surface of the metal. If it goes untreated, it will continue to eat away at the metal, eventually compromising its strength.

Find out

Have a look at some of the newly constructed houses in your location and see if you can spot some efflorescence appearing on new brickwork.

Figure 3.95 An example of efflorescence on brickwork

Remember

All of the above defects can be remedied through good design, quality workmanship and materials and effective maintenance.

Find out

What do the terms 'Grade A' and 'Grade B' mean on engineering bricks?

Find out

The Building Regulations specify the inclusion of DPCs and DPMs into the substructure construction. Find out which section of the regulations cover this aspect and establish exactly what is required.

Key term

Sand blinding – thin layer of lean concrete, gravel or sand applied to fill voids and provide a smoother, cleaner, drier and more durable finish.

Figure 3.96 The effects of spalling on brickwork

Damp

Damp can cause many problems in a building, and the damage it causes can be costly and difficult to repair. A range of methods and materials can be used to help stop damp getting into a structure.

- **DPCs** – placed within the skins of the external walls; always 150 mm above finished ground level.
- **Slate** – used traditionally as a barrier to resist the passage of moisture; still found in older external cavity walls; can still be used as a DPC, but commonly replaced by plastic DPC.
- **Engineering brick** – Grade A quality brick, so dense it naturally resists the passage of water, can be used below DPC to act as an additional barrier to rising damp.
- **Pitch polymer** – a bitumen-type DPC sometimes seen in external walls; can squeeze out of the joint due to pressure and heat; seldom used today.
- **PVC** – the most common type of DPC in use today; economical and easy to bed into the joint; often textured to bond to the mortar above and below the joint.
- **Injected** – a chemical DPC is injected into the wall to prevent the passage of moisture; used as a cheap refurbishment technique as you do not have to remove brickwork; internal plaster often removed up to 1 m high and wall replastered with a renovating plaster after injection work is complete.
- **DPMs** – placed under floors to prevent rising damp from entering warm floor; tucked into DPC within the external wall, thus 'tanking' the construction against damp.
- **Visqueen** – common trade name for a 1200-gauge plastic product tough enough to withstand tearing but which will bend around corners. **NB** hardcore beneath DPM should always be **sand-blinded** to prevent rupture of DPM.
- **Bituthene** – a sheet material manufactured from bitumen that can be laid in sheets, lapped, and used both horizontally and vertically; mainly used for waterproofing basement walls; must be used in accordance with manufacturer's instructions.

Effects of frost

Spalling

Spalling is the action of freezing water on the surface of a porous brick. The freezing action causes water to expand, pushing flakes of brickwork from the brick face. The photograph in Figure 3.96 clearly illustrates this action, which leaves the stronger mortar joints proud of the original brickwork face.

Thermal expansion

The Building Regulations clearly state the specification for expansion joints within brickwork external walls. These allow the brickwork to expand in the summer months and contract in the winter months without showing signs of cracking. Thermal movement may appear as complete cracks across bricks vertically.

Timber and concrete are good at resisting the effects of frost or freezing water. Exposed timber will maintain its structural integrity for many years. Concrete, once damaged, allows water to enter; if this meets any exposed reinforcing bars, then problems will occur.

Effects of chemicals

Concrete can be attacked by certain chemicals.

Carbon dioxide from the air can react with certain chemicals in the concrete. This decreases the protective alkali which ensures that the steel reinforcement does not rust. Once this bond is broken, then rusting can occur as the concrete expands and spalls away from the reinforcement bars.

Sulphates that come into contact with the cement in concrete can attack the chemical bond of the cement, affecting its strength. Sulphate-resistant cement (SRC) and not Ordinary Portland Cement (OPC) must be used where this is a risk: for example, where groundwater is contaminated.

Sulphates can also attack the brickwork cement mortar, especially with a chimney where coal is being burned. Sulphates eat away the cement mortar joints, the reaction causes the joint to expand and the chimney can start to lean over.

Chlorides have been used in the past to alter the setting times of concrete. Unfortunately, over time these affect the strength of concrete, which can have a disastrous effect if the material is under excessive loading conditions.

Alkali silicate is present in some concrete aggregates. This can react with the cement and water and expand, causing a pop-out of the concrete surrounding the reaction. This can have an adverse effect on structural concrete.

Acid rain – a product of burning fossil fuels – also has an effect on certain building materials. Natural stone is mostly affected, as acid rain eats away at the surface of the stone, causing long-term damage.

Did you know?

Brickwork expansion joints will need taking right through the cavity and the internal block skins.

Safety tip

With any chemical process, always refer to the supplier's safety data sheet for instructions.

Find out

Research the properties of SRC cement and when you need to use it instead of OPC.

Find out

The client is not happy with the efflorescence that is appearing on the first phase handover of homes and has asked for some remedial action. Research this effect and make recommendations to the client, justifying your remedy.

Effects of heat, fire and water

Masonry

Brickwork and blockwork cope well in a fire within a dwelling or commercial property. Extreme heat can cause masonry to expand and crack but this would be a substantial time after evacuation of a building. Fire is used in a kiln to harden bricks so they are more than capable of staying stable in a fire. Smoke does, however, cause blackening to the surfaces of bricks and blocks. This can to some degree be washed off but may leave a permanent stain that requires decoration internally and power washing externally.

Water, as we have seen previously, when combined with a frost, or freezing conditions, causes spalling to the surface of the brickwork or the breakdown of the mortar joint due to weathering.

Concrete

Concrete can spall under the influence of fire. If the reinforcement lies near to the surface of the concrete and this heats up then it will expand at a different rate from the surrounding concrete. This expansion can cause cracking to the concrete structure. Concrete is fairly resilient to water damage and will dry out after wetting; but if the water contains contaminants then this can lead to the chemical attack of the cement within the concrete.

Timber

Heat and the presence of oxygen cause the combustion of timber by fire. The surface chars and eventually breaks down the structural integrity of the timber until it is burnt right through. Smoke damage can discolour timber which will then require decoration if it has not caught fire and charred. Water can damage timber by wetting which expands the **hygroscopic** material and causes dimensional change to the timber, which will eventually rot if this wetting persists.

Metal

Metal does not react well in a fire. As it heats up, the molecular structure weakens and it loses up to half its strength at over 500 degrees. This can cause the collapse of structures as the steel melts slightly and warps under extreme heat. However, this does take some time and may not affect the evacuation of a structure. Water reacts with exposed metal, as we have seen, to form rust. Surface rust is not harmful but continual exposure to the elements of unprotected metal will result in severe corrosion.

Find out

Consult your local newspaper's website and look up a building fire that has occurred in your area. Look for photographs to see what damage was caused.

Key term

Hygroscopic – a substance that attracts or absorbs moisture from the air

Remember

Building Regulations will make provisions for the building structure in the event of a fire.

Treating building materials to prevent the effects of deterioration

Many building materials can be treated with chemical products in order to extend their lifespan and to reduce the effects of deterioration over time.

Intumescent paint

This is a chemical-based paint that reacts with high temperatures. It foams and expands around the steelwork it is painted upon to protect it from the heat – giving the occupants of the building time to escape during a fire.

Figure 3.97 Treated timber decking

Paints

These are used to protect timber, brickwork, and metal work from the effects of water. They form a microscopic seal across the surface, preventing water penetration past this layer.

Water repellent

This can be painted onto the surface of exposed brickwork to allow water to run off the brick face more easily. This prevents it standing and absorbing into the brickwork, because if it freezes it can become a problem, as discussed above.

Vac Vac and tanalising

These are chemical pressure impregnation systems to chemically treat timber from fungi and insect attack. They fill the pore holes within the timber and kill off any wood-boring insect that attacks its structure. Fungi includes the dry rot spores and other cellulose eating organisms.

This timber treatment alters the colour of the natural timber, often to a green shade.

Sulphate-resistant cement (SRC)

This is a type of cement, containing chemicals and mineral aggregates, which resists the attack of sulphates within concrete and is used where this is detected by testing.

Injected damp proof courses

These use chemicals of various kinds and mixtures to form a chemical barrier within the brickwork after they have cured and filled the pores in the bricks. They have to be injected through holes drilled into the outer wall and sometimes in inner walls.

Methods used to rectify and prevent deterioration

There are methods that can be used to protect and repair materials even after they have been put in place.

Masonry and concrete

Masonry and concrete make a movement joint that allows the brick and block panels to expand and contract under thermal movement. A compressible board (Flexcell) is used within the joint which is sealed with a polysulphide joint to prevent water ingress. Joints within concrete slabs are very similar but the Flexcell is replaced with a material that is more resilient.

> **Find out**
>
> Have a look around at the built environment where you live and work. Analyse the brick and concrete buildings and see where the movement joints have been formed.

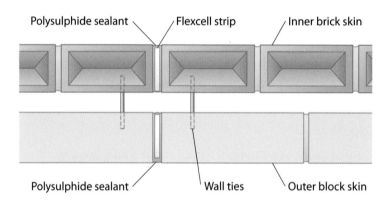

Polysulphide sealant — Flexcell strip — Inner brick skin

Polysulphide sealant — Wall ties — Outer block skin

Figure 3.98 Flexcell strip

Timber

Cutting and splicing in new timber is an age-old prevention method that saves having to remove the whole length of timber, manufacture a new piece and refit. Timber can be initially protected by pressure impregnation or it can be simply painted or stained using a flexible coating as the timber will expand and contract. This method of coating must be maintained to extend the lifespan of the timber and any damaged areas repaired quickly.

Insecticides or fungicidal washes will remove mould growth on timber but ventilation and quick drying of wet surfaces is the key to preventing this damage.

Methods used on metals to give galvanic protection and protective coatings

Galvanising using a hot dip process provides a good layer of protection to ordinary mild steel. The steel is fed through a bath of molten zinc, which coats the metal and gives it long lasting protection against water damage.

High-quality paints that are developed for bonding to steelwork should be used instead of galvanising where colour is required. A primer base coat is applied followed by several other coats that build up the film of paint. Powder coating steelwork is another process that can be used to coat the steel with a coloured protective layer.

Effects of adverse weather on building materials used in domestic and commercial dwellings

Water can be driven into a structure and this can occur in several ways: through the roof tiles and onto the underlay, through open windows or poor seals or through badly maintained brickwork mortar joints. This can lead to damage. The recent spate of floods within the UK have shown just what damage can occur to a property – even if the water did not enter the ground floor. Excessive rising damp can occur, which causes damage to internal finishes, timber wall plates and floor timbers if the water contains sewage particles. High volumes of floodwaters can cause buildings to move on their foundations from the water pressure or can, in fact, push over walls.

High levels of snowfall can produce heavy loads on structures that could lead to cracking or collapse of the roof structure. High winds each autumn also account for some damage to chimneys and walls as brickwork is blown over.

> **Find out**
>
> Find out the largest size of steelwork that can be powder coated, and gather some pictures of examples.

> **Functional skills**
>
> In answering the Check it out and Check your knowledge questions, you will be practising **FE 2.2.1** Select and use different types of texts to obtain relevant information, **FE 2.2.2** Read and summarise succinctly information/ideas from different sources and **FE 2.2.3** Identify the purposes of texts and comment on how effectively meaning is conveyed.
>
> You will also cover **FM 2.3.1** Interpret and communicate solutions to multistage practical problems.

FAQ

How do I know if the materials I am using are strong enough to carry the load?

The specification will give you the details of the sizes and types of material that are to be used. You will need to use this document when you need to know which materials to use.

Do I have to fix battens to the wall before I plasterboard it?

No, the method is called dot and dab and can be used where plaster is dabbed onto the back of the plasterboard and then pushed onto the wall.

How can I check my carbon footprint?

There are various websites that can allow you to calculate your own footprint, such as http://carboncalculator.direct.gov.uk. Use these to see how environmentally friendly you are being.

How do I know what the properties of materials are?

The supplier of the materials should be able to provide you with a data sheet that lists all the properties.

Check it out

1. Explain the reasons behind good environmental design and describe the key examples of this. Use the Internet and other sources of information to produce examples of each of these in practice.
2. In an area designated by your trainer, carry out a site survey. Make a detailed record of your results and complete a method statement explaining the process you followed.
3. Sketch the different ways of supporting trench excavations and explain the benefits of each.
4. Explain the factors that influence the design of a foundation and describe the benefits and features of each type of foundation.
5. Describe the difference between a single and a double floor on a suspended timber floor. Use sketches to illustrate your explanation.
6. With the aid of a sketch, explain the purpose of a joist hanger and how it functions.
7. Use sketches to show the different types of fall on a flat roof.
8. Describe why a cavity needs to be kept clean and outline the three steps to take to prevent damp penetration in a cavity wall.
9. Sketch sections through a suspended timber floor, showing how the flooring is supported.
10. Describe an 'I' type joist and the purpose of a roof ladder.
11. Explain how the effectiveness of insulation is measured and describe the qualities of the main types of insulation, explaining why insulation material is used.
12. A client is considering moving away from traditional brick cavity walls to produce domestic dwellings. Describe the benefits of two alternative methods that could be used and make a recommendation of which is best, explaining your reasons.
13. Identify key sustainable materials and explain their qualities, using sketches to illustrate their use.
14. Explain how to identify if a material is sustainable, and some of the methods used to protect timber and steel from decay.
15. You are working for a client who builds doctors' surgery centres. The current contract you are working on is a large medical centre. You have been asked by the client to recommend the finishes for the front of the centre due to your experience in using current sustainable materials. Assist the client by describing the advantages of cedar boarding over rendered blockwork.

Getting ready for assessment

The information contained in this unit, as well as continued practical assignments that you will carry out in your college or training centre, will help you with preparing for both your end-of-unit test and the diploma multiple-choice test. It will also aid you in preparing for the work that is required for the synoptic practical assignments.

The information in this unit will build on the information that you may have acquired during Level 2, Unit 2003, and will help you understand the basics of your own trade as well as basic information on several other trade areas.

You will need to be familiar with:

- new technologies and methods in construction
- energy efficiency in new construction buildings
- sustainable methods and materials in construction.

It is important to understand what other trades do in relation to you and how their work affects you and your work. It is also good to know how the different components of a building are constructed and how these tie in with the tasks that you carry out. You must always remember that there are a number of tasks being carried out on a building site at all times, and many of these will not be connected to the work you are doing. It is useful to remember the communication skills you learned in Unit 3002, as these will be important for working with other trades on site. You will also need to be familiar with specifications and contract documents to know the type of construction work other crafts will be doing around you on site. It is important that working drawings are precise in order to complete the structure accurately. You will need to be able to sketch a section through building elements and components.

A big focus of this unit has been on energy efficiency and sustainability in building. It is important to understand both the methods, and the benefits of these methods, when working on new constructions. For learning outcome three you will need to be able to select from and use a range of sustainable materials, choosing the correct equipment for the project. When working with these materials you will need to be able to identify how these can be affected by deterioration over long and short periods of time. As well as the impact of this on how the materials are used, you will also need to be able to organise the safe storage and protection of these building materials. Relating this information back into planning an environmentally friendly and sustainable project will be an important skill – both for your course and professionally.

This unit has explained a variety of different construction methods including modern, sustainable and energy efficient and the elements that are used in the construction. Although you will not be working on all these elements, you need to be familiar with the work undertaken on them in order to plan when to carry out your own work. You will need to be knowledgeable about different materials and their properties.

Good luck!

Knowledge check

1 Possible effects from global warming can be:

a) rising sea levels

b) increased temperatures

c) higher humidity levels

d) all of the above

2 What will investigation of the site prior to construction look at?

a) proximity of nearest bench mark

b) position of trees

c) the type of materials likely to be needed

d) all of the above

3 Which type of foundation should be used on sloping ground?

a) stepped

b) piled

c) pad

d) wide strip

4 What is a tamper board used for?

a) fixing joists

b) compacting concrete

c) levelling foundations

d) covering windows

5 In cavity walling where both the outer and inner leaves are 90 mm or thicker, you should use ties at what maximum horizontal distance?

a) 450 mm

b) 600 mm

c) 750 mm

d) 900 mm

6 Which value is used to describe insulation quality?

a) R-value

b) B-Value

c) I-Value

d) K-Value

7 Which material is described as 'Lightweight construction method, very fast to construct, thermally efficient, sustainable construction material'

a) bricks

b) blocks

c) timber frames

d) sheathing plywood

8 What is the timber component laid onto walls to support joists and trusses?

a) purlin

b) wall plate

c) sleeper plate

d) truss clip

9 What is strutting and bridging used in?

a) cavity walls

b) timber floor

c) metal studwork

d) rafter roof

10 What is spalling caused by?

a) freezing water

b) extreme heat

c) chemicals

d) dry rot

UNIT 3027

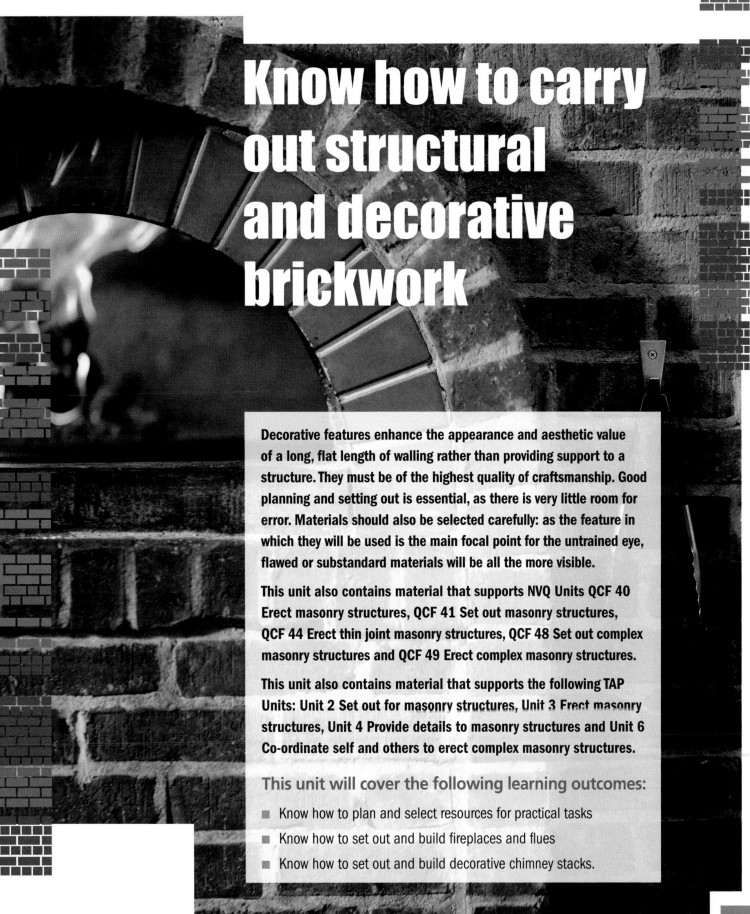

Know how to carry out structural and decorative brickwork

Decorative features enhance the appearance and aesthetic value of a long, flat length of walling rather than providing support to a structure. They must be of the highest quality of craftsmanship. Good planning and setting out is essential, as there is very little room for error. Materials should also be selected carefully: as the feature in which they will be used is the main focal point for the untrained eye, flawed or substandard materials will be all the more visible.

This unit also contains material that supports NVQ Units QCF 40 Erect masonry structures, QCF 41 Set out masonry structures, QCF 44 Erect thin joint masonry structures, QCF 48 Set out complex masonry structures and QCF 49 Erect complex masonry structures.

This unit also contains material that supports the following TAP Units: Unit 2 Set out for masonry structures, Unit 3 Erect masonry structures, Unit 4 Provide details to masonry structures and Unit 6 Co-ordinate self and others to erect complex masonry structures.

This unit will cover the following learning outcomes:

- Know how to plan and select resources for practical tasks
- Know how to set out and build fireplaces and flues
- Know how to set out and build decorative chimney stacks.

K1. Know how to plan and select resources for practical tasks

In order to plan and select resources for practical tasks, you will need to be familiar with the drawings, specifications and contract documents used in the construction industry. We looked at this material earlier in Unit 3002, so refer back to the following pages for more information:

- Drawings and specifications (pages 18–37)
- Contract documents (pages 41–5)
- Interpreting measurements from drawings (pages 38–40)

Remember, sometimes information given to you may be wrong or have mistakes in it. For example, oversights can be made on measurements or material requirements may not be suitable for the job. These inaccuracies should be reported immediately to your line manager and you will need to explain what the problem is. You should also report any defects in materials on site – these should be identified when unloading materials or as soon as possible afterwards.

Your manager may be able to give you the correct information straight away but, in most circumstances, they will probably need to speak to their line manager. This could be the site foreman. In turn they may need to speak to the clerk of works or the architect. Some issues may only be resolvable by the client. However, no work should be carried out until these issues are resolved.

Regular checks should always be made, whether it is to check dimensions, level, plumb, bond, or even the quality of the work so as to avert costly repairs or replacement. If the work is not to the correct standards it will have to be redone, causing waste and delay.

Resources required for structural and decorative walling

The main resources needed for walling are of course bricks and blocks. The type you will need to use depends on the job that will be carried out. There are several working characteristics that need to be taken into account when working on bricks:

- insulation
- solar gain
- resistance to moisture
- resistance to fire.

Most bricks and blocks have good fire resistance and provide thermal insulation. Some are also designed to provide good resistance of moisture. Particular qualities of certain bricks and blocks are described below.

Brick types

Clay bricks

The most common type of brick are clay bricks. There are three main types of clay brick.

Type of brick	Description
Engineering bricks	High compressive strength and low water absorption rates. Rated either as class A or B, with A being the strongest. Class B bricks sometimes known as semi-engineering bricks. Ideal for use below ground level and damp proof courses
Facing bricks	Literally bricks that 'face' the person looking at the building. Give the building a good look and designed to be used externally to provide an attractive appearance. Provided in a huge range of colours and sizes
Common bricks	Lower compressive strength and lower quality than engineering or facing bricks. Not decorative so no attempt is made to control their colour or appearance. Should only be used for internal brickwork

Table 27.01 Types of clay brick

Other types of brick

There are some other types of brick you will encounter.

- **Concrete bricks** are made from a mixture of fine aggregate and Portland cement pressed into steel moulds. They can be used as facings, commons or as engineering bricks and are either solid or have a frog. They are normally grey, but colour pigments can be used. They are heavy, must be kept dry, deaden exterior noise and provide good fire protection and thermal insulation.
- **Sand lime bricks** are decorative bricks sometimes used in place of facing bricks. Sand and lime is the common term for calcium silicate bricks, made from fine silica sand mixed with lime. The mixture is pressed into metal moulds, normally steel and then steam hardened in special chambers called autoclaves.

> **Remember**
>
> Bricks are largely pre-packed and banded using plastic or metal bands to stop them separating until ready for use. Plastic strips protect the edges to prevent damage.

> **Safety tip**
>
> Bricks should be stored on level ground and stacked no higher than two packs high. Once banding is cut, bricks can collapse so great care must be taken.

> **Find out**
>
> There are several different types of design and quality of clay bricks available – use the Internet to research this by looking at the websites of leading manufacturers.

This creates regular bricks with a smooth finish. The main colour is white but a colour pigment can be used when mixing. When used in warm, dry weather the bricks absorb moisture in the mortar very quickly. In wet conditions they need to be kept reasonably dry as the water within the mortar will start to run down the face of the brick if wet. When stacking or laying, avoid contact to the edges as these are easy to chip.

Types of block

Dense concrete blocks should be used up to DPC. These blocks are made from concrete and are strong so produce strong finished work. They are mainly used where a lot of weight will be put against, or on top of, the wall. They are often used as footings below ground, on walls that support steel, internal walls for car parks and shopping centres and retaining walls for embankments.

Lightweight insulation blocks should be used above DPC and provide good insulation qualities. These can be built higher than dense concrete blocks as they are lighter. The water content in the mortar is absorbed into the blocks, drying the joints faster and giving stability more quickly. These blocks are usually a uniform shape and size and are not normally used where heavy loads are to be transferred. Care needs to be taken when transporting and stacking as they can break more easily than dense blocks.

Stone

Stone is a natural resource that can be used as an external or internal finish, either cut into block or brick sizes or used in a larger form, like sheets. This material does not absorb water but may make a surface cold, especially if it is used internally as a finish, such as for floors.

Materials used for mortar

Mortar is used for bedding and jointing bricks and blocks. It is made from sand, cement, water and plasticiser. Mortar must be workable to allow the mortar to roll and spread easily. The mortar should hold onto the trowel without sticking.

Sand should be 'well graded', having large, medium and small grains (see Figure 27.01). If all the grains were of one size, this would be termed as 'poorly graded' and would require more cement to fill in the voids between each grain. Sand is dug from pits or dredged from the sea. In both cases it must be thoroughly washed to remove mud or silt.

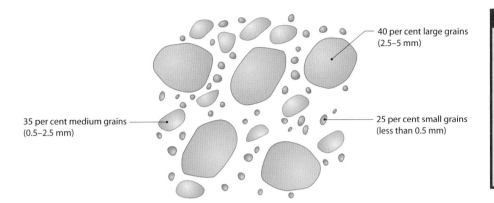

40 per cent large grains
(2.5–5 mm)

35 per cent medium grains
(0.5–2.5 mm)

25 per cent small grains
(less than 0.5 mm)

Figure 27.01 Graded examples of sand

Cement is made from limestone or chalk and is chemically controlled with added calcium, aluminium, silicon and iron. The materials are proportioned to form a raw mix and introduced into a kiln to create cement powder. It binds the grains of sand together. A layer of cement slurry coats the particles of sand and chemically sets after the addition of water, resulting in a hardened layer holding the bricks in place. The most common cement used is Ordinary Portland Cement (OPC), which is suitable for most general work and, if handled correctly, will produce mortar of a high quality and strength.

Masonry cement is often used for bricklaying mortar. It is similar to OPC but has a plasticiser added to the cement powder. As a bag of masonry cement contains 75 per cent cement powder and 25 per cent plasticiser, a higher proportion of cement must be used.

Water is used to make the cement paste and to cause the cement to set due to a chemical reaction (**hydration**).

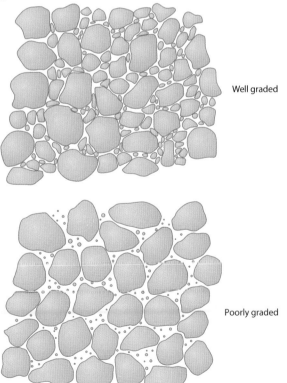

Well graded

Poorly graded

Figure 27.02 Well-graded and poorly graded concrete

Did you know?

It takes 1.65 tonnes of raw material to make 1 tonne of cement, with half of the weight of the limestone material being lost through carbon dioxide emissions during the manufacturing process.

Did you know?

Sulphate-resisting cement is suitable for use below ground, where high levels of sulphate may damage Ordinary Portland Cement. It is normally used for foundation works and drainage.

Remember

Cement is tested by British Standards and given a Kitemark and a number. Setting time for cement must not be less than 45 minutes before its initial set has started, and not more than 10 hours before its final set has taken place. Cement must be used before its initial set as any remixing or movement will prevent the mortar bonding or setting properly.

Key term

Hydration – the addition of water to cement paste to produce a chemical reaction to set mortar

This makes the cement 'workable'. Water is used in the production of concrete to enable the cement to set and also to make the concrete 'workable'. Water must not contain any impurities, which might affect the strength of the concrete. The general rule for the quality of water is that it should be drinkable (potable).

Damp proof course

Using correct insulation and damp proof course (DPC) is one of the main ways of ensuring that energy efficiency is maintained. Damp proof course or damp proof membrane (DPM) is a layer of non-absorbent material bedded onto a wall to prevent moisture penetrating into a building. DPC can be flexible, rigid or semi-rigid:

- **Flexible DPC** comes in rolls of various widths, with polythene the most common. It should always be laid upon a thin bed of mortar and lapped by a minimum of 100 mm on a corner or if joining a new roll.
- **Semi-rigid DPC** is normally made from blocks of asphalt, melted and spread in coats to form a continuous membrane for tanking for basements or underground work.
- **Rigid DPC** uses solid materials, such as engineering bricks or slate. Slate is more expensive and has no flexibility, so will crack under movement. Engineering bricks can be used for a garden wall, if DPC is required.

Local material used for walling

Materials available locally have always been used to construct buildings. The nature of these materials alters depending on the location. For example, buildings near woods or forests use timber as a large part of their structure. In other areas, stone or flint have been used as well as chalk.

This practice has continued, even after the point where clay could be hardened to form bricks (which introduced another type of material that could be used in several different locations). Small brickworks opened in areas where clay was located, producing local bricks. The growth of canals, and eventually trains and roads, allowed these bricks to be transported to further towns and cities.

This practice continues today – you will find in the areas where you work that there are some local materials used as part of the building processes. There are advantages to using local materials. They are generally cheaper to transport to the site. If matching to existing work, like an extension, local stone or bricks are more likely to be a better match as they are likely to be from the same brickyard or quarry.

Find out

What materials and supplies are local to your area? Use the Internet and information about local suppliers to find out more about materials that are unique to your area and the uses they have. What advantages can these bring to local building projects?

Functional skills

Researching information from local suppliers will allow you to practise **FE 2.2.2** Identify the purposes of texts and comment on how effectively meanings are conveyed.

Components, tools and equipment for structural and decorative walling

There are a number of different tools and equipment you will need to use to complete work on structural and decorative walling. In all these cases, you will need to collect together these materials and make sure that they are maintained correctly.

Portable power tools

Angle grinders

Angle grinders are cutting tools that run by electricity using 110 V and 230 V supplies or are battery powered. They cut using an abrasive or diamond-type disc. They range from 100 mm to 230 mm diameter disc size.

Angle grinders are used for cutting bricks, blocks, concrete and stone to size or for cutting existing material for alteration. Great care should be taken when using them as the disc travels at very high speed and takes time to slow down after release of the trigger, but can still cut.

Figure 27.03 100 mm/4 inch electric grinder

Owing to the cutting speed, large amounts of dust and particles are released from the material, so goggles and mask should always be worn in addition to the usual PPE. Ear defenders should also be worn. All leads should be checked before and after use for cuts or splits and, with a 110 V supply, a transformer must be used.

Figure 27.04 225 mm/9 inch electric grinder

Petrol disc cutters

This type of cutter is motorised, running on petrol. The disc size is 300 mm and runs at a faster speed than the angle grinder. It uses abrasive or diamond cutting discs and is used for heavier duty cutting. Fuel and oil levels should be checked regularly as should discs for wear or damage. The locking nut must be securely tightened to prevent movement when the disc is spinning. To help prevent this, the shim (a flat metal plate) should also be fitted over the main spindle either side of the disc.

Remember

The key hand tools you will need to use are:

- trowels (including pointing trowel)
- level
- line and pins
- club or lump hammer
- pointing iron
- tape measure.

Did you know?

In the construction industry only 110 V type or battery type angle grinders are allowed to be used on site by health and safety law

---

Safety tip

No person is allowed to change a cutting disc unless they hold an Abrasive Wheels Certificate.

Figure 27.05 Table mounted masonry saw

Functional skills

This section will give you the opportunity to practise **FM 2.1.1** – Identify and select mathematical procedures. It will also allow you to practise **FM 2.2.1a – h** and **FM 2.2.2** relate to applying a range of mathematics to find solutions and using appropriate checking procedures and evaluating their effectiveness at each stage. You will also be able to practise the *interpreting* elements of functional skills, such as **FM 2.3.1** Interpret and communicate solutions to multistage practical problems. **FM 2.3.2** Draw conclusions and provide mathematical justifications.

Key term

Volume – the amount of space taken up by a 3-D or solid shape

Table mounted masonry saws

This is an electric disc cutter fixed to a bench or table. It is used if a lot of cutting is required. This will normally be for brick or block cutting, with a water jet to cut down on the amount of dust generated with the cutting process. Some fireplace manufacturers use these types of cutter on stone and limestone.

Table mounted masonry saws should only be used by a competent trained person. This equipment should be used away from the main work area, with barriers erected to stop unauthorised people from getting too near, as fast moving blades can cause accidents.

Access equipment

The basic principles and health and safety issues of access equipment were covered in Unit 1001, pages 11–13. The key pieces of access equipment you will use are:

* stepladders
* ladders
* mobile tower scaffold
* trestles and staging.

Describe calculations and formulae for identifying quantities of materials and components

To make estimates of quantities of materials you will need to be familiar with some calculation techniques used in the industry. These methods will help you to calculate the amounts of materials you will need to use on a project.

Volume

Volume is measured in cube units, such as cubic millimetres (mm^3) and cubic metres (m^3). The volume of this cube is $1 cm^3$ or $10 \times 10 \times 10 = 1000 mm^3$.

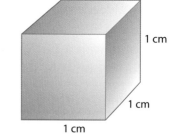

You can find the volume of concrete needed for a rectangular floor by measuring the length and width of the floor, and the depth of the concrete required and using the formula for the volume of a cuboid. For example, we can work out the volume of concrete needed for the floor of a rectangular room with length 3.7 m and width 2.9 m, if the depth of the concrete is to be 0.15 m.

Visualise the floor as a cuboid, like this:

The depth of the concrete (0.15 m) is the height of the cuboid.

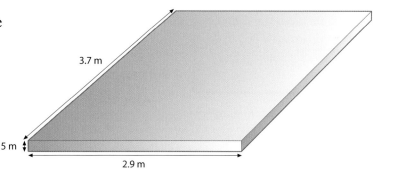

$$V = l \times w \times h$$

$$= 3.7 \times 2.9 \times 0.15$$

$$= 1.6095 \text{ m}^3$$

$$= 1.61 \text{ m}^3 \text{ (to 2 decimal places)}$$

Perimeters and areas

The perimeter of a shape is the distance all around the outside of the shape. To find the perimeter of a shape, measure all the sides and then add the lengths together.

The area of a 2-D shape is the amount of space it covers. Area is measured in square units, such as square centimeters (cm²) or square metres (m²). So for a square with 10 mm sides the area of the square is 10 mm x 10 mm, so 100 mm².

Area of a triangle

This is given by the formula:

A = ½ x h x b where h is the perpendicular height and b is the length of the base. The perpendicular height is drawn to meet the base at right angles.

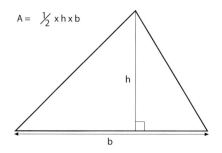

To find unknown lengths in a right-angled triangle, Pythagoras' theorem is used. In a right-angled triangle:

* one angle is 90° (a right angle)
* the longest side is opposite the right angle and is called the hypotenuse.

Pythagoras' theorem states $c^2 = a^2 + b^2$

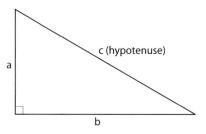

Areas of composite shapes

These are shapes made up from different squares, rectangles and triangles. To calculate the area of these shapes, split them up into smaller shapes, calculate the area of these individual shapes and then add them all together.

Did you know?

If you are given the diameter of the circle, you need to halve the diameter to find the radius.

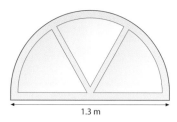

1.3 m

Area of a circle

The formula for the area of a circle of a radius r is:

$$\text{Area} = \pi r^2$$

We can calculate the area of a circle with radius 3.25 m as:

$$\text{Area} = \pi r^2$$
$$= \pi \times r^2$$
$$= 3.14 \times 3.25 \times 3.25 = 33.166\,25$$
$$= 33 \text{ m}^2 \text{ (to the nearest metre).}$$

Area and circumference of part circles and composite shapes

You can use the formulae for circumference and area of a circle to calculate perimeters and areas of parts of circles, and shapes made from parts of circles. For example, we can work out the perimeter and area of the semicircular window below.

The diameter of the semicircle is 1.3 m, so the radius is $1.3 \div 2 = 0.65$ m.

The length of the curved side is half the circumference of the circle with radius 0.65 m.

$$\text{Length of curved side} = \tfrac{1}{2} \times 2\pi r = \tfrac{1}{2} \times 2 \times \pi \times r$$
$$= \tfrac{1}{2} \times 2 \times 3.14 \times 0.65 = 2.041 \text{ m}$$

Circumference of the semicircle = curved side + straight side

$$= 2.041 + 1.3 = 3.341\text{m}$$
$$= 3.34 \text{ m (to the nearest cm)}$$

Area of semicircle = half the area of the circle with radius 0.65m

$$= \tfrac{1}{2} \times \pi r2 = \tfrac{1}{2} \times \pi \, r^2$$
$$= \tfrac{1}{2} \times 3.14 \times 0.65 \times 0.65 = 0.663\,325 \text{ m}^2$$
$$= 0.66 \text{ m}^2 \text{ (to 2 d.p.)}$$

To find the area of a quarter circle, use $\tfrac{1}{4}\pi r^2$.

To find the perimeter of a quarter circle, work out $\tfrac{1}{4}$ circumference + 2 × radius.

To find the area of a composite shape including parts of circles, divide it into circles and simple shapes and find the areas separately.

Predicting waste

When working out what materials you require to complete a job, add on a certain amount to your calculations for material waste. If you order the exact amount you require you are not considering any off cuts or damage to the material. Even when cementing or plastering, not all the plaster will go on the wall. Some will fall on the floor and some may go off too quickly if you mix up too much to use in one day. It is generally accepted that between 5 per cent and 10 per cent is added on to the total to allow for waste.

For adding on a percentage you simply need to divide the amount by 100 and then multiply by 100 + whatever the percentage is.

Material delivery

Most materials are delivered on site in lorries with crane off-loading equipment. This is a quick and efficient method of delivery as materials can be positioned anywhere required on site without manhandling. If materials are stored in specific areas (this is usual on larger sites), cranes are used to transport them around the site. If the correct procedures are followed there is little chance of injury to the workforce. The driver should be fully trained in the use of the equipment.

In some circumstances when materials are being delivered or moved on site, the driver may have problems seeing the position where the materials are to be placed. In these situations, a banksman is required to give hand signals to the driver to act as their eyes. The signals are normally for left, right, up, down and slow movement. The banksman should always stand in full view of the driver and the position the materials are to be moved to, or connected by means of two way radio. They should be fully trained in this role and hold a relevant and up-to-date certificate.

> **Remember**
>
> You also need to make allowance for mistakes, such as cutting materials incorrectly, as well as more natural waste.

> **Example**
>
> 300 metres of timber is the required amount and you want to add on 7 per cent for waste so:
>
> $$\frac{300}{100} = 3$$
>
> $3 \times 107 = 321$
>
> So with 7 per cent waste you would order 321 metres.

> **Working life**
>
> Lewis is given the job of building in an existing door opening. He is told all the materials he needs are in the back garden ready for use. He checks the amounts he needs and on counting the bricks, finds he has enough bricks, but some are of a slightly different type in colour and texture.
>
> Should he carry on and build the wall? What might be the implications if he does? Who should he consult on this situation?

> **Functional skills**
>
> Checking materials for use and deciding how to proceed with a practical task will give you the opportunity to practise the *interpreting* elements of functional skills, e.g. **FM 2.3.1** Interpret and communicate solutions to multistage practical problems. **FM 2.3.2** Draw conclusions and provide mathematical justifications.

Unit 3027 Know how to carry out structural and decorative brickwork

K2. Know how to set out and build fireplaces and flues

In the modern era most houses are heated by central heating installations which do not require a fireplace or chimney. However, it is once again becoming popular to have a fireplace as a feature in a house. Fireplaces consist of a hearth, breast and flue, with a chimney stack to carry the fumes away from the building.

Almost every home features a fireplace, either to heat the room or as a decorative feature. The main design is governed by the Building Regulations. However, the type of fuel used will determine the type of flue required, either during construction or any later work on the property.

There are four main types of fuel used for heating purposes: solid fuel, gas, oil and electric.

Solid fuel

Solid fuel is the use of wood or coal, or a combination of both. This is normally in the form of an **'open fire'** or it can be a 'wood burning' fire or stove.

Gas

Gas can be used for central heating purposes and with fires connected to lined flues within the chimney breasts.

Oil

Oil is mainly used for central heating purposes; it is very rarely used in conjunction with fireplaces.

Electric

Electricity can be used for central heating. Electric fires can also be fitted to chimney breasts but there is no requirement for a flue as there is no emission of fumes or smoke.

Methods of provision for services

When constructing fireplaces, it is important to make provision for other services that will need to be used in order to make the fireplace work correctly. The main elements you will have to make provision for are covered below.

Pipe ducts

Pipe ducts are areas allocated for the running of services. These may be underground or at ceiling level, depending on the size of the building. They are normally used by heating pipes or electrical

> **Key term**
>
> **Open fire** – form of heating contained within a fireplace recess

cabling. In general house construction pipework for heating is normally run on the surfaces of walls but, where it may need to cross a floor, a duct might be used. Access may be required to pipes for maintenance or repair. On larger constructions, such as blocks of flats or commercial buildings, larger duct areas will be needed for access.

Ventilation to fireplaces

Sometimes fireplaces need ventilation to help the fire smoke pull up the chimney. This is usually established by inserting airbricks at floor level and then using the draft to help push the smoke upwards.

Boilers

Boilers are used for heating commercial, industrial and domestic dwellings. The size of boiler required is determined by the **output** needed. Boilers are used to heat water and radiators, so the boiler size is determined by the amount of hot water required and the amount of radiators needed to heat the property.

> **Key term**
>
> **Output** – amount of energy (in this case, in the form of heat and hot water) required for the type of use.

All boilers should be installed by a specialist registered installer qualified to deal with boilers using the relevant fuel supply:

- gas boiler installers should be CORGI-registered engineers
- oil boiler installers should be OFTEC-registered engineers.

In most cases, boilers installed before 1989 had an output of up to 30 per cent more than was required – a larger drain on the energy supply and on people's finances. Today, efficiency calculations are usually made in order to establish what size of boiler is needed.

There are several different types of system that incorporate boilers:

- conventional heating systems
- system boiler heating systems
- combi boiler heating systems
- back boiler systems.

Different types of fuels can be used for boilers.

- gas (natural and LPG) – for gas boilers and condensing boilers
- oil   normally requiring a tank to store
- solid fuel - coal, wood, etc.
- electricity – storage heaters and blown-air systems.

Installing or replacing any of these systems will involve a registered installer, but for a solid fuel system a bricklayer may be required too.

Solid fuel systems come in two different forms: back boilers in chimney breasts and kitchen ranges.

> **Remember**
>
> If you are replacing old equipment or installing new equipment, you will need to know what types of fuel are available in the area.

Back boilers in chimney breasts

A back boiler is a box unit built into a standard chimney opening to produce hot water for general use and heating through radiators.

This type of boiler has a fireback incorporated within the unit, is positioned onto the back hearth and uses solid fuel. The fire looks like an ordinary open fire, with a fire grate and hearth but, as well as heating the room, the heat generated is transferred through the fireback to waterpipes connected to the side of the unit, which run through the side of the chimney jamb to the hot water cylinder and radiators.

The top of the 'box' is connected to the existing flue by means of a steel flue section running into the brick flue, or by inserting a stainless steel flue liner the full length of the stack. It has an 'open and close' moving plate at the top for air circulation, so that the fire can be lit initially from the front of the unit. Once the unit has been fitted, the space between the unit and the chimney should be filled with non-combustible material to prevent heat transfer. A solid fuel-type surround is then fitted to the chimney breast to finish as normal.

This type of boiler is mainly used in older houses and does have drawbacks: the pipework connections are difficult to access once installed, and there is unsightly pipework to the cylinder against the outside of the jamb, although this can be boxed in.

Pipes that need to run across floors will need to be laid in ducts below surface level to allow for floor finishes, but will require proper covers to allow future access. The ducts need to be set deep enough to accommodate the pipes required as well as sufficient ventilation and insulation space. This means that the ducts would usually need to be positioned, using timber or polystyrene section placed in the route positions, at the stage of pouring the oversite concrete.

The main problems with this system are that:

- it only works while a fire is burning
- it takes a while to warm up
- replacing the unit is a major task.

This type of system can also be used for gas fire finishes, where a specially fitted back boiler unit connects directly to the fire. Here, the flue should connect to a flexible twin-skinned stainless steel flue liner, running the full length of the chimney stack and sealed correctly to the unit by a specialised installer.

Figure 27.06 Back boiler

Figure 27.07 Kitchen range

Kitchen ranges

In older cottage-type dwellings and farmhouses, the kitchen was a major focal point and the warmest room of the house – and this was due in part to the kitchen range.

As with a back boiler, a kitchen range can supply heat to some of the other rooms as well as hot water for the whole house. The old ranges were made of cast iron and had a central solid fuel fire, with either one side oven or twin ovens for cooking or making bread, and cast-iron rings on the top for cooking with pots and pans.

Many larger new homes are now installing modern ranges as a central feature in the kitchen. These do not normally incorporate a back boiler, and can run on solid fuel, gas or electricity.

Working life

James is helping to take out and replace a solid fuel back boiler. He has removed the fire surround, and the unit seems to be loose in the opening – he can pull it forward slightly, but it will not come out.

What could be the reason? James will have to be careful he does not cause any damage. How could he repair any problem or fault?

Remember

You may need to cut bricks and blocks for erecting fireplaces. You will need to use a hammer and bolster with the cutting position marked on all sides. Then tap sharply with the bolster on the cutline, face side first. Work around until the brick or block cuts. The face edge is the most important so make sure that the cut here is good quality. You can also use the disc cutter for cutting bricks and blocks.

Remember

You will also need to include a damp proof barrier in the construction of fireplaces. Look at pages 170–71 for more information on this.

Industrial standards for brickwork and blockwork

Industrial standards are the standards and tolerances allowed on site, or in the workshop, covering plumbness, level and finish of a wall, the gauge, the joints on courses running true and plumb and as the cleanliness of the wall once built.

For fireplaces and flues, you will also need to follow government regulations covering the building of these features.

The design and construction of fireplaces are controlled by Part J of the Building Regulations as well as guidance and advice being found in the British Standards 6461. The main areas covered are:

- the installation of chimneys and flues for domestic appliances using solid fuels
- BS 1251 specifications for the installation of open-fireplace components
- BS 1181, the specification for liners and terminals
- Part 1 of the codes of practice for chimneys and flues.

These cover the installation in domestic homes for class 1 appliances with an output up to 45 kW. The regulations are mainly concerned with avoiding the spread of fire to the surrounding areas or structures and the release of combustible material into the atmosphere.

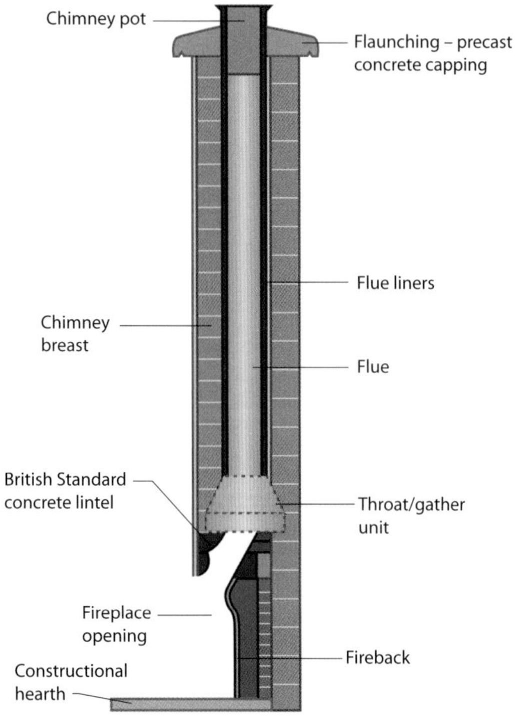
Chimney pot
Flaunching – precast concrete capping
Flue liners
Chimney breast
Flue
British Standard concrete lintel
Throat/gather unit
Fireplace opening
Fireback
Constructional hearth

Figure 27.08 Constructing a fireplace

Methods of erecting fireplaces

A typical fireplace consists of:

- a constructional hearth
- a chimney breast with incorporated flue
- a chimney stack.

Figure 27.08 shows how this fits together and names the different parts involved.

There are many terms used in the construction of a fireplace. They are listed below so that you can understand their meanings before we go any further.

Component	Purpose
Chimney breast	projection on a wall which encloses a fireplace or flue
Flue	a channel or duct leading from a fireplace for smoke or fumes to escape
Flue liner	a circular or square liner placed inside a flue to prevent condensation or gases escaping
Constructional hearth	a structural hearth or base under a fireplace to prevent fire spreading
Fireplace opening	the opening that contains the fire or heating appliance
British Standard splayed fireplace lintel	a concrete lintel with a cut out used over fireplace openings
Gather/throat unit	corbelling of brickwork to reduce a fireplace opening to flue size. Can be pre-cast
Chimney stack	the brickwork above roof level which contains the flue
Necking course	a projecting course of brickwork part way up a chimney stack
Oversailing	the projecting brickwork at the top of a chimney stack for weather protection
Flaunching	the sloping weathered finish to the top of a chimney stack
Chimney pot	the end of the flue, very often tapered to accelerate the escape of gases
Flashing	waterproof material (usually lead sheet) used at the joint of a roof and chimney stack
Midfeathers	brickwork between flues
Class 1 appliance	an appliance not giving an output in excess of 45 kW (an open fire)
Fireback	an ornamental iron slab against the back of the hearth

Table 27.02 Main components of a fireplace

To construct fireplaces you will need to form builder's openings in masonry walling. As with any opening in brick and block work where masonry is above, a lintel must be inserted to carry the weight. This can be made from either concrete or steel. In some instances, especially with large fireplace construction, a timber beam may be used. This is normally made of solid oak as it will provide a decorative finish as well as be load bearing. The temporary support that needs to be put into place when creating openings is covered in Unit 3028 on pages 192–97.

Construction techniques for fireplaces and flues

Fireplace construction

A fireplace should be constructed using a brick wall around its entirety to prevent the spread of fire. This can be done using four main methods that comply with Building Regulations:

1. in conjunction with an external straight cavity wall

2. with the breast external in a cavity wall

3. in conjunction with an internal wall

4. built as a double breast, back to back.

Figure 27.09 An external straight cavity wall

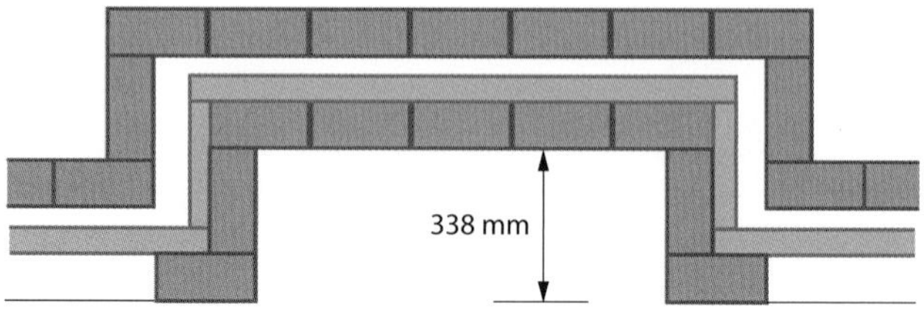

Figure 27.10 The breast external in a cavity wall

338 mm

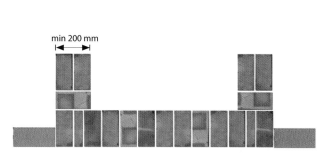

min 200 mm

Figure 27.11 An internal wall

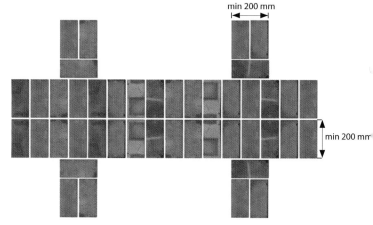

min 200 mm

min 200 mm

Figure 27.12 A back to back fireplace

More modern or extravagant fireplaces can be built as a corner feature, again using solid brickwork, or circular, self-supporting brickwork, as a central feature to a room.

Building the chimney breast

The sides or jambs of the chimney breast must be a minimum thickness of 1 brick (215 mm) and extend from the back wall by a minimum of $1\frac{1}{2}$ bricks (338 mm). The width of the opening will depend on whether or not a fitted appliance is to be used but the minimum opening size is $1\frac{1}{2}$ bricks (338 mm). This can allow for a change of appliance being fitted at a later date.

The fire opening must be closed at the top to ensure the appliance is fully encased within the chimney breast. This is done by the use of a splayed reinforced concrete lintel to support the brickwork above. This forms the start of the 'throat' of a chimney.

The internal area of the chimney breast now needs to be closed to form the 'flue'. The flue allows the fumes or smoke to escape into the atmosphere. In older properties, the flue was made by corbelling the brickwork on both sides on the inside of the chimney breast until the flue size (a minimum 215 mm) was reached. This is called the 'gather'. The flue was then corbelled forward on one side and corbelled back on the other, keeping the flue size the same, until reaching the side of the breast. This gave the flue an approximate 45° angle within the chimney to help 'draw' or pull the fumes up into the finished flue. Figure 27.13 illustrates this.

Once this was achieved, the flue was then built straight to the top. This could also accommodate a fireplace in a first floor room above, meaning the flues would run parallel so that only one double chimney stack would be required at the top.

In more modern homes, a prefabricated unit made from fireproof material (normally refactory concrete) is used (see Figure 27.14). This has the gather incorporated within the unit itself. These come in standard sizes to suit different openings as well as different flue sizes and flue shapes to suit what has been specified.

> **Remember**
>
> The opening can be made smaller but it cannot be made bigger at a later date to accommodate a larger appliance. Therefore, if it is not known what type of appliance will be used, it is better at the building stage to have a slightly larger opening.

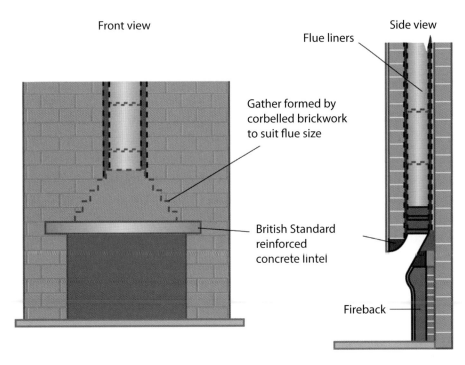

Figure 27.13 Construction of a fireplace gather using brick corbelling

Front view

Side view

Flue liners

Gather formed by corbelled brickwork to suit flue size

British Standard reinforced concrete lintel

Fireback

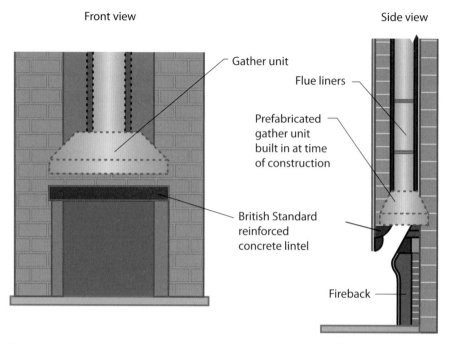

Front view | Side view

Gather unit

Flue liners

Prefabricated gather unit built in at time of construction

British Standard reinforced concrete lintel

Fireback

Figure 27.14 Construction of a fireplace gather using a prefabricated unit

Flue liners

Flue liners were not really introduced until the 1960s. Until then flues were built square with bricks and the inside of the flue was rendered as it was being built with sand and lime mortar; this was called 'parging' the flue. This was to stop the solid fuel wastes, mainly sulphur, from attacking the bricks.

The other problem came from condensation forming when the hot fumes travelling up the flue met with the cold air from the outside atmosphere. This moisture then ran down the inside of the flue, mixing with the deposited sulphur and forming sulphuric acid and carbonic acid. These could attack the mortar and eventually seep into the bricks and mortar joints. This caused crumbling of the bricks and weakness to the structure, as well as staining to internal walls and ceilings. The flue could also become blocked as a result of parging falling away from the bricks.

The Building Regulations made the use of liners compulsory to avoid this problem to chimneys in the future.

What are flue liners made of?

Flue liners are made from factory manufactured concrete or clay, both of which are non-combustible and resistant to damage by acid attack. They are either round or square and come in various sizes.

Figure 27.15 A typical flue liner

How do flue liners fit together?

Flue liners are manufactured with a rebate or socket at one end and a spigot at the other. When joined to another liner, it forms a perfect seal. These have to be installed the correct way up and the socket/rebated end should always be at the top. This stops any moisture running down the inside from penetrating into the surrounding brickwork. The joint between two separate liners should consist of either mortar of the same consistency as the brickwork, a sulphate-resistant mortar or a manufacturer's sealant.

All liners should be checked for damage and cracks before use to avoid problems after construction. The area between the outside of the built-in liner and the brickwork should be filled with a material, allowing the liner to expand without causing damage to it or the surrounding brickwork. This can either be a weak lime/sand mortar or a weak vermiculite concrete mix.

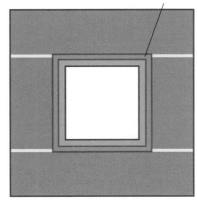

Weak lime mortar or insulating concrete

Plan view of chimney stack

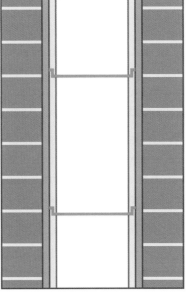

Section through lined flue

Figure 27.16 A section of a flue

> **Remember**
>
> Make sure joints are left flush in the flue to prevent any obstructions.

The finishes to the chimney breast and hearth

The chimney breast at ground floor level is normally the main feature of the room. Therefore, in most modern homes, great thought will go in to the type of finish to complement the fireplace. In the case of open fires which burn solid fuel, some may have 'face' brickwork specifically designed to a customer's specifications across the whole of the breast. Alternatively, they may have partial brickwork with a **'mantelpiece'** (the rest of the wall having a plaster finish).

Stone could also be used as a chimney breast finish, particularly in areas which have plenty of this natural material.

> **Key term**
>
> **Mantelpiece** – a shelf made of wood, tile, stone or brick to finish the top of a fireplace

> **Remember**
>
> Great care must betaken to protect the finishes until handover to the client.

Figure 27.17 Fireplace finishes

The finished hearth is positioned, normally using the same material (for example, brick or stone). Again, this is for decorative purposes as well as for protection. In the case of an open fire, it is to avoid hot material having contact with the flooring finish.

With gas appliances, where the fire requires specific sealing requirements, other finishes may be used. These can include timber surrounds with marble hearths and 'back panels' in many colours and designs.

First floor construction

Once the chimney breast has been built to first floor level, the overall size is reduced to the width of the flue and surrounding brickwork. This is so that it does not take up so much space in the room. It would then have a plastered finish. If a fireplace was to be constructed in the room at first floor level, the construction process would be the same as on the ground floor.

If a chimney breast is built then the reduction will be made at the point the chimney breast reaches the roof space, to start the chimney stack.

Points to remember

* Make sure the foundations for walls meet correct building regulations and specifications.
* Make sure the construction of the brickwork/blockwork is well bonded and flushed up in accordance with your drawings and specifications.
* Remember the fireplace must contain the fire or appliance and it must also prevent the fire spreading to other parts of the building.

- The flue must be soundly constructed to enable the smoke and gases to be safely carried away to the outside atmosphere without endangering health.

- It must be remembered that fireplaces and flues are hidden behind finished brickwork or plastered walls, etc. They are extremely difficult to put right if poorly constructed.

Working life

Sarah is building a chimney breast and flue for a new open fire. She is inserting flue liners as the work progresses. As she is inserting the liner she notices the liner has a crack in it down the side. She decided to still use it, as the liner was surrounded in brickwork.

Will this matter? What could happen because of Sarah's decision? What might happen to the fireplace and its surroundings? You will need to think about the possible effects of using this liner in the fireplace.

The constructional hearth

This is a solid base under a fireplace to prevent the spread of fire. It is made of concrete with a minimum thickness of 125 mm. It must extend fully into the depth of the fire opening as well as projecting a minimum of 500 mm in front of the fireplace jambs. It is also a requirement to extend a minimum of 150 mm either side of the jambs.

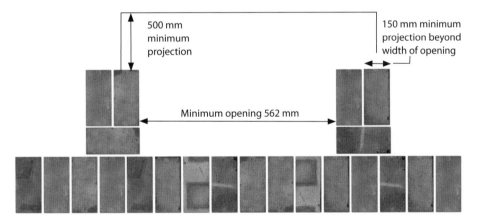

500 mm minimum projection

150 mm minimum projection beyond width of opening

Minimum opening 562 mm

Figure 27.18 A plan view of a constructional hearth

The fitting of a hearth and surround

The surround and hearth are fitted after the main construction has taken place. At this point in the construction process, unless the internal brickwork is to be 'faced', the internal opening needs to be finished to take the required appliance.

Stage 1 Positioning the surround

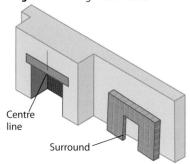

Centre line

Surround

Stage 2 Fixing the back hearth

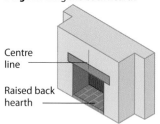

Centre line

Raised back hearth

Stage 3 Fixing the fireback

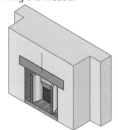

Stage 4 Checking the position of the fireback

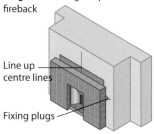

Line up centre lines

Fixing plugs

Stage 1

The first stage is to position the surround close to the opening to avoid excessive lifting. Be careful not to damage the edges of the surround or finished decoration. Measure the chimney breast and mark a centre line with a pencil or a cut line in cement screed. Measure and put a small mark on the centre of the surround on the top edge with a pencil. Use a marker that can be wiped off and make sure not to scratch the surround.

Stage 2

The back hearth within the fireplace opening has to be raised to the thickness of the hearth to allow it to take the fireback. This can be done by using split bricks and then covering with a thickness of sand/lime mortar, or fully with mortar, making sure the finish is level both ways. In some instances, firebricks may be used as the finished back hearth.

Stage 3

Lift the fireback into place within the opening and set central to the line marked on wall.

Stage 4

Reposition the surround and line up the two centre lines. Check and make sure it is level and plumb on the face side. Move the fireback so it is positioned almost against the surround (leaving a gap of approximately 25 mm to allow for the expansion rope). Mark the positions of the fixing plugs on the surround onto the chimney breast wall ready for drilling. Then remove the surround to its resting position.

Stage 5

Drill the fixing holes using an electric drill or battery operated drill to take red or brown fixing plugs, making sure the depth of the holes are correct. A minimum size of 50 mm screw should be used.

Stage 5 Drilling the fixing holes

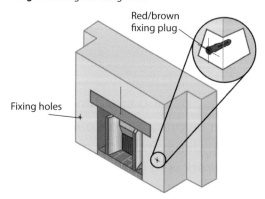

Red/brown fixing plug

Fixing holes

Remember

If the wall has been finish plastered, the area of the fixing lugs should be cut out with a hammer and chisel to allow the fixing to be covered at completion.

Stage 6

The next stage is to build in the fireback. Corrugated paper should be positioned around the rear of the fireback to allow for any expansion while in use. The gaps on each side should be filled first with bedded bricks or cut bricks to stop any overspill. The void at the back should then be filled with lightweight vermiculite concrete or sand/lime mortar. If mortar is used, make sure it does not push the fireback forward under the pressure.

Stage 7

Repeat the sequence detailed in stage 6 until the top of the fireback is reached.

Stage 8

The space between the top of the fireback and the back wall, a distance of about 100 mm, should now be filled with sand/lime mortar at an angle of approximately 45° to give maximum draw for the smoke and gases to escape.

Stage 9

Lift the surround into position and line up the centre marks and fixings, level and plumb in position. Next, fit the fire resistant rope into the gap along both sides between the fireback and the surround and across the top between the surround and chimney breast, making sure it is approximately 25 mm behind the face line. Then position the screws into the lugs and tighten until fully secured.

Stage 10

Bed the hearth into position ensuring it is level both ways and point the gap where the rope is fitted with fire cement to ensure a seal between the surround and fireback. The chimney breast should now be plastered or if this has been carried out, the gap sealed with mastic. Clean off the surround to remove any excess material and protect with paper or bubble wrap on completion.

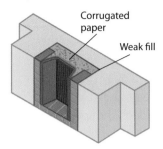

Stage 6 Building in around the fireback

Corrugated paper

Weak fill

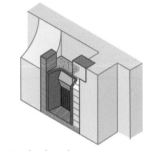

Stage 7 Continue to build up the fireback

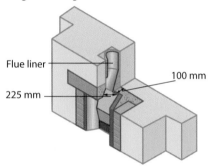

Stage 8 Forming the thread

Flue liner

225 mm

100 mm

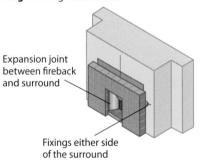

Stage 9 Fixing the surround

Expansion joint between fireback and surround

Fixings either side of the surround

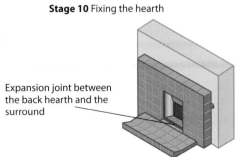

Stage 10 Fixing the hearth

Expansion joint between the back hearth and the surround

Figure 27.19 The stages of fitting the hearth and surround

Did you know?

Stages 9 and 10 may be done in reverse order depending on the type of hearth used. When stage 10 is carried out first, the bedded hearth must be fully dry to take the weight of the surround.

K3. Know how to set out and build decorative chimney stacks

A chimney stack is the terminal of the flue or flues. It is very open to the weather so very careful construction is necessary to avoid costly maintenance later. A chimney stack can be very plain or very decorative (this is often seen in older buildings) and can contain one or several flues. The purpose of the stack is the same, whatever the design, and the following points should always be observed.

- As the chimney is one of the most exposed parts of a building, a suitable brick must be used as well as a high standard of workmanship.
- A good chimney pot should be tapered at the top to induce the fumes or smoke to escape and it should be bedded into the brickwork to ensure that it is not likely to be moved by high winds.
- A stack must be high enough to clear the roof to discharge the smoke, etc safely. It should be at a height that does not affect the health of the occupants or present a fire risk.
- A sound waterproofing of the stack is essential to keep out rainwater.
- The flue liners must carry through to the full height of the stack to meet the chimney pot.
- The joint made by the stack and the roof should be watertight. This is done using what is known as flashing (see page 171), usually formed in lead sheet by a plumber.
- A DPC should be inserted to prevent moisture passing downwards into the building. Lead sheeting can be used (or engineering bricks as an alternative).

The bond of a chimney stack will generally be dictated by the size and thickness of the stack. If the stack is only half a brick thick then a stretcher bond is normally used. If the stack is one brick thick, an English or Flemish bond may be used. In some instances, particularly with older chimneys, decorative brickwork may be incorporated.

Building the chimney stack

The brickwork and flue should be carried up through the roof space and on to meet the roof. The brickwork should be raised 150 mm or two courses at the front or lowest point of the roof pitch, above the roof.

This is the position where the lead tray should be inserted, to prevent water penetrating down the chimney from saturation of the exposed brickwork above. See Figure 27.20a. The tray should be made of sheet lead and be a minimum of 50 mm wider on each side of the stack size. It should be bedded onto the existing brickwork.

The flue area is then cut out smaller by a minimum of 25 mm all round; this is so that the lead can be turned up, in order to stop moisture running down the flue.

The brickwork is then continued to form the exposed stack. The joint under the lead at the front and sides outside the roof should be raked out to a depth of approximately 30 mm for future use. Weep holes are installed on the first course above the lead on the exposed front side. The lead overhanging the stack on the outside should be turned up tight to the stack but, where it is inside the roof, the overhang should be turned down on the front and side areas above the rafter line after the front apron is fitted. This is to force any water that penetrates the stack to run out at the front of the chimney through the weep holes situated in the perp joints. See Figure 27.20b.

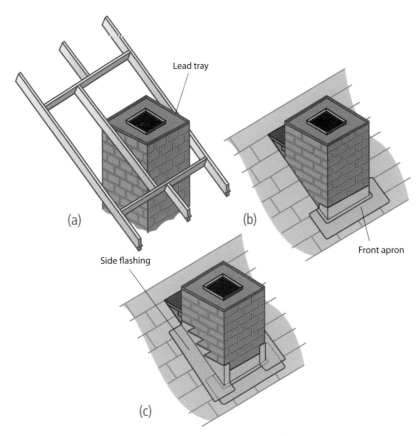

Figure 27.20 Lead positioning on a chimney stack

The brick joints should be raked out in readiness for the lead flashings to be inserted in order to waterproof the sides and back as the stack is built. See Figure 27.20c.

Once the brickwork has reached a height of 150 mm (two courses) above the roof at the back, a second DPC tray can be fitted and the joint raked out to take the back lead apron. (This is the same operation that was previously carried out with the front apron to prevent water penetration.)

Remember

If you are unsure of the exact position, rake out more than is required. It is easier to re-point than to have to cut out hardened joints at a later date when there is a chance of stack damage.

The stack is then built up to the height specified or to Building Regulation heights as shown in Figure 27.21, allowing for oversail courses to be built.

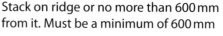
Stack on ridge or no more than 600 mm from it. Must be a minimum of 600 mm

600 mm

600 mm

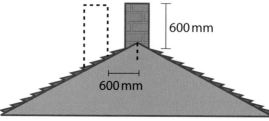
Minimum height of stack 2300 mm or less from rooflight 1000 mm

1000 mm

rooflight

2300 mm

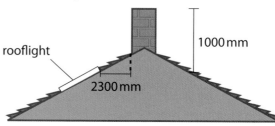
Stack 1000 mm minimum above roof level

1000 mm

Figure 27.21 Regulated heights of chimney stacks

Decorative chimney stacks

These days, chimney stacks are usually built to be functional, taking into account costs and using standard materials, so very few new decorative chimneys are built. Many old decorative chimneys have been replaced over the years by modern, traditional stacks. The new stacks tend to use newer, traditional bonds including Flemish and English bonds for stacks of 1-brick thickness or more.

Many old Tudor houses had decorative stacks. As these stacks were built of soft brick and soft mortar, they suffer from weathering and erosion, so restoring a decorative stack takes a lot of time and money. Most old decorative stacks were replaced during Victorian times, and thankfully many still used the same traditional methods and designs.

Most bricks made at this time were traditional shapes, and as they were soft, they could be cut to most shapes. Some were made in special moulds, sometimes made just for the specific house – at the time there were many brickmakers using local materials. Replacing these stacks today would require extensive photographing of the stack, course by course as it is dismantled, as well as the creation of templates of the shape at each stage. Each sound brick would need to be cleaned and numbered, then placed in padded trays and crates for protection until reuse.

New handmade bricks would need to be made well in advance of the work, as they take a long time to produce. Originally, brickmakers cast the bricks in the general shape, then allowed them to dry and harden, and only then cut them to the required shape using a knife. Finally, the bricks were fired in a kiln.

The technique used today follows the Victorian way of production. Textured red bricks are handmade in the traditional manner and fired as oversized blanks, ready for cutting. Templates of the existing bricks and cutting blocks are made for each profile. New bricks are then cut by hand to each required shape and size needed using a bow saw, and rubbed to take out any irregularities and to refine any curves of the profile.

The stack is then rebuilt using the new and old bricks, using the templates and photographs taken as a guide. The bedding and pointing mortars would be analysed and reproduced to match the existing texture, colour and finish as closely as possible.

> **Remember**
>
> The height at which the lead tray should be inserted in a new chimney stack is 150 mm above the rafter line on the front side.

> **Did you know?**
>
> A variety of decorative patterns are used at Hampton Court – it has the largest number of decorative chimney stacks in the UK.

Figure 27.22 Decorative chimney stacks

Figure 27.23 Bricks are cut using a bow saw, here being carried out by traditional methods

Remember

When assembling flue liners, the rebate should always be at the top fitting into the spigot of the flue liner above.

Did you know?

Necking courses can be used on stacks. There are oversailing courses in the middle of the stack that prevent water flowing down the whole stack.

Methods for providing oversail and capping

Oversailing is the projecting brickwork at the top of a chimney stack which helps to protect the stack from the elements. A minimum of one course is set out overhanging the stack on all sides. The remaining course or courses, depending on the feature at the top, are then completed and the chimney pot is incorporated.

The top is then sealed with mortar raised at the pot edges to allow water to run away from the top. This is called 'flaunching'. The water will then run off the top and past the chimney stack and not down its length.

An alternative finish to the top would be a purpose-made capping made of concrete that is bedded on. It has a central hole to allow the pot or liner to pass through to the required height; this would then be sealed with mortar between the pot and capping.

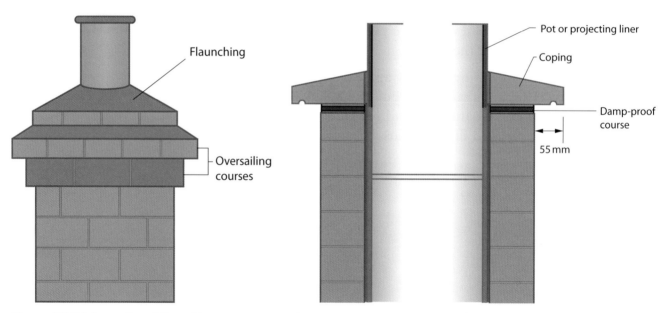

Figure 27.24 Oversail and flaunching

Figure 27.25 Concrete capping finish

Methods for applying chemical cleaning agents to remove mortar smudges

When completing structures, smudges can occur from the mortar over the brickwork. You will want to remove this from the final build to leave an attractive finish. Cleaning agents are usually applied by brushing onto the affected areas and then washing or spraying with clean water.

When working with fireplaces, pre-wet the bricks with fresh, clean water before any cleaning agents are used. This is because all bricks are absorbent, and a dry brick may absorb the cleaning agent and create new stains and smudges. Cleaning agents will need to be washed out immediately if they come into contact with skin or clothing. Always read the manufacturer's instruction on the amount to be used and what precautions to take.

Types, uses and limitations of joint finish

Jointing is carried out to make sure that the mortar joint is completely filled and in contact with each brick. This will prevent rainwater penetration and damage from frost, which would crumble the joint. Once the jointing is completed, rainwater should run down the surface of the wall and not into any gaps left in joints.

One of the most important things to consider is at what time jointing should be carried out. As the brickwork is carried out over the course of the day, lower courses will dry out, but other factors need to be taken into consideration.

- **The type of brick used** – stock or engineering bricks do not absorb moisture as fast as some softer bricks. Therefore the joints will take longer to dry to the required texture for jointing.
- **The moisture content** – the bricks may be damp before use. Therefore moisture absorption will be slow.
- **The weather** – when working in summer the heat will dry out joints faster, due to the warmth of the bricks, than in damper conditions, when moisture stays in the air.

Joints need to be checked by touching to see if they are ready for jointing. If they are too dry, it will be difficult to carry out jointing and if too wet the joint mortar is inclined to 'drag', giving poor adhesion to the bricks and a poor quality appearance.

Ironed or tooled joint

This type of joint is the most commonly used as it covers up slight impurities in the brick arrises and is the quickest to carry out (see Figure 27.26). There are different sizes so care should be taken to use the same size each time. Smaller sizes give a deeper profile whereas the larger diameters give a shallower, rounded look.

Safety tip

When applying cleaning agents always make sure protective clothing is worn including the appropriate mask as well as goggles.

Did you know?

Some bricks can 'swim' with water and may require pointing the next day. To 'swim' means to float on the bed joint due to delayed drying out time.

Remember

The drying out of mortar has no given time span, so understanding and experience are key to knowing when it is the right time for jointing.

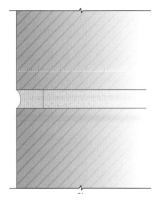

Figure 27.26 Tooled joint

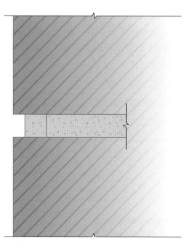

Figure 27.27 Recessed joint

Key term

Rustic – old and natural looking; traditional

Figure 27.28 Flush joint

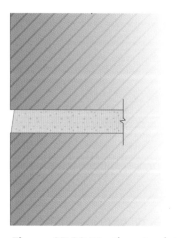

Figure 27.29 Weather struck joint

Recessed joint

With this type of joint the mortar is dragged out to a maximum depth of 4 mm and then ironed to compress the joint's surface. Great care should be taken to ensure that all of the joint is removed. A recessed joint is used when bricks are a more frost-resistant type as water can lie on the edge of the recessed arris on the brick.

Flush joint

This type of joint gives a simple look but it is quite difficult to keep a complete flush surface finish (see Figure 27.28). If modern type finishes are not required, it gives a **rustic** look. A hardwood timber or plastic block is used to smooth and compact the surface of the mortar into place.

A flush joint is not ideal if the bricks used are not regular in shape as the joints will show any deviation and could look wider than they are.

Weather struck joint

This type of joint is slightly sloping to allow rainwater to run down the face of the brick rather than lie at the joint (see Figure 27.29). The mortar is smoothed with a trowel, with the mortar the thickness of the trowel below the top brick and flush with the brick below. The same process is carried out with the perps and the left side of the joint is below the surface.

Weather struck and cut pointing

This is the most common type of jointing carried out on previously raked out joints (see Figure 27.30) and can cover any irregularities to bricks. The mortar is smoothed flush to the brick at the top of the joint and about a trowel thickness proud of the brick at the bottom. The mortar is then allowed to dry slightly and is then 'cut' in a straight line using a tool called a Frenchman.

The straight edge should be kept off the wall using cork pads, nails or screws, so that the cut excess can drop and not be squashed against the face of the wall. Perps are again angled to the left and finished in the same way as the bed joints, but cut with a pointing trowel. All perps should be completed before the bed joint so as not to mark the beds with the trowel and to keep a continuous joint to the bed. This should then be lightly brushed sideways so as not to drag the edges of the bed joints.

Reverse struck joint

This type of finish is normally used for internal walls, giving a smooth finish to work that is not plastered as no shadows appear at the joint area (see Figure 27.31). Care must be taken to ensure the bottom edge is flush to the brick to stop the joint becoming a dust trap when work is complete. The wall would then be given a paint finish.

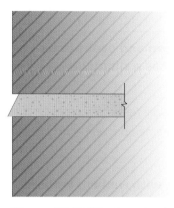

Figure 27.30 Weather struck and cut joint

Figure 27.31 Reverse struck joint

Did you know?

Sometimes a glue (PVA) can be added to the mortar to give a better adhesion to the brick and help bond to the existing mortar.

Working life

James is building a chimney stack and working from a platform scaffold. He has built the brickwork courses and three oversail courses at the top. The chimney is now ready for the chimney pot to be placed. The pot is quite tall and James can see he will have problems reaching and keeping the balance of the pot. He considers borrowing a chair to provide extra support.

Would this be alright as he will only be on the chair for a short time? What could be the result of using this chair? What should James actually do?

Functional skills

In answering the 'Check it out' and 'Check your knowledge' questions you will be practising **FE 2.2.1–3** covering using texts and understanding and summarising their meaning. You will also cover **FM 2.3.1** Interpret and communicate solutions to multistage practical problems and **FM 2.3.2** Draw conclusions and provide mathematical justifications. This may also involve giving oral answers to questions from your tutor and is practise for **FE 2.1.1–2.1.4** Make a range of contributions to discussions and make effective presentations in a wide range of contexts.

FAQ

What happens if the fireplace finish has not been decided and I obviously have to build the chimney breast to tie into the structural wall as I go?

This is not a problem. Build as normal and if there is a chance that a full or part brick fireplace may be built, wall ties should be built into the breast and left to tie in the new breast. If this doesn't happen they can be cut off at a later date and plastered over. Just make sure you put in enough ties to start with.

I am using a petrol disc cutter with a fibre blade. The blade has worn down and needs to be replaced but no diamond blade is available. The only other blade I have has a slightly larger centre. Would this be okay to use?

No, this blade should not be used on the machine. If it does not fit correctly the blade will not rotate properly and will shatter. This could cause injury to the user or any persons who might be near by. Remember only a fully trained person is allowed to change the blade.

I am cleaning down a brick wall using chemical cleaner. The nearest area with running water is on the other side of the site. Will any small splashes be okay if I wipe it off with a rag or cloth?

Any contact to the skin will cause burning, irrespective if the skin is wiped as the chemical will still penetrate the skin. Clothing will also burn and rot over a short time. What you should do in this situation is carry a bucket of clean water to the area to use immediately if required.

Check it out

1. Put together a possible materials list for a new fireplace you may build in a home, making calculations for quantities and possible waste.
2. Prepare a method statement describing the best method to be used for setting up and using a portable power tool of your choice, making special reference to the health and safety issues involved.
3. State which part of the Building Regulations covers chimney work and describe the factors you will need to take into account when working on chimneys.
4. Describe the four main types of fuel used for heating, and explain the different uses for them.
5. Describe why it is important to have access to pipework and other services and the methods that can be used to ensure that this access is in place.
6. Explain the minimum thickness of chimney jambs and explain why this is.
7. Prepare a method statement explaining the stages that need to be followed when fitting a fireplace into position, including reference to health and safety and potential problems. Include sketches for each stage, explaining the information each sketch contains.
8. Explain what a chimney stack is, stating when and where it would be used and why.
9. Describe the materials needed to create flue liners and explain the benefits of these materials.
10. Explain why it is important to undertake regular checks on all work and draw up a method statement describing how to report any defects found.

Getting ready for assessment

The information contained in this unit, as well as the continued practical assignments that you will carry out in your college or training centre, will help you with preparing for both your end-of-unit test and the diploma multiple choice test. It will also aid you in preparing for the work that is required for the synoptic practical assignments. The information contained within this unit will aid you in learning how to carry out structural and decorative brickwork, particularly in reference to setting out and building fireplaces, flues and decorative chimney stacks.

You will need to be familiar with:

- planning and selecting resources for practical tasks
- setting out and building fireplaces and flues
- setting out and building decorative chimney stacks.

This unit will have made you familiar with the methods of constructing fireplaces and flues. For example, learning outcome two will require you to set out brickwork and blockwork to construct fireplaces and flues and select materials suitable for the purpose of constructing these components, positioning them ready for use. You will then need to prepare and cut components safely, erecting fireplaces that incorporate a flue. You will also need to work with other occupation to ensure that you are producing structures that allow access and openings.

Similarly for learning outcome three you will need to set out brickwork, select and position materials, prepare and safely cut components and construct single- and double-flue chimney stacks, incorporating decorative features. You will also need to produce joint finishes, maintaining industrial standards and conducting accuracy checks to ensure that work meets industrial and organisational standards and tolerance, reporting any problems.

Before you start work on the synoptic practical test it is important that you have had sufficient practice and that you feel that you are capable of passing. It is best to have a plan of action and a work method that will help you. You will also need a copy of the required standards, any associated drawings and sufficient tools and materials. It is also wise to check your work at regular intervals. This will help you to be sure that you are working correctly and help you to avoid problems developing as you work.

Your speed at carrying out these tasks will also help you to prepare for the time limit that the synoptic practical task has. But remember, don't try to rush the job as speed will come with practice and it is important that you get the quality of workmanship right.

Always make sure that you are working safely throughout the test. Make sure you are working to all the safety requirements given throughout the test and wear all appropriate personal protective equipment. When using tools, make sure you are using them correctly and safely.

Good luck!

Check your knowledge

1 How is the area of a circle calculated?

- **a)** πd^2
- **b)** $d\pi^2$
- **c)** πr^2
- **d)** $r\pi^2$

2 A ladder should be:

- **a)** securely tied at the top
- **b)** footed or tied at the bottom
- **c)** not rested against guttering
- **d)** all of the above

3 When working from a mobile tower scaffold, you must not:

- **a)** climb up the outside
- **b)** move it when there are people on it
- **c)** throw things from the platform to the ground
- **d)** do any of the above

4 What should sand for mortar be made up of?

- **a)** mainly small size grains
- **b)** mainly large size grains
- **c)** well-graded grains
- **d)** mainly medium size grains

5 What type of fuel is rarely used in conjunction with fireplaces?

- **a)** electric
- **b)** gas
- **c)** solid fuel
- **d)** oil

6 What is the concrete section called at the start of a flue?

- **a)** flaunching unit
- **b)** flue unit
- **c)** gather unit
- **d)** hearth unit

7 When connecting a flue liner, which part should be at the top?

- **a)** socket
- **b)** sprigot
- **c)** spigot
- **d)** stocket

8 What are flashings made of?

- **a)** plastic
- **b)** clay
- **c)** concrete
- **d)** lead

9 What is the minimum height a chimney stack should be if the stack is near or on the ridge?

- **a)** 300 mm
- **b)** 500 mm
- **c)** 600 mm
- **d)** 900 mm

10 What is the gap between the surround and the fireback sealed with?

- **a)** fire resistant rope and mastic
- **b)** sand and cement mortar
- **c)** sand and lime mortar
- **d)** plastic

Know how to repair and maintain masonry structures

Some home owners carry out alterations to their home to improve it, either by adding extra space or by changing the current layout of the property. This can include taking out walls or putting openings into existing walls to create more space in certain rooms. Home owners may also want to carry out simple repairs or maintenance.

This unit also contains material that supports NVQ Units QCF 48 Set out complex masonry structures and QCF 50 Repair and maintain masonry structures.

This unit also contains material that supports TAP Unit 5 Carry out masonry cladding to timber-framed structures and Unit 6 Co-ordinate self and others to erect complex masonry structures.

This unit will cover the following learning outcomes:

- Know how to select required quantity and quality of resources for the method of work to be carried out

- Know how to carry out repairs and maintain existing brickwork or vernacular style structures to contractor's working instructions.

Safety tip

Carelessly discarding fixings, such as nails, can be costly, but can also create health and safety hazards. Broken fixings should be disposed of carefully.

Figure 28.01 Different types of fixings should be stored separately

K1. Know how to select required quantity and quality of resources for the method of work to be carried out

Many of the processes used to select the required quantity and quality of resources for a method of work were covered in Unit 3027. Turn back to pages 146–69 for more information. To complete work you will need to be familiar with mathematical calculations and formulae used for identifying quantities. These were covered on pages 152–55. This unit also looked at carrying out checks on resources and reporting faults and problems on page 155.

Resources required for carrying out repairs and maintenance

Many of these resources were looked at in Unit 3027. Material on the following can be found there:

- bricks and blocks (page 147)
- stone (page 148)
- local materials (page 150)
- mortars, cement and lime (pages 148–50).

Fixing devices

Each type of fixing is designed for a specific purpose and includes nails, screws, pins, bolts, washers, rivets and plugs. As with door furniture, fixings tend to disappear if their storage is not supervised and controlled by a store person.

Fixings must be stored appropriately to keep them in good condition and to make them easy to find. Where possible, they should be kept in bags or boxes clearly marked with their size and type. This enables easy and fast selection and prevents the wrong fixing being used.

Window and door frames

Frames and linings are fitted around openings and are used to allow components such as windows and doors to be fitted. The frame or lining is fitted to the wall and usually finished flush with the walls; the joint between the frame or lining and the wall is covered by the architrave. Before being built into brickwork they are supported by planks weighted down with blocks.

It is very important to make sure that the frame or lining fits the opening well and that it is level. If this is not done, you will end up with doors and windows that don't hang properly and don't open and close properly.

Door linings are of a lighter construction than frames and are only used on internal doors. Door frames are more substantial and are made from **heads**, **jambs** and **cills**. They usually have a rebate cut from the solid timber.

The majority of modern window frames are casement windows. This means they are hinged on the side, allowing them to swing open vertically (similar to the way a door opens) A window frame also contains **mullions** and **transoms**. Frames can be made from softwood, hardwood, uPVC, aluminium and galvanised steel.

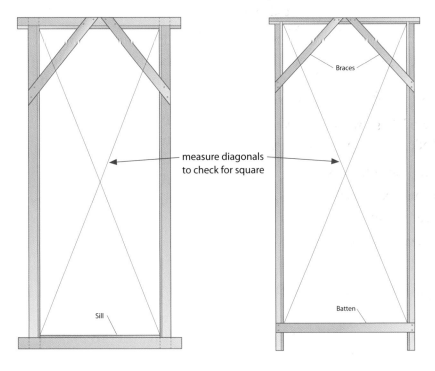

Sill
measure diagonals
to check for square

Figure 28.02 Door frame

Braces
Batten

Figure 28.03 Window frame

Key terms

Heads – the top horizontal part of the frame

Jambs – the vertical sides of the frame

cills – the bottom horizontal part of the frame; can also be spelled 'sills'

Mullion – vertical dividers in a window frame

Transoms – horizontal dividers in a window frame

Remember

A temporary frame used before final frames are fixed is called a dummy frame.

Wall extension profiles

In some instances, proprietary wall connectors may be used rather than cutting out the brickwork toothing (see page 202). There are several different types available and they are made of galvanised steel or stainless steel. If used on external walls, only the stainless steel type should be used. They are fixed to the wall by coach bolts and wall plugs. Therefore the wall requires drilling, normally with a 10 mm masonry drill.

This system is used because it is quicker to fix than toothing and causes less vibration or damage to the existing brickwork. The cost of buying the connectors outweighs the time and effort required for toothing. However, permission must be granted before use so look on the drawings to see if they are specified or ask the local authority if they can be used.

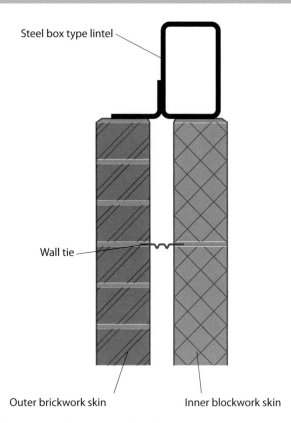

Steel box type lintel

Wall tie

Outer brickwork skin

Inner blockwork skin

Figure 28.04 Box type lintel in situ

Steel and concrete lintels

Lintels are compartments placed above openings in brick and block walls to bridge the opening and support the brick and blockwork above. Lintels made from concrete have a steel reinforcement placed near the bottom for strength, which is why pre-cast lintels have a 'T' or 'Top' etched into the top surface. Pre-cast lintels come in a variety of sizes to suit different opening sizes.

Horizontal brick reinforcement

Brick reinforcement is used in mortar joints to help bond and strengthen brick or blockwork and increase resistance to tensional stresses in areas where vibration or change in temperature may occur. Most brick reinforcement comes in rolls ranging from 50 mm wide up to 300 mm and 20 m long. Any joints must have an overlap of a minimum of 75 mm. This type of reinforcement is mostly used above windows and doors.

Functional skills

Estimating materials that might be needed is an opportunity to practise **FM 2.2.1–2** relating to applying a range of mathematics to find solutions and using appropriate checking procedures and evaluating their effectiveness at each stage.

Remember

You will need to make sure you have all the required materials *before* you start the work, as the last thing you want is to be looking for a brick match after you have removed the broken bricks.

Estimation of materials that might be reclaimed from repair work

Before carrying out any repair work look at what materials will be needed to repair or replace the existing structure. To make a correct estimation of the materials you need to complete repair work, you will need to be certain exactly how much repair work is required for a job. Questions you will need to ask include:

- How many bricks may have to be removed and replaced?
- How much of the original structure can be salvaged and reused, not just what can be replaced?
- Can you match the colour and texture of the bricks and blocks still in place?
- Are the mortar joints soft enough to take out the bricks or blocks without damaging them or will they need to be broken out?

This will determine what materials are able to be salvaged and re-used. Once you know how many materials you can re-use you can make a more accurate estimate of the amount of new material you will need. You can then contact suppliers and cost up the estimate in order to make an informed decision about what is required and the likely expense connected to it.

Tools and equipment required for repairing and maintaining brick and block walling

Many of the tools and equipment you will need to use were covered in Unit 3027, pages 151–52. There are some additional pieces of equipment you will need to work with when working on repairing masonry.

Shoring equipment

Shoring is used where an existing building or component is supported to prevent falling or collapse during modification or removal work. Our example here is the removal of a load-bearing stud partition.

Proper shoring is vital, and is most commonly done with **telescopic** props adjusted to take the weight of the floor above.

Removal of a load-bearing partition

First determine which way the joists on the upper floor run, to make sure your props will support the weight.

Ideally, the props should be placed as close to the partition as possible without being in the way of operations, with the upper floor propped on both sides of the partition. The props should be placed onto a board, acting as a sole plate, and a board should also be positioned where they meet the ceiling, to spread the load.

Now the work can commence. The props should only be removed once the work is complete and a suitable support system such as a steel beam is in place.

More information on support for walls and floors, including mechanical aids for support, can be found later in this unit on page 192.

More information on support for walls and floors, including mechanical aids for support, can be found later in this unit on page 192.

Figure 28.05 Right and wrong way to set up props

Safety tip

Props must *not* be over tightened as this could cause the upper floor to lift slightly, causing damage to the ceiling and floor above.

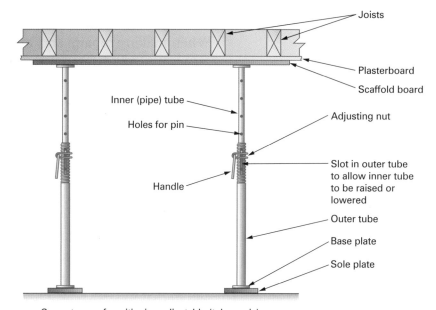

Correct way of positioning adjustable (telescopic) prop

Labels: Joists, Plasterboard, Scaffold board, Inner (pipe) tube, Holes for pin, Adjusting nut, Slot in outer tube to allow inner tube to be raised or lowered, Handle, Outer tube, Base plate, Sole plate

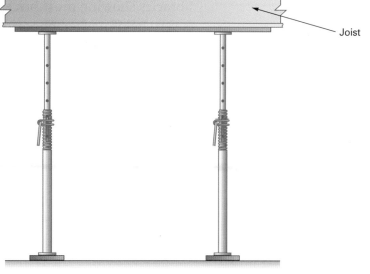

Wrong way

Label: Joist

Manufacturer's recommended checks

Checks required on props should be clearly set out in the manufacturer's manual and instructions. However, it is advisable to make sure that any props used are tightly secure at every point where they are being used. You will need to check this on a regular basis as the weight of the structure being supported is gradually taken on by the props.

K2. Know how to carry out repairs and maintain existing brickwork or vernacular style structures to contractor's working instructions

When making repairs and maintaining existing brickwork there are a number of different jobs which you may need to carry out to ensure that the quality of the building is not allowed to decline. Some of the most common repairs and jobs are looked at below.

Need to maintain standard of existing work

The appearance of new work must match the existing property, so make sure any brick or block you use is as close a match as possible. The brick type may be stated in the specification or it may state 'to match existing'. If you are unsure of the type of brick, take a sample to a builders' merchant and ask them if they can match the brick or tell you what type it is. If it is an older property, the company that made the original bricks may no longer be in production. Some merchants have their own brick libraries showing most bricks that are manufactured today which is very helpful when choosing bricks.

All windows must also match existing profiles and materials used (wood or uPVC being the most commonly found, although some properties may have wood frames with aluminium infills). These would generally be stated in the specification for the work or on the drawings supplied.

The standard of work should also match the existing work so any joint finish should match as well as the colour of the mortar joint. This could be achieved by producing several different mix proportions in small quantities, leaving them to dry and then choosing the most suitable.

Functional skills

Maintaining the standard of existing work will require you to read through specifications and other resources to determine the correct materials needed which will allow you to practise **FE 2.2.1** and **FE 2.2.3**, which cover reading sources for information and identifying their purpose.

Remember

You will also need to match to the same brick sizes as older properties would have used imperial bricks which are different from the metric sizes produced today.

Lime mortar

Lime mortar has porous properties that provide advantages when working with softer building materials such as natural stone and terracotta. Lime mortar is used on older properties for repairs in order to match the existing mortar colour. It has had a reputation for being a soft mortar and not very durable but the number of older buildings still in place that used this mortar has shown this to be a myth.

There are two types of mortar lime used:

- **Non-hydraulic lime** – made from pure limestone, heated to a high temperature, driving off carbon dioxide to produce quicklime (calcium oxide). This is done in a lime kiln. The quicklime is then mixed with water (slaked) to produce lime putty.
- **Hydraulic lime** – this means lime that hardens under water. The limestone used contains quantities of clay or silica, producing dicalcium silicate as a final product. It is slaked with enough water to convert the calcium oxide to calcium hydroxide, but not enough water to react with the dicalcium silicate. When the powder dicalcium silicate is mixed with water, this causes it to set producing hydraulic lime.

Specialist bonds

Rat trap bond

Rat trap (or Chinese) bond is used in the construction of garden walls. It is similar to Flemish bond but the bricks are laid brick on edge to form the bond. In this bond, the stretchers are called shiners and the headers are called rowlocks.

When under construction the wall gives an internal cavity, bridged by the rowlocks. The main advantage of this type of wall is that the overall cost is approximately 25 per cent less than if built in English or Flemish bond. The amount of bricks used per metre is reduced from 350 per cubic metre to 280. This also reduces the joints by 25 per cent and amount of mortar used by 54 per cent.

Rat trap bond was in common use in England for building houses of fewer than three storeys up to the turn of the 20th century and is still commonly used in India as an economical bond. It also offers insulation via the air cavity.

> **Did you know?**
>
> Dutch bond is another variation on Flemish bond and has always been considered the most decorative bond used.

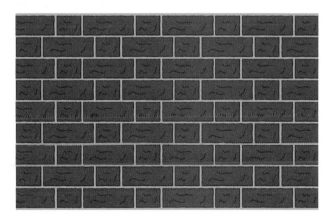

Figure 28.06 Rat trap bond

Monk bond

Monk bond is another variation of Flemish bond. This type of bond has two stretchers between the headers in each course with the header centred over the joint between the two stretchers in the course below. Another variation of this is Wessex bond which has three stretchers between each header.

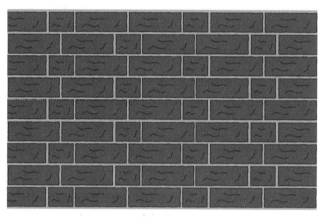

Figure 27.07 Monk bond

> **Key term**
>
> **Blown** – plaster or render no longer adhering to the interior brick or block wall

Figure 28.08 Effects of damp

Methods for replacement and repair of damp proof barriers

Damp penetration can be a major problem, causing staining to interior finishes, bubbling of paintwork to walls and even plaster which is powdering and **blown** on walls.

Other areas that can be affected by damp include timber such as floorboards, joists, skirting boards, window frames, fascia and soffit boards which can all rot.

Internal damp is caused in two different ways:

1. moisture travelling horizontally
2. moisture travelling vertically.

Horizontal moisture

This is normally caused when the cavity is bridged, allowing moisture from the external wall to cross through the cavity into the internal wall. Bridging is usually caused by pieces of brick, block or mortar dropping down the cavity, either during the original construction or through work carried out later. Breakdown of mortar over the course of time can also fill the cavity above the DPC and allow moisture to penetrate across.

Rectifying the problem depends on the area affected. If the damp is part way up the wall and affecting a small area, then it could be just a single piece of brick/mortar causing the problem. In some cases, small pieces of timber have also been found to be the cause. These will have to be removed by cutting out a brick or two (see page 190) on the outside wall to investigate. The bridge is then removed and the bricks replaced.

If the damp is at floor level or just above, the problem could be horizontal or vertical. The cavity could be bridged or filled with mortar above the DPC. To rectify, cut out bricks just above DPC level to see if the cavity is full. If so, the cavity needs to be fully cleaned to a minimum of 150 mm below DPC level.

Cleaning out must be done carefully. In some cases, mortar may be soft and easy to remove but in others it could be firm and hard to remove. As the cavity is very narrow (probably 50 mm wide) there is not much room to work, meaning very basic tools have to be specially made in order to drag out the mortar.

Obviously you may only be able to reach a small area at a time, so more bricks will need to be removed to complete the job. When you do this, make sure the holes are positioned so you can clean both left and right within the cavity as far as you can reach.

Remember the stability of the wall is paramount. Only cut out two to three bricks long per section and leave at least four bricks before cutting the next section. It is advisable to only cut out four sections, if needed, on a wall before reinstatement. When replacing bricks (see page 190) an airbrick may be put in at intervals to allow more ventilation to the cavity and to help prevent future problems.

Another problem area for horizontal damp is at reveals due to splits or holes in the vertical DPC. In these cases, cut out the brickwork and replace the affected section of DPC, making sure to lap the DPC by a minimum of 100 mm top and bottom.

Did you know?

If cleaning to a minimum of 150 mm below DPC level, this cleaning may have to be carried out along the whole length of the wall if the findings are bad.

Safety tip

Gloves must be worn at all times as other materials could be under the initial surface such as nails, wood, even glass fragments. You must also take care around wall tie areas. It is very easy to catch your hand or part of your arm on a wall tie.

Vertical moisture

Vertical damp problems are normally due to a breakdown of the horizontal DPC, causing moisture to draw up through the ground into the brick or blockwork. If the external DPC is replaced, brickwork is removed in sections in the same way as for cavity cleaning. If the whole wall is replaced, break the sections into four and name them sections A, B, C and D. Cut out all section As first. Lay the new DPC to the cut out opening, allowing for a minimum of 100 mm turn up at each end to allow lapping when those sections are replaced. Replace the brickwork but don't mortar the perp joints against the existing brickwork – wedge it (see page 197). Then replace all section Bs, making sure the DPC is lapped with the previous section. Continue for the remaining sections until the wall is completely replaced.

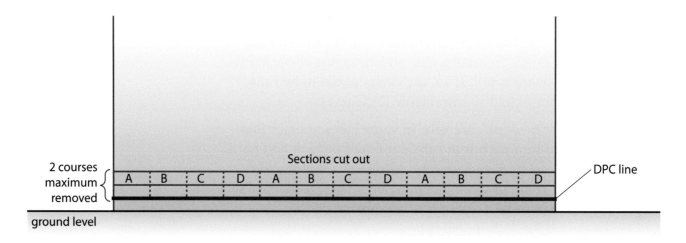

Figure 28.09 DPC sections

If the horizontal DPC has broken down on the internal wall, it is normally rectified by injecting a silicone-based liquid DPC.

Remove the skirting boards and plaster 1 m up from the floor. A series of holes are drilled into the wall just above the existing DPC. The liquid is pumped in and absorbed into the bricks. Once dry, re-plaster the wall with a moisture resistant plaster. Sometimes liquid bitumen or sealer is painted onto the exposed brickwork prior to the plaster to stop any further problems. This is normally carried out by a specialist company giving a minimum of a 10-year guarantee, but they may require the original plaster to be removed by the contractor.

If damp shows over a lintel, it could mean the cavity is bridged or no DPC tray has been fitted. Cut out the brickwork in sections as before (probably not as many sections will be required) and clear if bridged, or fit a DPC cavity tray in sections, making allowance for lapping as previously described.

Also available is a plastic tray system, with each tray being two bricks long with interlocking edges to connect to the next section. A flapped back edge adjusts to meet the internal wall, stopping any moisture in the cavity from going behind the tray. Care must be taken with the measuring and placement of further trays, as the trays joining the sections may be too long or too short to fit into their correct position. The bricks are actually bedded into the tray, with plastic weep holes placed in the joint between the two bricks to allow any moisture to run back outside the building.

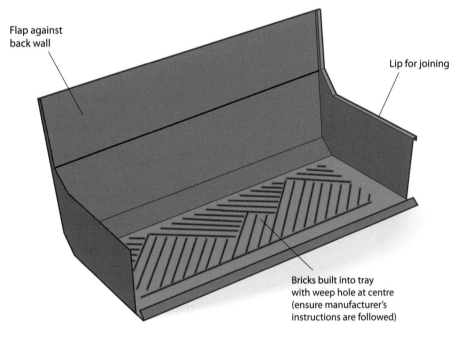

Flap against back wall

Lip for joining

Bricks built into tray with weep hole at centre (ensure manufacturer's instructions are followed)

Figure 28.10 A cavity tray

Working life

You are replacing a horizontal damp proof course using a plastic-coated flexible DPC. You are aware that the minimum overlap of the DPC should be 100 mm. However, you have come to the end of the roll, and only have sufficient DPC left to give you a 50 mm overlap. The experienced bricklayer you are working with assures you that this will be sufficient and will save you opening a new roll just for an additional 50 mm.

What do you do? Should you open a new roll to comply with the information on the drawing? Or do you avoid opening a new roll and use what you have left? What are the possible consequences of using a smaller piece than that required?

Functional skills

Calculating the requirements of a particular work situation will allow you the opportunity to practise the *interpreting* elements of functional skills, e.g. **FM 2.3.1** Interpret and communicate solutions to multistage practical problems and **FM 2.3.2** Draw conclusions and provide mathematical justifications. You may also be able to practise **FE 2.2.1** and **FE 2.2.3**, which cover reading sources for information and identifying their purpose.

Methods used to temporarily support existing walls and floors

When working on brickwork you will often need to work on walls and floors that bear weight. The weight above the opening must be supported by a lintel and the bearing of the lintel must be sufficient to take the weight that has been transferred.

To form any new opening in existing brickwork, the wall above needs to be supported. Checks need to be made to ascertain the extent of the weight to be transferred. The main areas to look at include:

- Does the wall continue above on the next floor or, if it is an upstairs room, into the roof space?
- Do the ceiling joists above sit onto the wall, transferring the weight of the room's furniture onto the wall?

How do we check for this?

Visual inspection will show if the wall above is load bearing. In the case of a standard size door opening, there will be brickwork in the existing room that will require supporting as well as anything above. If it is impossible to tell then the original drawings with measurements will provide this information.

A quick visual check to see which way ceiling joists run is to check the direction of the upstairs floorboards, as the joists will run the opposite way. If the flooring has been replaced with chipboard sheeting, the lines of nailing will show the joists. This check gives a lot of information about how the weight needs to be temporarily supported.

The temporary support system is called dead shoring and carries vertical loads. The system uses props that support timber or steel positioned either on both sides of the wall, or through the wall, depending on the way the joists run. Props used to be made of timber but now are likely to be steel props. Steel props are adjustable by means of holes and pins similar to trestles and

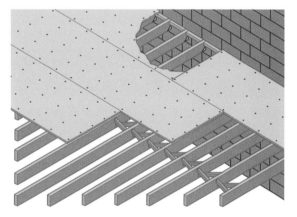

Floor sheeting

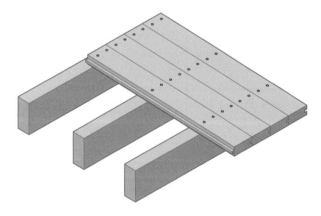

Floor boards

Figure 28.11 Floorings and fixings

have a lever screw system to fine adjust for tightening. They come in different sizes and can be hired from most plant hire companies.

Positioning of props

Before any work is carried out, all furniture etc. must be moved from the areas so that it is not damaged by the work in progress. Carpets must also be removed or rolled back away from the area and covered. You want to avoid costly repairs to furniture or carpets.

When you have found out which way the joists run, you will know how the propping needs to be positioned. There are two different ways to carry out the system based on the way the joists run.

1. Parallel to the wall

2. Through the wall

Parallel to the wall

If joists run directly into the wall to be worked on, two sets of props will be required, one set each side of the wall. Props are placed parallel to the new opening area and need to be set back to allow sufficient space to work.

Props should be placed on a scaffold board which must be laid directly onto the floorboards or screed. The scaffold board should be long enough to run past each side of the new opening by at least 1 m. In the case of a standard size door, opening two props each side should be sufficient to carry the weight – they should be positioned no more than 1.5 m apart. A second scaffold board of equal length is to be positioned directly above the floorboard, against the ceiling, with the two props acting as wedges tight between the two boards.

To carry out this operation safely three people will be needed, two to hold and adjust the props and one to hold the board to the ceiling.

The sequence runs as follows:

1. Place the board onto the floorboard or screed, parallel to the wall.

2. Set up the props with the pins roughly in the correct position for the height required.

3. Place the props on the base board and hold in position.

4. Place the second board on top of the two props and temporarily hold from the underside, so as not to trap fingers.

5. Tighten up the props using the lever until the board is tight to the ceiling.

> **Remember**
>
> Be careful if the flooring has been covered with hardboard as this will be fixed down onto the existing flooring but the fixings could be randomly set giving no indication of the positions of the joists. In this instance, an area of the hardboard will need to be removed to confirm the correct joist positions.

Figure 28.12 Adjustable props

> **Safety tip**
>
> Working platforms will be needed to give enough height to install the lintel when required.

> **Remember**
>
> Do not lay base board on to carpets as this will cause damage and allow movement on the props.

6. Plumb the props to ensure they are fully upright both ways.

7. Tighten slightly to take up any slack but do not over tighten as you will lift and crack the ceiling line area.

8. Repeat the sequence to the other side of the wall.

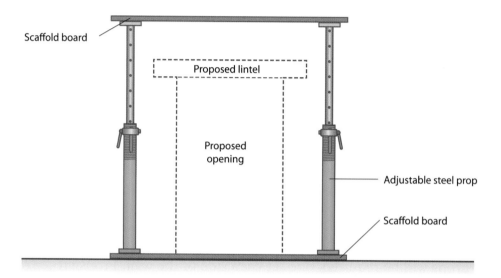

Figure 28.13 Props in position

Through the wall

If the joists run parallel to the wall, no weight from the room is transferred to the wall. The weight that needs to be supported is only above the immediate area so the props are set to carry this weight. Only two props will be needed to carry out this operation and, instead of a ceiling board, a piece of stout timber (150 mm x 100 mm) or small steel (RSJ) about 2 m long will be needed. This is called a 'needle'.

The sequence for propping is as follows:

1. Mark out the position of the proposed opening on the wall.

2. Mark the lintel position (for this size of opening a standard 100 mm x 65 mm x 1200 mm is adequate) ensuring equal bearings on both ends.

3. Above the lintel line, mark for a hole at the centre of the opening – it must be large enough for the RSJ or timber to go through.

4. Carefully cut the hole through the wall.

5. The needle is then pushed through the hole leaving equal distance on both sides.

Remember

If an RSJ is used as a needle, a timber block needs to be placed between the RSJ and prop to stop any sliding (metal against metal) and for securing the prop.

6. A base board needs to be set on the floor on both sides of the wall. If the floor is wooden, make sure the base board runs across the joists to transfer any weight.

7. Set up the two props, one on each side of the wall, and adjust the height of the prop to suit the height that the needle comes through the wall.

8. Gently tighten the props until they meet the needle, ensuring that the needle is in a level position. Re-check and adjust the props until the needle is correct.

9. Plumb the props both ways.

10. Finally, tighten both props together so they are firmly in place.

11. Place nails into the prop top and base to stop any movement.

Did you know?

Another method that can be used is using strong boys. These are steel props which have steel support struts which are knocked into the mortar joint above the point where the masonry is to be removed, taking the weight.

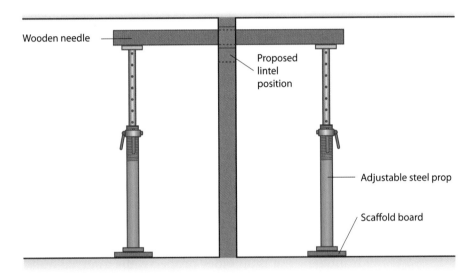

Wooden needle

Proposed lintel position

Adjustable steel prop

Scaffold board

Figure 28.14 Props and needle through wall

Working life

You are required to form an opening between two rooms in a domestic dwelling. You are unable to find, without further inspection, whether or not the wall in which the opening is to be formed is a load-bearing one.

An electrician working on the same job tells you that the wall is not carrying any load and is purely a partition wall, so you do not need to provide support for the floor above, just for the brickwork above the opening.

Taking this advice will save a lot of time, prevent any unnecessary moving of furniture and carpets in the room above, and will remove the possibility of damaging existing floor coverings, such as floorboards.

Do you take the advice given by the electrician? If not, why not? What could the consequences of your decision be?

Forming openings in existing masonry walling

Altering the inside of a property can give more space to areas which are used more than others. For example, older properties may have a separate lounge and dining area and this can be changed to make one larger room by taking out the adjoining wall, or by forming an opening to allow access from one room to the other. The layout is designed to suit the customer but the changes are based on the same construction principles – taking out existing brick or blockwork without affecting the structural stability.

Cutting out the opening

The cutting method is determined by the circumstances of the property. If the property is empty, it may be possible to use a disc cutter (but tape the doors to stop the dust travelling right through the property). The dust and fumes (if using a petrol cutter) produced will replace the oxygen in the area, so correct PPE must be combined with regular breaks outside. A cutter is the quickest method but not always the cheapest, as the area will need to be ventilated after work. Another method is to use hammer and bolster or drill lots of holes along the marking prior to cutting (though this can be time-consuming).

The main thing you must take into account is keeping damage to the surrounding wall to a minimum. The type of material the wall is made of may work to your advantage – if it is an older property, the internal walls are likely to be made of brick but may have sand/lime joints which will be fairly soft. Newer properties may have lightweight blocks meaning that they will be easier to cut.

Cutting by hand tools

Carefully take off the skirting board on both sides of the wall and store it for future reinstatement. Always start the cutting from the top – cut away the plasterwork to the marked lines to the whole of the new lintel area. This will expose the material that the wall is made of. Carefully cut a hole using the nearest joint at the top left- or right-hand corner near to the plumb line.

If the mortar joint is soft, it may be possible to cut the bed joint right across the top of the proposed lintel and then cut the brick

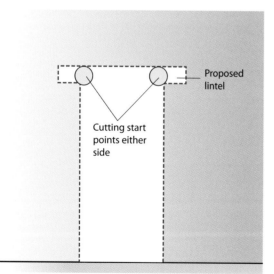

Figure 28.15 The start point for cutting

Labels within figure:
Proposed lintel
Cutting start points either side

Find out

Find out how loads are calculated and what type of lintels you should use for a specific job.

Remember

You will have to complete any propping before you will be ready to start the cutting out.

Remember

Do not cut out the lintel bearing at this stage.

course out from the bed joint below. If not, the course must be cut out in small sections of brickwork so as not to crack or damage the whole wall. In both cases, cut out full bricks only.

Once you have reached the sides, cut the plumb line vertically with a hammer and bolster. If two people are available, this can be cut simultaneously from both sides reducing vibration and damage.

Whole bricks can be cut out course by course. A saw could be used to cut out a soft perp joint each time to make things easier, and the plumb line cut the same as stated until reaching floor level. A plugging chisel can also be used to cut bricks.

At this point, carefully cut out the bearings, making sure no damage is done to the course below as this will eventually take the weight from the lintel area.

If the wall is made of insulation blocks, once a hole has been cut it could be cut with a masonry saw down the plumb lines, as well as horizontally, for the lintel and bearings.

The lintel is then bedded into position. At this point don't bed joint the top of the lintel – allow it to set. Once the bed has set, the top joint should be wedged to the existing brickwork with slate all the way along and then pointed.

The opening is now ready for finishing.

Finishing the opening

Any opening can be finished in two different ways:

1. by plastering all the exposed edges
2. by fitting a lining around the edges.

The lining is normally made of timber.

Plaster finish

If plaster is to be used on all edges as a finish, all the corners must be fitted with a metal angle bead to give a smooth edge to finish the plaster to. There are several different types of beads used in plastering. The main ones are:

- plaster beads
- plasterboard beads
- stop beads.

They all have different uses but produce the same finish, creating an edge to plaster to. Plaster should always be stored in a dry place and used in date order so that it does not harden in the bags before being used.

> **Did you know?**
> The brickwork will need to be cut to below the floor level to allow for finishing at a later date.

> **Remember**
> If the joint is filled at the time of bedding there is a chance of shrinkage of the joint, causing later movement.

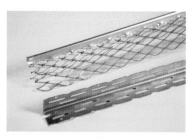

Figure 28.16 Different types of plaster beads

Remember

Ensure that the beads are parallel on both sides of the wall.

Did you know?

Nowadays, multi-finish plaster is used in most cases. This means that the thickness can be achieved in one coat, gradually building up the thickness as coats are applied and finishing in the same way as previously described.

Plaster angle beads

Plaster angle beads will need to be used. These have a galvanised metal edge connected to galvanised wire mesh and are approximately 50 mm wide on each angle. They are fixed into position on the wall by plaster dabs which set quickly to secure them in place.

To fix them there must be sufficient brickwork exposed and, as the opening plaster was cut flush, you may need to cut the plaster back about 50 mm to take the angle bead. The corner edge of the bead must be set in line with the existing plaster finish and plumbed on the opening internal edge, allowing for at least 15 mm cover of plaster to the wall. This sequence is carried out to all the edges including the underside of the lintel.

Plaster

Once all the beads are dry and secured, the plaster can be applied. This is normally in two coats, the first approximately 12 mm thick (but this could depend on the thickness of the existing plaster – it may need to be slightly thicker). Thin coats are applied and built up to the required thickness.

If using sand and cement, or bonding, plaster is used for the first coat and must be levelled and plumbed using a straight edge or rule. Before the material has set rub it over with a wooden float, with nails protruding, to form a key for the finishing plaster. Once dry, the finish plaster is applied and smoothed with a steel plastering trowel. As the plaster dries, slightly damp the surface with water and re-trowel to give the finish. The correct timing for this is important to give a smooth sheen to the plaster.

The floor area where the bricks were cut out now require finishing with a grit/cement mix of about 1:4 ratio. It must be a minimum of 75 mm thick so that it does not crack and must be finished smooth to both room levels. DPC may be required below the screed to prevent damp rising. If the finished floor is timber, the boards must be extended between the last joist in each room. Make sure that the wall below this area does not touch any of the timber as this could cause damp and rot.

When the plaster is dry and the floor is completed, the skirting board can be re-fixed and mitre jointed to the corners on both sides of the wall and through the opening.

Once the plaster is completely dry, that is the plaster colour has changed to a very light colour, the wall is ready to be painted. A mist coat should be used first as the plaster will draw the paint in, then a minimum of two further coats should be applied.

Lining finish

Rather than having a full plaster finish to the opening, a timber lining can be fitted in the same way as a standard door lining (the difference is that no door stops are fitted). The lining is fitted by the carpenter and the plaster finished as previously described. Once dry the architrave can be fitted.

Larger openings

In the case of larger openings through walls, or complete wall removal, the weight distribution works on the same principles. However, more props need to be used and longer lintels are required. If a whole wall is to be removed, an RSJ/**BSB** will be needed or very substantially sized timber, normally oak. This may need to be situated on brick piers to take the weight. In cases like this, you may need a structural engineer to determine the size of steel or timber, and the size of piers if required, plus bearings needed (a **padstone** could also be needed). If a full wall is being removed, the steel or timber is normally situated tight to the ceiling line to give maximum headroom to this area. Once situated, the steel is boxed in and can either be plastered or timber lined to create a timber effect.

Key terms
BSB – British Standard Beam
Padstone – a reinforced area in a wall, built to distribute pressure from a concentrated load onto a larger area of wall. The padstone is usually made from concrete

Remember
Do not forget to place the RSJ/BSB next to the wall before props are positioned, as the props may prevent moving the beam into the correct position once support has been set up.

Working life
You have positioned/bedded a steel lintel above a newly formed opening and you are now ready to fill in the void between the top of the lintel and the brickwork above, which is to be supported by the lintel.
You do not have sufficient packing material, as specified by the architect, to complete the work. The bricklayer you are working with has suggested you use additional mortar to fill the rest of the void, but make sure it is a stronger mix than that used so far.
Do you take this advice? If not, what is your alternative?

Replacing lintels to existing walling

There are two main reasons for repairs to lintels or cills. One is edges breaking away and shear breaks. Lintels and cills are generally made of reinforced concrete. The front edge of a lintel or cill is the most exposed to the elements. Moisture absorbed into the concrete can freeze, causing expansion, or the reinforcement gets damp and rust forms on the steel, which also expands, causing the concrete to break away from the mass. The other reason for repairs to lintels and cills is cracking due to pressure from the weight above or movement around this area.

In the case of expansion, the affected material could be removed, the exposed reinforcing coated with a rust treatment and rendered to finish, depending on the amount of damage.

An alternative is to replace the lintel. If the lintel or cill is cracked or broken then this is the only option. The lintel will require dead shoring through the wall and the course of bricks above the lintel cut out. The lintel can then be carefully removed and replaced. A continuous DPC tray should be fitted on top of the lintel and the bricks reinstated, joint wedged and pointed. Weep holes should be positioned along the line of bricks to allow for any water drainage.

In the case of a cill replacement, care must be taken not to damage the frame.

1. The bricks below the cill are removed, taking care to ensure the cill does not suddenly drop trapping fingers.

2. A section two courses in depth should be cut out at each end under the cill.

3. Once removed, replace with dry bricks or timber blocks and wedge tight.

4. Remove the rest of the two courses of brickwork below the cill.

5. Slowly take out the wedges and allow the cill to sit on the blocks.

6. Gradually remove the blocks end by end until the cill is clear of the frame. Take out the cill and dispose of it correctly.

The new cill should be fitted following the steps to remove the old cill in reverse order. Once in position build back the central brickwork and allow to dry – then wedge. Remove the end wedges and rebuild the remaining brickwork as before.

Reasons for walling extension provision

There are several ways in which a property can have space added. These could include:

- building an extension to give extra space or an extra room or rooms
- adding a conservatory
- converting roof space (the loft)
- changing the use of a garage or **outbuilding**.

Did you know?

In the case of a boot lintel, both internal and outer skins need to be removed.

Safety tip

This operation should use the correct type of scaffolding to ensure operatives are not put at risk.

Key term

Outbuilding – a shed or storage area which can be connected to the main building

Figure 28.17 An extensin both during and after initial construction

Extensions

This is where an extra room or rooms are added to the current structure. If an extension is to be built, planning permission or building regulation approval must be gained from the local council prior to the start of any work.

Foundations must be dug to meet local authority approval, as with any new building with a cavity wall construction.

The extension must be joined correctly to the main structure with the cavity continuous throughout; this process is usually started just below DPC level as the damp course also requires lapping to the existing to prevent moisture rising up at the joining point. The mortar joint at DPC level must be cut out with a brick saw or disc cutter to allow the DPC to be slid into position and the join repointed.

Prior to the joining of the DPC, the cavity must be extended. This is done by marking the existing wall at the back of the face brick line and plumbing and marking this line vertically to the height required for joining. From this line the cavity width size is marked and the same process carried out. These two lines are then carefully cut using a disc cutter, ensuring that the material is cut right through to the cavity to ensure less vibration of material at the next stage. The material is then cut out to leave an open cavity which is the size required for the extension.

> **Remember**
>
> The brick needs to be matched before the work is priced as it could prove very costly if you have not allowed enough money. The local authority could reject the bricks if they are not correct.

Key term

Toothing – cutting out existing brickwork to join new

Now the cavity has been cut, the new external brickwork has to be joined as well as the internal blockwork. This process is carried out by **toothing** the external face brickwork and internal blockwork.

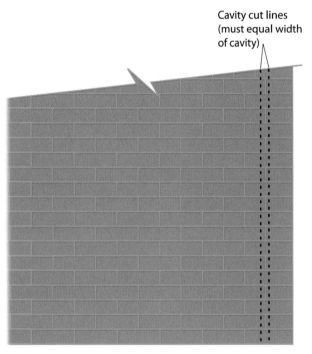

Figure 28.18 The marking of cavity position

Cavity cut lines (must equal width of cavity)

Remember

With all toothing, always start from the top and work downwards.

Joining the face brickwork by toothing

The face brickwork is joined to the existing wall by toothing. The amount to be cut out is determined by the type of bond used on the existing brickwork and the position of the extended wall. If the new wall is built to an existing corner on a stretcher bonded wall (half bond), the half batt remaining from the original cavity cutting is removed, allowing for new brickwork. If the existing wall is built in Flemish or English bond (quarter bond), then the half batt and closer is removed. The toothing will determine the bonding of each course. This must be decided at an early stage to ensure brickwork showing above ground level works to the toothed brickwork for bond or, if this is not possible, suitable cuts are used within the new wall.

If the toothing is to be elsewhere along the wall, then only the width of the brick plus a joint thickness needs to be cut on alternate courses (you will still need to think about which course to cut out).

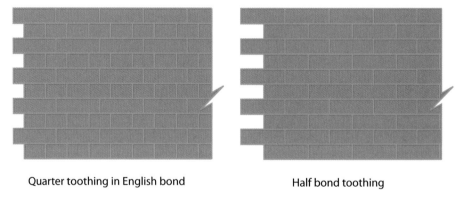

Quarter toothing in English bond

Half bond toothing

Figure 28.19 Toothing for half and quarter bond

Cutting the brick toothing

Take care not to damage the remaining brickwork around the area when toothing for the new wall. If the brickwork is older with a sand and lime mix, the joints may be fairly soft. Therefore, it may be possible to cut the bed joint with a masonry saw and to tap the brick out carefully. If the joint is made of sand and cement, a small disc cutter will be required. The cutting must be carried out very carefully to avoid damaging the surrounding bricks – remove any remaining brickwork if the blade touches it. Chipping bricks is also a hazard. In some instances, a hammer and sharp chisel may be used but, again, great care must be taken not to chip or crack and break the surrounding brickwork.

The blockwork

The cutting process for blockwork is almost the same as for brickwork except that three blocks are cut out each time and the width may vary to suit different thicknesses of blocks. This is called block toothing or block bonding. The toothing must work out to accommodate the block courses so that they line up with the brickwork.

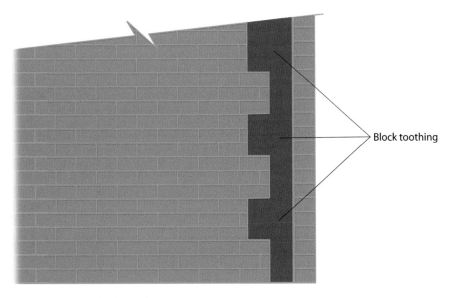

Figure 28.20 Block toothing

> **Remember**
>
> Bricks should be cut by gradually cutting one small section at a time, angling the chisel to cut the middle and back areas first and then the front area so not too much pressure is applied to the surrounding brickwork.

> **Working life**
>
> You are carrying out some work on a small extension to a domestic property. The specification for the job states that the new brickwork should be toothed into the existing brickwork with matching facing bricks.
>
> A work colleague informs you that they have noticed some proprietary wall connectors in the stores and that these would be a much easier way of doing the job, and would also be a lot quicker. Also, these would also eliminate the possibility of existing bricks being damaged when cutting out the toothing.
>
> What do you do? State the reasons for your choice.

> **Functional skills**
>
> Working with specifications is an excellent opportunity to practise **FE 2.2.1** and **FE 2.2.3**, which cover reading sources for information and identifying their purpose.

Remember

These techniques will be identical to carrying out repairs in decorative features. Decorative features are classed as decorative panels, soldier courses, corbels and any other design or brick layout that is not straight forward brickwork.

Jointing and pointing and replacing bricks

All properties need repairs as they get older. The lifespan of some materials runs out and they have to be repaired or replaced. Some areas that involve the bricklayer are:

- pointing
- cracked bricks or blocks (caused by movement).

If we break these down we can investigate the causes and the solutions to correct these problems.

Pointing

The mortar used to build older properties was made up of sand and lime. This is a very soft mortar and, due to weathering or attack, breaks down. This can happen in small areas or whole walls but must be rectified.

Repointing is the process carried out on older properties where mortar joints have broken down due to rain, wind or frost exposure over many years. This could be because the original mortar was very soft with no cement being used.

Another reason for repointing could be because of insect attack. Soft joints allow small insects to burrow into the joints, the worst being *Osmia rufa* or the mason bee, which burrows into soft joints to lay its eggs. This type of bee can literally demolish a building by removing enough mortar to make it dangerous to enter. Walls can be spray-treated to deter this type of attack and if repointed with cement-based mortar attacks cease as the new joints are not as soft.

Did you know?

Mason bees do not like cement-based joints.

Figure 28.21 Mason bee in soft joint

Remember

Replacement bricks need to match those bricks already in situ. Some of the methods of doing this were covered on pages 186–88.

Cracked or broken bricks

Cracked or broken bricks look unsightly in a wall, but before replacement the cause for the damage must be found. If a large area has been affected, it could be due to movement of the building through subsidence, or it may only be a single brick that was cracked when first laid or had a slight flaw which was not noticed originally.

In the case of large areas, investigation needs to be carried out, especially if there is sizeable cracking and gaps in the bricks and mortar joints. Cracks may have small glass plates screwed across them which are monitored over a set period to see if movement is still happening. These plates are called 'telltales' and they do what they say; some have a measuring gauge to show movement and others may be plain but if movement occurs they will crack.

Structural engineers are generally involved when a large area is affected, so if you are asked to look at a problem like this it is advisable to inform the client straight away. This problem is probably due to movement in the ground causing the concrete foundation to shift, normally through a crack or sheer. The main reason for movement could be due to:

- shrinkage of the ground structure
- tree roots
- leaking or broken pipes.

However, there are other factors that could cause movement such as:

- underground railways
- mining
- ground erosion
- long-term bomb damage.

An expert will find the cause and suggest the best way to repair, normally through underpinning the foundation and rebuilding the wall or walls. Underpinning is carried out by specialised companies to specifications set by a structural engineer, or jointly with an architect.

When just single bricks are the cause of the problem, the remedy is to take them out and replace them. Great care is needed when cutting, as well as when matching the brick and mortar colour and finish. Cut small quantities at a time and chip carefully away at the brick to avoid damaging the rest of the wall.

Working life

Amir has been asked to cut open and repoint a section of wall on an old property that has been patched by the previous owner using nearly neat cement.

What tools should Amir use to cut the pointing and what problems could arise?

FAQ

I am building in a door frame and I have run out of frame ties. Can I use 100 mm nails as a replacement?

No. The correct fixings must always be used.

I am inserting a new concrete lintel into an opening that has just been formed. On measuring the size of the lintel it is found to be only 75 mm bigger than the opening. Will this be okay to use?

No. The minimum bearing for a concrete lintel is 100 mm – if steel is used then it is 150 mm bearing at each end.

Can you use screws for fixing proprietary wall connectors?

It will depend on what type of connector is used. Some manufacturers supply screw bolts with washers but some supply screws and washers. If a replacement is required due to loss etc., then the same type and size should be used.

Check it out

1. Using a repair job that might need to be carried out in the building you work in, put together an estimate for materials, including amounts for waste.
2. Prepare a method statement explaining the process used to shore up structures during building, using diagrams to show the best practice which should be used.
3. Explain the possible implications of damp appearing over a lintel and the reasons behind this appearing.
4. Explain the principles behind placing and lapping of DPC when dealing with moisture.
5. Explain why the standard of existing work must be maintained, explaining what techniques and information you will need to do this.
6. Describe three materials that can support an opening, explaining why each may be used and when.
7. Explain why props should not be over tightened.
8. Describe the two methods that can be used to finish an opening ready for decoration, using diagrams and sketches to show the stages followed.
9. Explain the advantage of using multi-purpose finish plaster.
10. Explain two methods to join brickwork on an extension to an existing property, using diagrams to illustrate how each method works.

Getting ready for assessment

The information contained in this unit, as well as the continued practical assignments that you will carry out in your college or training centre, will help you with preparing for both your end-of-unit test and the diploma multiple-choice test. It will also aid you in preparing for the work that is required for the synoptic practical assignments. The information in this unit will help you to learn how to repair and maintain existing masonry structures, in particular carrying out repairs to the contractor's working instructions.

You will need to be familiar with:

- selecting required quantity and quality of resources for the method of work to be carried out
- carrying out repairs and maintain existing brickwork or vernacular style structures to contractor's working instructions.

This unit has looked at the work needed to repair and maintain existing structures. For example, for learning outcome two you will need to be able to select the materials required for producing a specified mortar mix to match the existing mortar. You will also need to position bricks, blocks and components ready for use, preparing and cutting components to existing walls, working safely. You will need to be able to form toothings, indents and block bonding by hand or by disc cutter or table mounted saw. Among the tasks you will need to be able to perform are repairing brickwork to match existing bonding, dressing and forming finishes to match existing walling and producing jointing and pointing finishes to match existing walling. You will need to protect resources and work areas during work and after completion.

Before you start work on the synoptic practical test it is important that you have had sufficient practice and that you feel that you are capable of passing. It is best to have a plan of action and a work method that will help you. You will also need a copy of the required standards, any associated drawings and sufficient tools and materials. It is also wise to check your work at regular intervals. This will help you to be sure that you are working correctly and help you to avoid problems developing as you work.

Your speed at carrying out these tasks will also help you to prepare for the time limit that the synoptic practical task has. But remember, don't try to rush the job as speed will come with practice and it is important that you get the quality of workmanship right.

Always make sure that you are working safely throughout the test. Make sure you are working to all the safety requirements given throughout the test and wear all appropriate personal protective equipment. When using tools, make sure you are using them correctly and safely.

Good luck!

Check your knowledge

1 What is a proprietary connector used for?

a) providing space for electric supply

b) joining a new wall to existing

c) joining DPC

d) fixing windows in existing openings.

2 What should be done before setting up props inside a room?

a) check dimensions of area to be propped

b) take off skirting

c) remove carpet from area

d) close up door

3 What is fitted to the bottom of a wall once plaster has dried?

a) floorboards

b) architrave

c) dado rail

d) skirting board

4 What is another name for a steel lintel?

a) BSA

b) RJS

c) RSJ

d) RSB

5 What should be used to stop damp penetration above a lintel?

a) insulation

b) skirting

c) damp proof course

d) cavity tray

6 Why, in most cases, should you not use a disc cutter for forming internal openings?

a) not accurate enough

b) too large

c) too dusty

d) too heavy

7 If extending a property, what type of window should be used?

a) wooden

b) uPVC

c) same match

d) latest modern type

8 What should be put on top of props where they meet the ceiling?

a) scaffold tube

b) lintel

c) scaffold board

d) batten

9 What is the minimum number of courses of bricks you should remove when replacing a cill?

a) 4

b) 3

c) 2

d) 1

10 What is the minimum thickness for floor screed when brickwork has been removed to make good?

a) 0 mm

b) 75 mm

c) 65 mm

d) 100 mm

UNIT 3029

Know how to erect complex masonry structures

The term 'complex masonry structures' refers to any brickwork or stonework that requires intricate, and sometimes difficult, setting out procedures. Many of these complex masonry structures are vital to the structure and support of a building, and are a principal part of its design and function. Others are only intended to be decorative.

This unit also contains material that supports NVQ Units QCF 40 Erect masonry structures, QCF 41 Set out masonry structures, QCF 44 Erect thin joint masonry, QCF 48 Set out complex masonry structures and QCF 49 Erect complex masonry structures.

This unit also supports the following TAP units: Unit 4 Provide details to masonry structures, Unit 5 Carry out masonry cladding to timber-framed structures and Unit 6 Co-ordinate self and others to erect complex masonry structures.

This unit will cover the following learning outcomes:

- Know how to set out and build arches
- Know how to set out and build brickwork curved on plan
- Know how to set out and build ramped brickwork
- Know how to set out and build reinforced brickwork
- Know how to set out and build obtuse and acute angle quoins
- Know how to set out and build brickwork incorporating features.

K1. Know how to set out and build arches

Arches have been used for many centuries in bridges, viaducts, aqueducts and castles, as well as many modern and simple housing structures.

The curved shape of an arch allows the weight of the masonry above it (the load) to be distributed evenly down through the walls at each side. The arch is not exposed to tensile stresses (forces that pull apart) because it is wedged between the walls on each side and therefore will not collapse when a load is placed above it.

There are certain terms used when referring to parts of an arch, particularly during its construction, all of which you will come across in this unit. Figure 29.01 shows many of the different parts of an arch and Table 29.01 describes what these are.

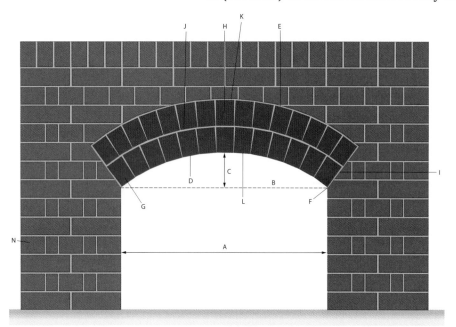

Figure 29.01 The parts of an arch

Letter	Part	Letter	Part
A	**Span** – the distance between the **abutments** (N) that support the arch	G	**Springer** – the first brick of the arch seated on the springing line
B	**Springing line** – the line at which the arch sits on the **abutments**	H	**Key** (or **key brick**) – the central brick or stone at the top of an arch
C	**Rise** – the height of the arch from the springing line to the soffit	I	**Skewback** – the angle at the springing point, on the abutments, at which the arch ring bricks will be laid
D	**Intrados** – the interior lower line or curve of the arch ring	J	**Collar joint** – the horizontal or bed joint separating the arch rings
E	**Extrados** – the outside line of the arch ring	K	**Crown** – the very top point of the extrados
F	**Springing point** – the point at which the arch meets the abutments	L	**Soffit** – the underside face of the arch

Table 29.01 Arch construction terminology

Some other important arch construction terminology includes:

- **Haunch** – the bottom part of the arch ring from the springing point to half way up the ring.
- **Radius** – the distance from the central point on the springing line (known as the striking point) to the intrados.
- **Striking point** – the central point of the springing line from which the arch radius is struck.
- **Voussoirs** – the wedge-shaped bricks/stones of which the arch is made.

Setting out arches and providing templates

Often when arch construction is incorporated into a building, purpose-made bricks are used. Purpose-made bricks remove the need for bricks to be cut on site which can be time-consuming and generate a high percentage of waste. Another major advantage with using purpose-made voussoirs or arch-bricks is their shape is uniform and dimensions accurate.

When there is a requirement for voussoirs to be cut by hand, a template must be made to establish the shape of them. The template itself will need to be traversed across the face of the arch in order to provide the exact shape required for each of the voussoirs.

The traditional method of producing axed brick arches is to cut bricks to shape using a hammer and bolster, measuring them against a tempate of the voussoir shape required.

Figure 29.02 An axed arch

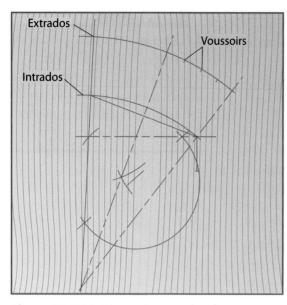

Figure 29.03 Setting out an axed arch

> **Remember**
>
> You only need to set out half of the arch, to include the key brick.

> **Remember**
>
> Once the dividers have been set, do not open them any further as any template based on this voussoir shape will be incorrect and any bricks cut to this template will be too narrow to fit the actual arch.

How to make the template

The tools required to make an accurate template:

- trammel heads
- dividers
- bevel
- traversing rules
- measuring rule
- straight edge
- carpenter's tools for cutting wood template.

The template is usually made from timber of between 6 mm and 12 mm thickness.

The first step is to draw the arch full size on a sheet of plywood.

Set out a centre line and then another line at right angles to this (known as the 'springing line'). Find out the springing point and draw intrados, extrados and skewback lines.

Set the dividers to the size of the brick being used in the arch, and mark out voussoirs on the extrados.

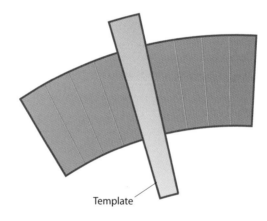

Figure 29.04 Template

Based on the full size drawing of the arch, mark out the template onto plywood, to project approximately 50 mm above the extrados and 150 mm below the intrados, which will allow for any adjustment that may need to be made when traversing the arch.

Providing temporary support for arches

An arch centre is used to support the brickwork while the arch is being built, and is usually left in situ until the key brick is fitted and the mortar has set.

Arch centres are usually made from timber. If the span of the opening is larger than 1.5 m, a stronger metal centre is used. The arch centre has several parts:

- **ribs** – usually made from 19 mm plywood, MDF or 22 mm solid timber, these form the outer part of the centre, giving the outline for the rest of the framework
- **ties** – horizontal members attached at the bottom of the ribs to prevent the load pushing the ribs out of shape
- **struts** – vertical members used to transfer the weight and spread the load
- **bearers** – flat members fixed to the bottom of the ribs to tie the ribs together
- **bracing** – timber fixed at an angle on the inside of the arch to give support and keep the arch square
- **laggings** – either thin sheets of hardboard or plywood nailed across the top of the ribs, or small timber laths nailed at right angles to the ribs.

When setting out for an arch centre you need to know the span, arch radius and so on. You can get this information from the bricklayer or from drawings.

First draw out the arch full size. Use the drawing to make templates out of hardboard, which can then be traced onto the ribs. The way the ribs are made up depends on the size and radius of the arch: some arches use two ribs per side while others use four.

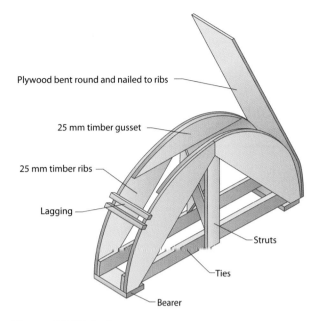

Figure 29.05 Arch parts

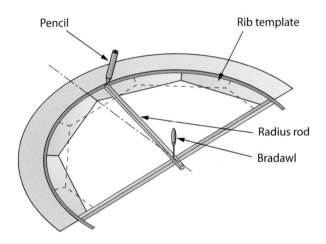

Figure 29.06 Marking out the arch

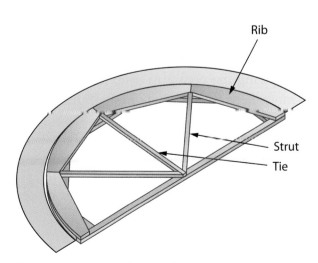

Figure 29.07 Brace ribs together

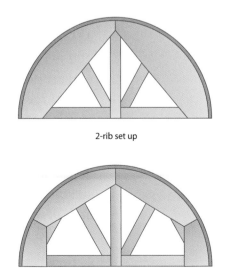

Figure 29.08 Two-rib and four-rib set-ups

2-rib set up

Remember

When marking out the ribs, you must allow for the thickness of the lagging, otherwise the arch will be too big.

Now nail the ribs together using gusset plates, fixing them where the gusset overlaps the ridge, then fix the struts and ties. Usually both ribs are made as a pair and checked together against the drawing made earlier.

The bracing is fixed next, bringing both ribs together, then the bearers can be fitted.

Finally fit the lagging, which is nailed down through the tops of the ribs. The arch centre is now ready to be used.

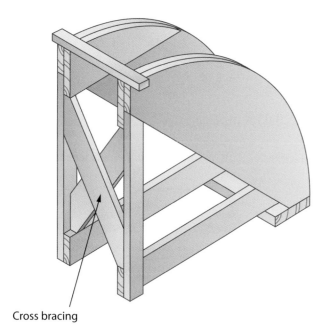
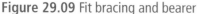

Cross bracing

Figure 29.09 Fit bracing and bearer

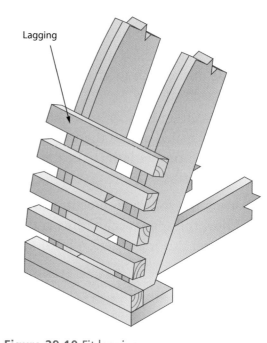

Lagging

Figure 29.10 Fit lagging

Props and wedges

Props are used to support the arch centre while the arch is built. More information about props can be found in Unit 3028, pages 192–95. Folding wedges are used to level the arch centre into the correct position before building commences. Once the arch is built the wedges are removed allowing the centre to drop down without causing any pressure or movement to the newly built arch.

Proprietary arch formers

These are made from steel or plastic and incorporated into the structure as a permanent fixture. They are used in place of an arch centre. They come in different sizes and widths to suit most standard size openings and serve two main purposes:

1. they act as an arch former

2. they act as a lintel over the opening.

The arch former in Figure 29.11 is a plastic arch former resting upon the flange of a steel lintel. The former can be removed when the arch is formed and the mortar is set, but in most cases it is left in as a feature. It is ideal for when flat-topped windows or door frames are fitted into the main structure.

Some formers incorporate a cavity tray as all openings require this to stop moisture penetration.

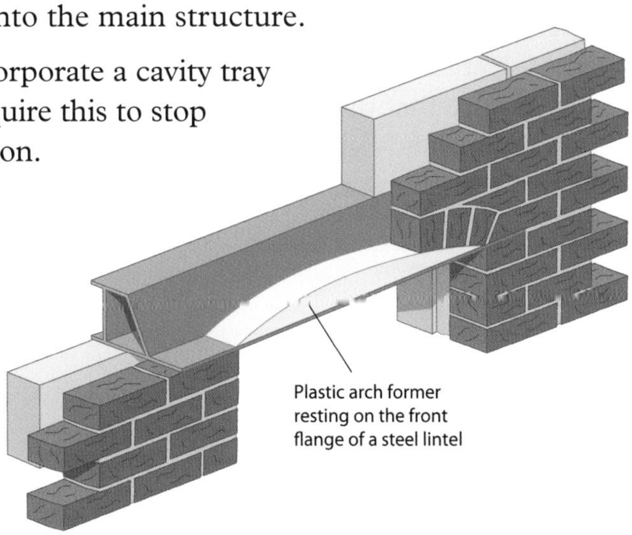

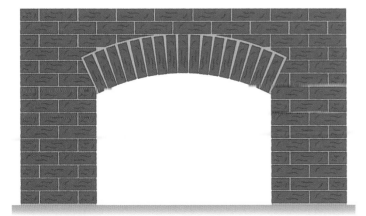

Plastic arch former resting on the front flange of a steel lintel

Figure 29.11
Plastic arch former

Construction methods used to build arches

The templating and support methods will be used to construct all types of arches. This section will look at the construction of simple and more complex arches.

Methods of constructing simple arches

Two of the most common shapes of arch are the segmental (Figure 29.12) and semi-circular (Figure 29.13). Both shapes can be constructed by using either the rough ringed arch or axed arch methods. We looked at the geometry methods used to set out segmental arches in Unit 3002 pages 34–35. Refer to this section for more information.

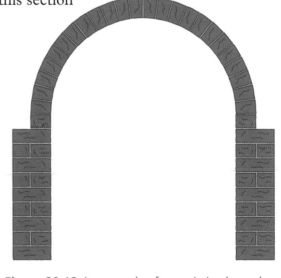

Figure 29.12 An example of a segmental arch

Figure 29.13 An example of a semi-circular arch

> **Did you know?**
>
> The methods used to bridge openings for arches are the same as those used to prevent damp from penetrating cavity walling.
>
> Cavity trays are not made to match shaped lintels, such as the curved lintel for an arch, so a gap will occur between the lintel and the cavity tray.

> **Remember**
>
> Openings are the only points where moisture can penetrate. However, the use of a cavity tray over an opening drains any moisture that does settle out of the wall, preventing the moisture from penetrating and bridging the cavity.

Turning piece – the temporary timber support for the arch ring on segmental arches during construction. It is constructed from a single piece of timber

Rough ringed arch method

This method uses wedge-shaped joints with standard sized bricks to form the arch ring. The size of the joints is determined by the arch centre or **turning piece**. The bricks used in the arch ring are normally laid as headers as opposed to stretchers (see Figure 29.14); if stretchers were used, the joints would need to be much wider to ensure that the desired shape was obtained which could result in an unsightly appearance. The overall height of the arch is reached by using a number of arch rings.

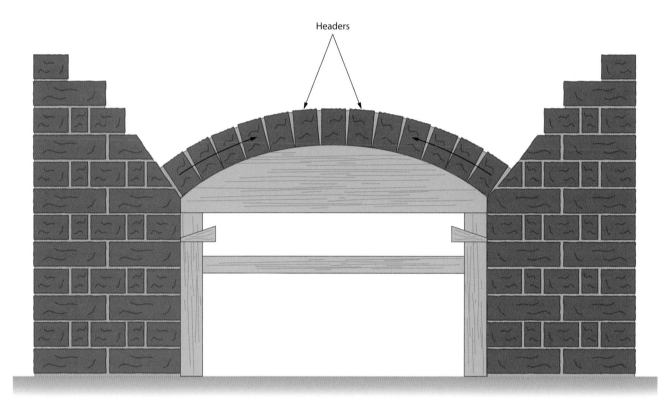

Headers

Figure 29.14 Headers used to form an arch ring

Identify the striking point on the timber turning piece or arch centre and plumb a vertical line up from this point to the top of the support. This will give you the centre point of the key brick's position. Mark the width of the key brick on the arch centre or turning piece. Then on either side of the key brick proceed to mark out, down the length of the intrados, equal brick spacings.

Note that these spacings must include allowance for mortar joints. The size of the joints may need to be altered slightly during bedding to allow for any deviation of brick size or to enable equal brick spacing around the timber support. Normally the joint size is slightly reduced from that of the standard 10 mm mortar joint in order to compensate for the widening of the joint at the extrados.

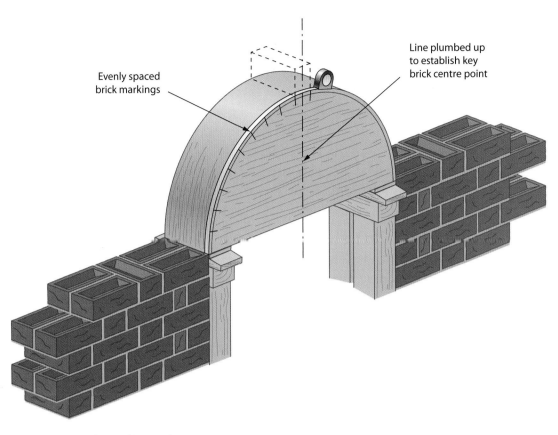

Evenly spaced
brick markings

Line plumbed up
to establish key
brick centre point

Figure 29.15 The striking point

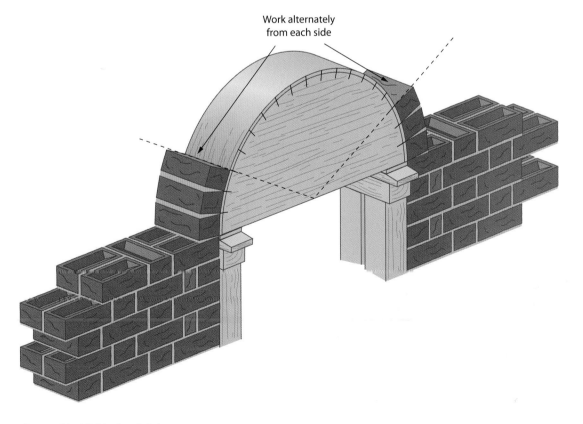

Work alternately
from each side

Figure 29.16 Placing bricks

Commence with the placement of the bricks forming the arch ring, with the first brick being laid against the skewback angles on either side of the key brick.

It is important to ensure that there is no bedding between the brick and the timber centre as this will result in difficulty in maintaining the correct curve of the arch bricks during construction and also stain the face of the bricks exposed once the support is removed. Lay bricks face down on the centre. Packing may be introduced at the base of the joint being formed to allow for ease of pointing once the support is removed.

Bricks should be laid alternately on either side of the key brick to ensure that there is no overloading on any particular side of the support. Once the key brick position has been reached ensure this brick is placed accurately in the marked position on the centre and there are fully compacted joints either side of it.

Throughout the construction of the arch rings you must maintain the face plane of the brickwork using a suitable, accurate straight edge or by erecting temporary line supports on each of the abutments. These can be built in brick and are known as dead men (see Figure 29.17) or consist of timber or metal profiles, accurately gauged and plumbed.

Remember

Arch supports must not be removed until the bedding mortar has fully hardened.

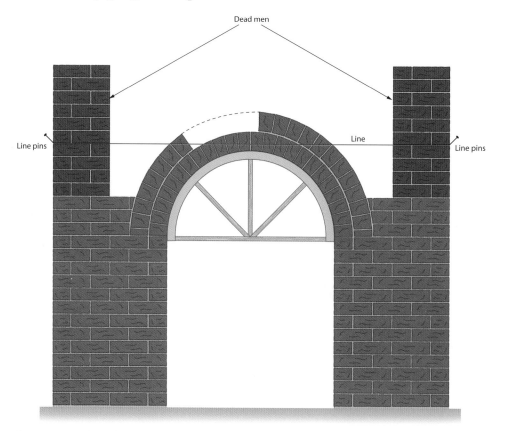

Figure 29.17 Dead men in use on a semi-circular arch

Max is setting out a semi-circular arch to form an archway to a garden wall. He has set the arch centre in place and is marking out the brick positions on the arch centre using a gauge of 75 mm. However, that creates a 15 mm gap to place a brick into.

How can Max get over this to make the arch correct? He will need to consider all the parts of the construction process. What might he need to do if the gap was larger?

Setting out arches is a good opportunity to practise **FM 2.2.1a–h** and **FM 2.2.2** relating to applying a range of mathematical procedures to find solutions and using appropriate checking procedures and evaluating their effectiveness at each stage.

Constructing an axed arch

Before constructing an axed arch, you will need to create a template. This provides a rough guide for the shape of the arch. To obtain an accurate shape, the template must be **traversed** over the face of the arch, to highlight any small errors in the shape.

To traverse the arch, follow the steps below.

1. Place the traversing rule A to the key brick.
2. Arrange the template to fit a voussoir and mark a line on the side of the template to coincide with the intrados. This is called the 'traversing mark'.
3. Place the traversing rule B.
4. Remove A and the template.
5. Place A to B
6. Remove B and again fit template, allowing traversing mark to coincide with the intrados.

If the template reaches the top of the skewback (the extrados) before it reaches the bottom (the intrados), it must be made smaller at the top. If it reaches the bottom before the top, then it must be planed down at the bottom. If there is space left over between the template edge and the skewback, then the template must be lowered so that the traversing mark is higher up the templet. If it overruns the skewback, then the template needs to be raised so that the traversing mark is lower down.

Traversing the arch must be repeated until the template fits exactly between the key and the skewback. This means the template will be accurate and the voussoirs cut using it will be the exact shape required to complete the axed arch.

Once the exact shape of the voussoirs has been established, construction of the arch can begin. Set up the arch centre and mark the position of the key brick. Then use dividers to mark the remaining brick spaces, plus one joint, either side of the key brick.

Unit 3029 Know how to erect complex masonry structures

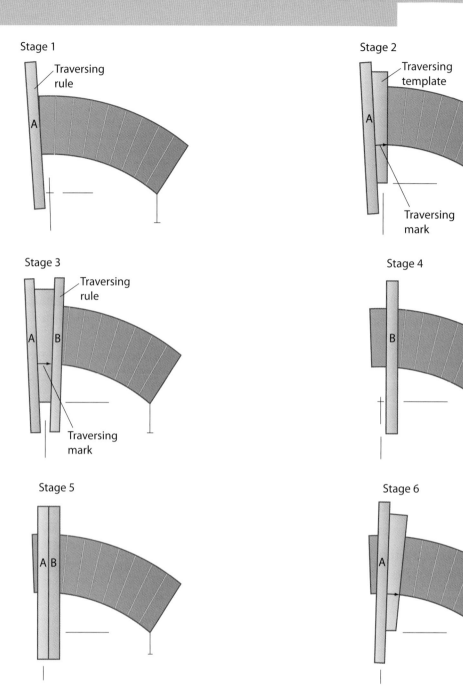

Figure 29.18 Traversing a template for an axed arch

The first brick is bedded against the skewback and lined in from the striking point through the voussoir gauge mark, identified on the arch centre. Continue to bed the remaining voussoirs alternately on either side of the key brick to prevent any unnecessary overloading on either side of the arch centre.

The arch bricks should be frequently checked for square with a straight edge or, alternatively, a line should be used across the face of the arch.

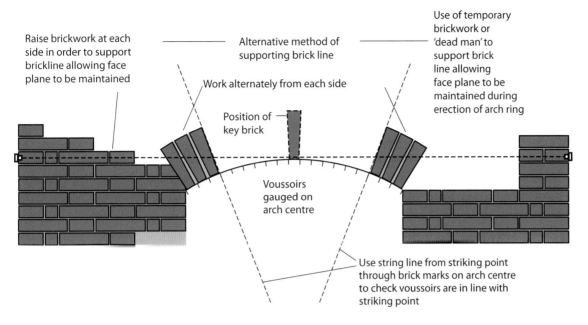

Raise brickwork at each side in order to support brickline allowing face plane to be maintained

Alternative method of supporting brick line

Use of temporary brickwork or 'dead man' to support brick line allowing face plane to be maintained during erection of arch ring

Work alternately from each side

Position of key brick

Voussoirs gauged on arch centre

Use string line from striking point through brick marks on arch centre to check voussoirs are in line with striking point

Figure 29.19 Bricks being laid from alternate sides of the key brick

Cambered arches

A camber arch is a one centred arch. This means it has only one striking point. It is sometimes known as a square arch, flat arch or Georgian arch.

The soffit of the arch is given a slight rise or camber to prevent the illusion that the arch is sagging. This rise is inserted from the centre of the springing line up to the centre of the intrados and is normally 1 mm for every 100 mm of span. The camber arch is not normally used as a load bearing arch, but is normally built above a window or door as a feature using the main structure to transfer the load from above. The span of the arch should not exceed 1350 mm without being supported by a steel or concrete lintel. Each voussoir in a camber arch has three cuts and the depth of the arch is normally a minimum of 300 mm or four brick courses.

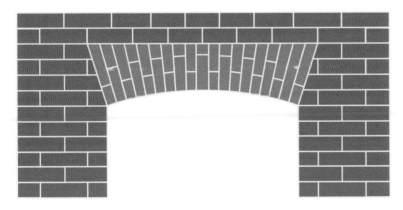

Figure 29.20 Cambered arch

K2. Know how to set out and build brickwork curved on plan

Brickwork curved on plan can be used in a number of situations, including supporting bay windows, boundary walls following the curvature of roads and pathways and for numerous decorative features such as flower beds, etc. There are a number of methods used in constructing this type of walling. The method used depends on the size of the wall to be built and the work space available.

Whichever method is used, the rules for both plumbing and levelling the brickwork remain the same. With walls curved on plan it is essential that plumbing and levelling are accurate throughout the construction of the walling. If accuracy is not maintained, the end product will be unsightly and the desired curvature of the wall will not be achieved.

On any curved wall, plumbing points will need to be established at various intervals around the length of the curve. Although the length of the curve will determine the amount of plumbing points required these should be no more than 1 m to 1.2 m apart. Levelling across the top of the wall should always be carried between the plumbing points.

Constructing curved brickwork

Where the curves to be constructed are relatively small, a small timber template can be used. This template is accurately cut to fit around the curved face of the wall and must be cut to a length which allows it to fit between the plumbing points.

Remember

No matter what type of template is used, it is essential that you ensure that all bricks sit against the template when you are carrying out checks using it.

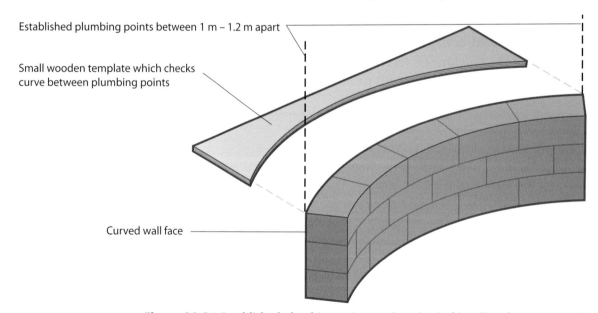

Established plumbing points between 1 m – 1.2 m apart

Small wooden template which checks curve between plumbing points

Curved wall face

Figure 29.21 Established plumbing points and method of levelling for curved walls

Larger templates can be produced for constructing bay windows. These templates are designed to sit on the top of each course to be built and give both the curve for the outside face of the curved bay and the line of the main wall.

Although stretchers are used in curved walling, the most common bond used is header bond. Stretcher bond can be used in curved walls. However, the stretchers may have to be cut on the back face, where the curve is too tight to allow the use of full stretchers, so as not to affect the trueness of the curve.

Using a trammel

The other method used to help in the construction of curved walls is the trammel. This is a short length of timber pointed at one end and fixed to the face of the wall.

The point at which the trammel is fixed to the face of the wall is known as the pivot point.

The trammel can be fixed to a timber plate, which is secured to the brickwork with the use of nails driven into the bed joints. When fixing the trammel to the timber plate you must ensure that it is not fixed tightly against the plate, preventing it from turning easily.

The bricks to be cut in order to form the curve are placed in position, dry and on top of a piece of timber or other suitable

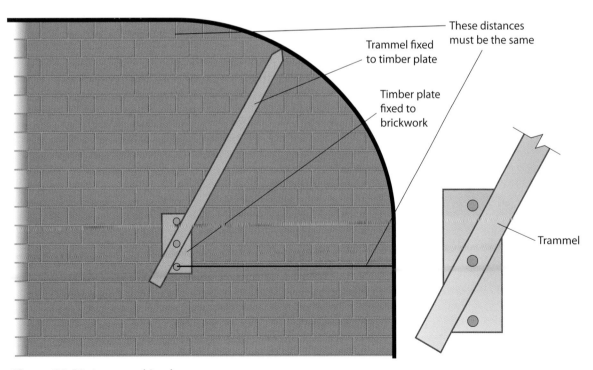

Trammel fixed to timber plate

Timber plate fixed to brickwork

These distances must be the same

Trammel

Figure 29.22 A trammel in place

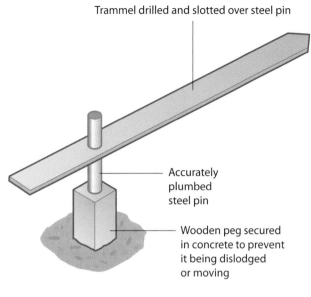

Trammel drilled and slotted over steel pin

Accurately plumbed steel pin

Wooden peg secured in concrete to prevent it being dislodged or moving

Figure 29.23 A trammel fixed over a steel pin

material at a thickness of 10 mm to simulate the bed joint thickness. The vertical joint thickness must also be allowed for.

The trammel is then swung round across the face of the positioned brick and marked with a pencil or suitable marker. Once the brick has been cut it can be laid and checked for accuracy by again swinging the trammel across the face.

The trammel is fixed by one end being drilled to allow it to be dropped over a steel pin representing the pivot point. This steel pin should be seated in the top of a wooden peg, which in turn is set in concrete to prevent it from moving while in use.

A trammel can only be used where there is sufficient space to establish the pivot point. The position of the pivot point can be determined from the detailed drawings provided on site. The trammel can be used for either the internal or external face of the curve.

Header bond

Depending on the severity of the curve, full headers can be used throughout the length of each course. However, where the curve is smaller or tighter, snap headers have to be used in order to maintain a true curve. Where this is the case, a full header is used every third brick. This prevents oversized V-shaped joints which make the wall look unsightly.

Where both sides of a curved wall need to have a good face, it is advisable to use purpose-made Radial bricks. These are available in both headers and stretchers.

Remember

The use of these bricks also removes the need for V-shaped joints.

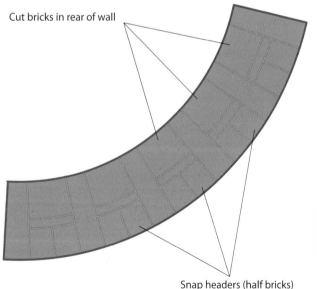

Cut bricks in rear of wall

Snap headers (half bricks)

Figure 29.24 Using snap headers when constructing curved walling in header bond

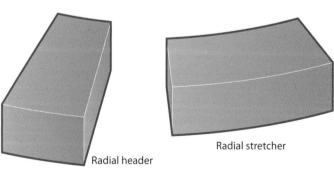

Radial header

Radial stretcher

Figure 29.25 Radial header and stretcher bricks

Figure 29.26 Bay window

Bay windows

A bay window projects out of the front of the main walls of a house. This type of window became popular in the late 1800s as they give the room the appearance of being larger and also allow more light in. Bay windows are either square or polygonal in plan.

The foundations are laid at the same time as the main house to gain maximum strength and stability. They need to be set out carefully, especially in the case of the polygonal type. In modern construction of bay windows, special templates are produced to help set out the construction of these. Special bricks called **cants** or **squints** (see pages 241 and 243) are required to build polygonal bays. This helps to gain the angles required and to give strength to the corners and to join to the main wall.

Bay windows can also be fitted to floors above ground level, and are then known as oriel windows. Oriel windows became popular in the late Victorian era. At this time, houses were rows of terraces so the oriel window was designed to give a better view of the street.

An oriel windows projects out from the upper story of a building and is supported on brackets or corbelled brickwork (see page 228–31). They are mainly constructed from timber to help with weight distribution, as there is no solid material below them.

Did you know?

Some bay windows are built circular and these are called bow windows.

Figure 29.27 Oriel window

Elevation – refers to a vertical face of a building

Concave – means rounded inwards

Convex – means curved outwards

K3. Know how to set out and build ramped brickwork

Ramped brickwork is also known as curved brickwork. Brickwork can be curved either on plan or in **elevation.** Arches are a typical example of brickwork curved in elevation. This section will deal with how to create other curves in brickwork.

Brickwork curved in elevation

There are two methods of constructing curved brickwork in elevation:

1. convex
2. concave.

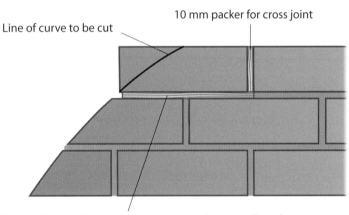

Line of curve to be cut

10 mm packer for cross joint

Figure 29.28 The use of a 10 mm packing to allow for joint thickness (a trammel would also need to be attached)

Constructing convex curved brickwork

This type of curved work is produced with the aid of a trammel, in the same way as the brickwork curved on plan (see page 223).

A brick laid on edge is the most common way to provide the finish or capping to this type of curved brickwork, unless of course it is used as a decorative feature within a length of walling which is to be continued in height

Depending on the severity of the curve, the brick-on-edge can either be laid with V-shaped joints or the bricks are cut to a V shape to prevent oversized joints.

Constructing concave curved brickwork

Again, a trammel will need to be used to establish the cuts required to form the curve. However, the trammel needs to be positioned and secured in a completely different way.

Before the trammel can be positioned, the main walling will need to be built to the height of the striking point. Once this height has been reached the trammel can be positioned.

The trammel is fixed onto a timber support held in position on the top course by either a brick or block weight.

The same principles used in forming the convex curve are then applied to this type of construction. This also includes the forming of the brick-on-edge course.

Figure 29.29 Concave curved brickwork

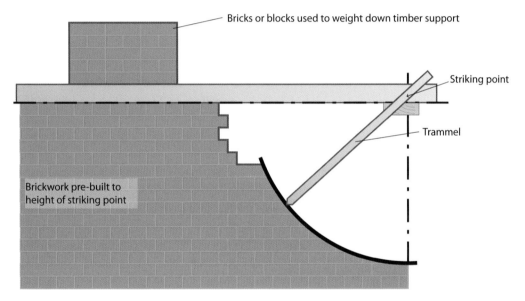

Bricks or blocks used to weight down timber support

Striking point

Trammel

Brickwork pre-built to height of striking point

Figure 29.30 The positioning of a trammel, and its timber support, for the construction of a concave curve

Working life

You are half way through the construction of a curved section of walling and you are using a timber trammel to aid with the marking of the bricks to be cut. Due to a knot in the timber the trammel breaks and can no longer be used. The alternatives are to either spend time producing a new timber trammel or use a bricklaying line of the same length as the trammel and attach this to exactly the same point as the trammel was attached.

Which of the alternatives would you choose and why?

Serpentine walls

This type of walling turns in and out along its length giving a snaking effect. The curves are set out and constructed using the methods for convex and concave curves.

Serpentine walling snaking in and out throughout its length

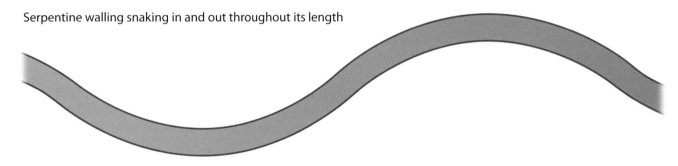

Figure 29.31 A plan view of a serpentine wall

Corbelling

Traditionally, corbelling was used as a method of providing structural support for brickwork extending in front of the main walling. However, corbelling details are also used to enhance the appearance of brickwork structures, and have been for many years.

In fact, corbelling has been used since Neolithic times. In medieval times, it was widely used to provide support for upper storeys, parapets or turrets projecting from strongholds. Early forms of corbelling were made from stones keyed deep into the main walling, often carved with elaborate designs, depicting human faces, animals, demons or floral themes.

Figure 29.32 Corbelling used as the shoulder of a gable end

Figure 29.33 Corbelling at a certain position in a length of walling

More recently corbelling has been used to reduce the opening size at the top of manholes and sewer chambers, to accommodate standard-sized covers and frames. However, this is achieved using precast concrete reducing slabs. A bricklayer may still be required to form corbelling at the heads of manholes where existing corbelling has been partially dislodged, or has perished over the years and requires repair or reinstatement.

Corbelling can be used at certain positions in a length of walling or can be continuous throughout the length of the walling. All corbelling work must be carefully planned and carried out to satisfy both the structural design requirements of the project and the British Standards Institution Codes of Practice.

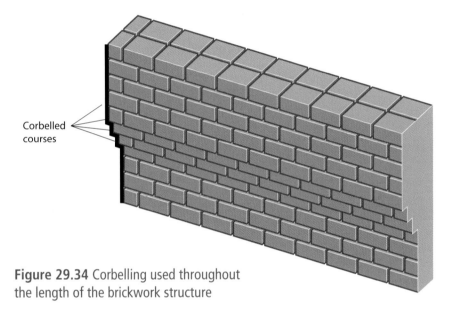

Corbelled courses

Figure 29.34 Corbelling used throughout the length of the brickwork structure

Methods for constructing traditional corbels

The overhang measurement for each course of a brick corbel should be equal. In all instances, the measurement shown on the detailed drawing provided by the architect should be adhered to. However, the two most common measurements used for the overhang of individual courses is either 28 mm or 56 mm.

It is essential when constructing a corbel that plumb and level are accurately maintained. It is also important to maintain equal projections for each course and as a rule of thumb, the total projection of the entire corbel should not exceed the thickness of the main wall.

When tying the corbel bricks into the main wall, try to achieve the maximum lap with the course below and wherever possible headers should be used for the corbelled bricks, particularly for a corbel where larger projections are used (quarter brick overhang).

Did you know?

Corbelling is commonly used to form the shoulders of gable ends.

Remember

Failure to plan effectively and follow the requirements for bonding of corbelling bricks can result in weak support for the structure and, quite possibly, collapse of the corbelling feature and any work it supports.

Find out

With your colleagues, list five instances you know of where corbelling has been or could be used, either as support in a structure or as a decorative feature.

Functional skills

After researching you may need to present your findings, allowing you to practise **FE 2.1.1–2.1.4** Make a range of contributions to discussions and make effective presentations in a wide range of contexts.

Remember

The greater the overhang the more difficulty there is in preventing tipping of the bricks during construction.

Tipping – this is where, if care is not taken during the laying process, the whole corbel may tip forward and quite possibly topple over

When building any corbel it is important to lay the bricks from the back of the main wall through to the front of the corbel. This allows the back of the corbelled bricks below to be held or weighted down as quickly as possible to prevent them **tipping** forward.

Figures 29.35–29.38 show the preferred bonding arrangements for a corbel with a quarter brick overhang per course.

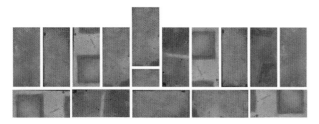

Figure 29.35 Course 1

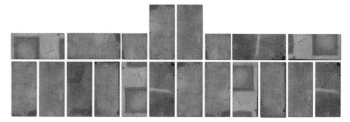

Figure 29.36 Course 2

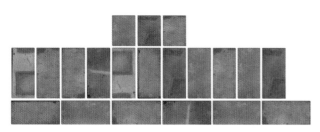

Figure 29.37 Course 3

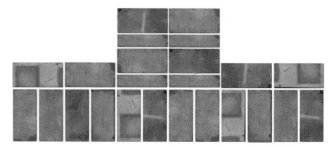

Figure 29.38 Course 4

Did you know?

Always tilt the front corbel bricks backwards slightly as they are laid – this can help prevent tipping. The brick can be truly levelled in as the next course is laid.

Remember

Always ensure that all bed joints and cross joints are completely full within the corbel to ensure both strength and stability.

Figure 29.39 Completed corbelling

As each course is constructed the bricklayer must ensure that corbel is square to the main wall. This can be achieved with the aid of a building square. It is also important that each course is levelled on the underside of the corbelled bricks as this is the line that will be seen. This is called the eye line. Where a continuous corbel is being built, a line is used on the underside edge of the corbel to maintain a face plane.

Corbelling in timber- and steel-framed buildings

Traditional methods of constructing corbels cannot be applied successfully in many modern construction systems, such as timber- and steel-framed buildings, where brickwork cladding is used to form cavity walling. These need specially designed brickwork support systems, along with purpose-made bricks, in most instances, to form the corbelled feature and mask the support system adequately.

Additional care must be taken when forming corbelled features using this method. Temporary support for the purpose-made bricks will need to be provided during construction to prevent 'tipping' of the bricks. Each corbel course is required to be tied back to the structure at every bed joint. Any brickwork laid above the corbelled course will be carried by a suitable type of support system.

Figure 29.40 Using a building square

> **Working life**
>
> You are in the final stages of constructing a brick corbel and have cut one of the bricks, which ties into the main wall, too short. You have just put away all your cutting tools, as this was the last cut.
>
> Should you use the brick you have cut and fill the void with strong mortar, or should you cut a new brick to the correct size? What are the consequences of each of the actions you may choose?

> **Functional skills**
>
> Deciding on the best course of action when faced with a problem during construction may require you to read through specifications and site documentation, allowing you to practise **FE 2.2.1–2.2.3** which covers selecting and using texts to obtain information and summarise and identify their purpose.

Tumbling-in

Although not commonly seen in modern building projects, tumbling-in was an effective decorative method of reducing the width of supporting piers or buttresses on retaining or large boundary walls. It was also used in reducing the width of external chimney breasts.

One simple method of reducing the thickness of a wall or pier is to use plinth bricks. The face of the angled brickwork is not as appealing to the eye as it is with tumbling-in using standard cut bricks. This is because the face of the work completed with plinth bricks will have small ridges formed by the shape of the plinths.

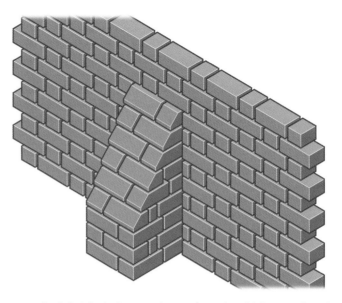

Figure 29.41 Plinth bricks being used to reduce the thickness of a pier

Method of tumbling-in using standard cut bricks

Where tumbling-in is only required for a short reduction, the angle and cuts can be set out on a large piece of plywood. The angle can then be maintained with the use of a small template cut in the shape of a gun, to the angle required.

For larger reductions where the work cannot be set out on a board, position lines at either side of the tumbling-in. These lines are fixed in place with the use of battens. The positioning of these battens, along with the lines, is shown in Figure 29.43.

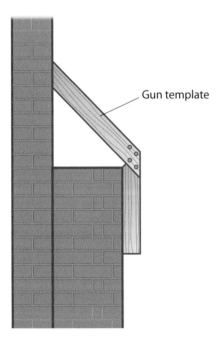

Gun template

Figure 29.42 'Gun' template used to maintain slope of reduction

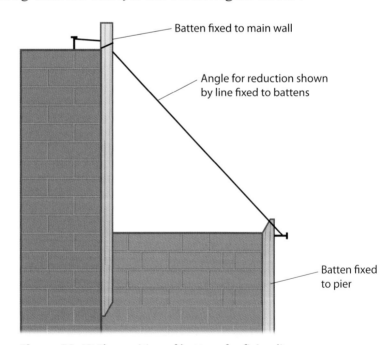

Batten fixed to main wall

Angle for reduction shown by line fixed to battens

Batten fixed to pier

Figure 29.43 The position of battens for fixing lines

Once the lines are fixed, a gun template can be made to the angle required and this is used to check and maintain the correct angle throughout the run of tumbling-in.

When starting it is essential the first course is laid so that it overhangs the brickwork below in order to provide a weathering. This overhang must be provided for when positioning the batten, by extending it past the actual striking point.

It is important as the work proceeds that a gauge rod is used throughout the length of the tumbling-in: failure to maintain gauge would result in unsightly split courses at the top of the tumbling-in.

Where there is a large length of tumbling-in, it is best practice to extend the horizontal brickwork of the pier or buttress to give the impression of both the tumbling-in and the pier brickwork blending into each other. This is shown in Figure 29.44.

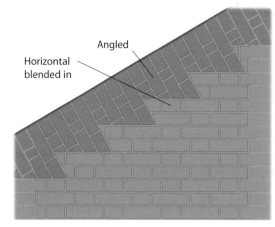

Figure 29.44 A preferred method of blending in the horizontal and angled brickwork

Raking cutting

The most common situation where raking cutting is used is when constructing a gable end.

When constructing a gable end, temporary profiles are required to establish the angle of the raking cut and provide a guide for the bricks to be cut. These profiles are in the form of temporary roof trusses or rafters and are positioned immediately behind the wall to be built. The height and pitch of the truss or rafters will have already been determined and this information will be included on the relevant drawings.

A bracket or short length of ridge board is fixed at the top of the profile in order to extend the point of the apex out far enough so that lines can be attached to establish the cutting line. Once the lines have been set up and the angle of the raking cut has been established, the main walling is constructed and raked back to leave just the spaces for the bricks to be cut.

Temporarily bed the brick to be cut. Mark the brick with a pencil at the points, top and bottom, where the line crosses the face of the brick.

Figure 29.45 A typical brick gable end

Once marked, draw the cutting line across the face of the brick by joining the two previously marked points together. The marking must be transferred to the back face of the brick to ensure that an accurate cut is obtained across the width of the brick.

Trim any excess from the top of the brick using a scutch hammer. Now the brick is ready to be laid to the line.

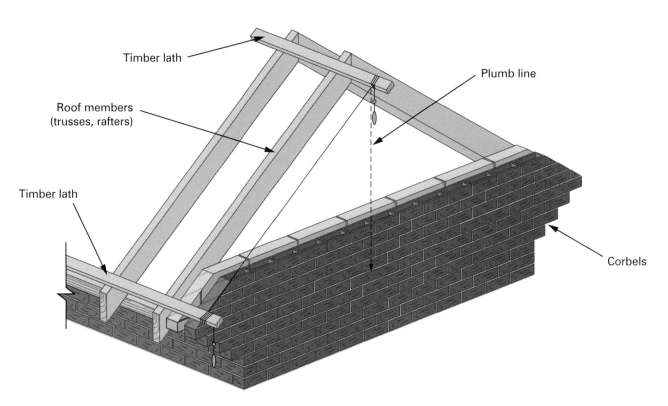

Timber lath

Roof members
(trusses, rafters)

Timber lath

Plumb line

Corbels

Figure 29.46 The position of temporary profiles (truss/rafters) and lines with a plumb line to maintain accuracy and corbelling built into wall

Functional skills

To carry out maintenance work on tools you will need to be familiar with the manufacturer guidance. This will allow you to practise **FE 2.2.1** and **FE 2.2.3**, which cover reading sources for information and identifying their purpose.

Working life

Joe, a recently qualified bricklayer, is working with a gang constructing a boundary wall, one end finished with a curved ramp feature. Joe has been asked to mark and cut the bricks for the curve. He has been told that the bricks can only be cut using the mechanical table saw on site. Although he has been trained and deemed competent in the use of the table saw, he has never been trained in the process of changing a saw blade.

Halfway through the cutting job, the saw blade starts chipping the face of the bricks, and is taking longer than normal to cut through the bricks.

What is the possible cause of the bricks becoming damaged and the process taking longer? How should the problem be rectified? Should Joe carry out any necessary remedial work on the saw?

K4. Know how to set out and build reinforced brickwork

Under normal circumstances brickwork, if bonded correctly, is more than strong enough to carry **compressive loads** without the need for additional reinforcement. However, brickwork structures can also be subjected to **tensile stress,** where lateral loads or forces are imposed on the brickwork structure, such as high winds, or heavy loads that must be supported by the face of a structure.

Where brickwork structures are exposed to tensile stress, the brickwork must be strengthened to prevent it failing, which could result in cracking and even the collapse of the structure. Steel reinforcement is one of the most common ways of providing additional strength. However, structural engineers are needed to determine the right method for each situation.

One of the most commonly used types of steel reinforcement is bed joint reinforcement. This is laid in the mortar bed to counteract movement in the brickwork. When laying steel reinforcement in the bed joints, it is important that a minimum of 15 mm space is left between the face of the brickwork and the edge of the reinforcement mesh. This is to ensure that the steel is fully surrounded by mortar to protect it from exposure and subsequent corrosion.

Steel reinforcement has limitations, and is not suitable for structures subject to persistent and severe tensile stresses, such as retaining excessive volumes of soil, or where boundary walls may be subjected to impact. In these types of situations, you will need to use other methods of providing lateral support to the structure.

One bonding arrangement that incorporates steel reinforcing rods is Quetta bond reinforced brickwork.

Quetta bond reinforced brickwork

This method uses vertical steel reinforcement rods contained in 'pockets', formed in the middle of solid walls using either Flemish or Flemish garden wall bond on the face of the wall.

Vertical steel reinforcement rods should be attached to starter bars, incorporated at the base of the wall to tie the vertical bars within the wall to the foundation. As construction of the brickwork progresses, the pockets containing the rods are filled with a particular mortar or concrete mix to stabilise the rods and form a bond between the rods and the brickwork. Mortar should be compacted well around the rods so that the pocket is fully filled and there is sufficient bond between the rods and the brickwork.

> **Key term**
>
> **Compressive loads** – loads that bear down on the brickwork
>
> **Tensile stress** – where lateral loads or forces are imposed on the brickwork structure

> **Find out**
>
> In a group, use the Internet and other sources to least at two examples of:
>
> - brickwork being put under compressive loads
> - the face of a structure being expected to support a heavy load or impact.

> **Remember**
>
> When doing the reinforcement work, it is vital that you follow all instructions and construction details precisely: poor workmanship can result in serious failure of the structure.

This method has its limitations, and can only be used where the walls are of a $1\frac{1}{2}$-brick thickness.

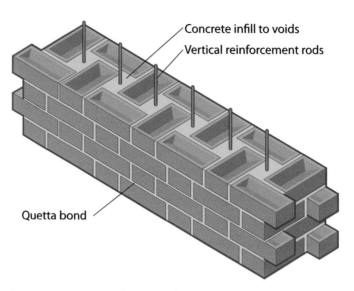

Figure 29.47 Quetta bond reinforced brickwork

Other methods of construction

Pockets on the retaining side of the wall

An alternative to Quetta bond is to provide pockets containing reinforcement rods encased in concrete on the retaining side of the wall. These pockets will not be visible as they will be covered by the soil being retained. This method allows a solid wall to be reduced in thickness towards the top of the wall, saving on the amount of materials that need to be used without affecting the stability of the structure.

As with Quetta bond, the vertical steel reinforcement rods are fixed to starter bars incorporated in the foundation concrete. The vertical reinforcement rods can be left until the construction of the brickwork is complete. Shuttering is then placed against the pocket and filled with a suitable concrete mix. This concrete must again be compacted to make sure the steel rods are properly protected.

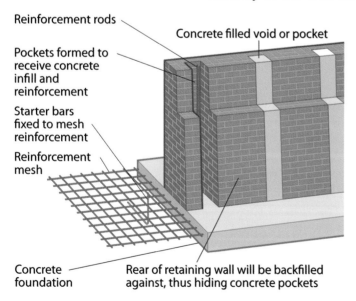

Figure 29.48 Method of pocket reinforced brickwork

Cavity method

One other method of providing reinforcement in brickwork involves constructing an inner and outer leaf of brickwork with a cavity between them. Reinforcement rods or reinforcement matting are positioned and secured in the cavity, then the cavity is filled with suitable concrete mix.

When building the inner and outer leaves, make sure the cavity is kept clean of mortar droppings – apply the same measures used when constructing normal cavity walling. Failure to keep the cavity construction clear of mortar will result in a poor bond between the concrete infill and the brickwork.

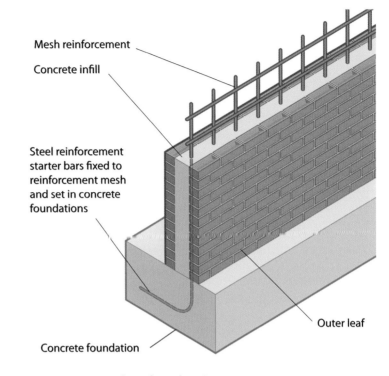

Figure 29.49 Typical reinforced cavity structure

In some building situations, the inner and outer leaves of brickwork can be built against or around hollow concrete blocks, which replace the need for the cavity to be filled with concrete. Vertical reinforcement rods are positioned in the hollow pockets of the blocks, and these rods are fixed to starter bars incorporated into the foundation concrete.

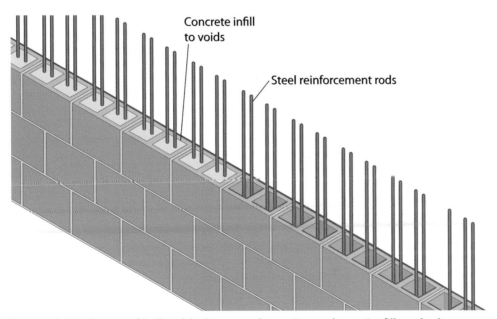

Figure 29.50 The use of hollow blocks as an alternative to the cavity fill method

Working life

You are constructing a section of walling that incorporates bed joint reinforcement mesh in every third course. You have completed the first five courses and notice that the reinforcement laid at course three is protruding slightly from the bed joint.

What do you do? Do you wait until the work is completed and the mortar joints have fully hardened and then cut off the protruding reinforcement with a bolster chisel? Or do you take off the fourth and fifth courses you have just laid and reposition the reinforcement correctly? What are the issues with each of the alternatives?

Parapet walls

Parapet walls are a continuation of the main wall structure above the roof level. They are mainly intended as a safety barrier at the edge of roofs. A low parapet wall may be in place to allow work to be carried out on the roof safely. A high parapet wall may be in place on flat roofs to prevent people falling where the area is used as a sun area or roof-top garden. Parapets are also used as a low wall division between two houses to separate the roofs.

All parapet walls should be designed to resist strong winds, rain, change in temperatures, and the weight of people leaning

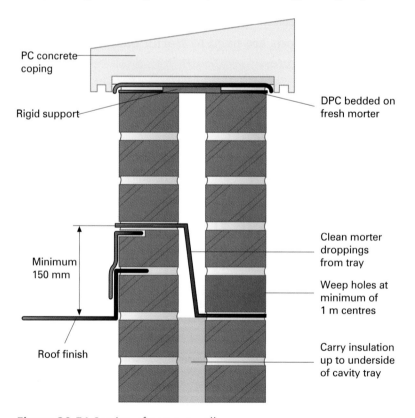

Figure 29.51 Section of parapet wall

PC concrete coping

Rigid support

Minimum 150 mm

Roof finish

DPC bedded on fresh morter

Clean morter droppings from tray

Weep holes at minimum of 1 m centres

Carry insulation up to underside of cavity tray

against them. The best method for building them is cavity wall construction, but most older properties were built with solid walls.

Water penetration was and still is a major problem and some parapets are rendered, causing costly repairs when replacing areas or all render due to frost and water penetration. DPC trays and flashings need to be built in above the roof structure and below the top capping to prevent water penetration.

Coping stones are normally used to finish the top of the wall as this is more resilient to the elements. However, in some cases, particularly in older properties where solid wall construction was used, brick on edge was often used to finish. These are always affected by frost attack and, if you look at most properties with parapets you will be able to see some form of attack.

K5. Know how to set out and build obtuse and acute angle quoins

Not all buildings, boundary walls and garden walls are built with 90-degree or right-angled returns. It is sometimes necessary to build walls at angles to each other in order to follow the lines or boundaries of the site.

Angles at which walls are built other than 90 degrees are known as either acute or obtuse angles.

Where **acute** or **obtuse angles** are to be used on site, the angles have normally been established by the architect. In most instances special-shaped, purpose-made bricks will be supplied for the construction of angled walls. It is not uncommon to see acute angles constructed from bricks cut on site. It is highly unlikely a bricklayer would be expected to cut these angled bricks with normal hand tools as this would undoubtedly result in a large number of wasted bricks. Where these bricks are required to be cut on site, a table saw would be used. It is important to note that where bricks are cut on site, these should be solid, as bricks with a frog or holes would be impossible to cut to the desired angles.

Acute angles

A number of bonding arrangements for acute angles are shown in Figures 29.52–29.56. In walls of 1-brick thickness, acute angles can be produced by bringing the corner of the angled brick structure to a sharp point or they can be produced by using special-shaped bricks to remove the sharp point. The method used will be determined by the architect.

Key terms
Acute angle – this is an angle less than 90 degrees
Obtuse angle – this is an angle greater than 90 degrees

Method 1 – corners produced with a sharp point

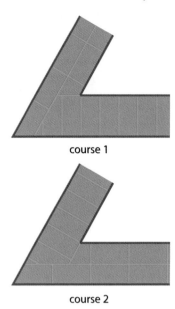

course 1

course 2

Figure 29.52 Bonding arrangement for 1-brick thick wall in English bond

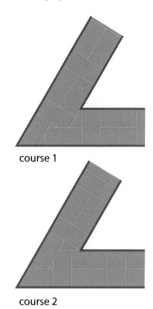

course 1

course 2

Figure 29.53 Bonding arrangement for 1-brick thick wall in Flemish bond

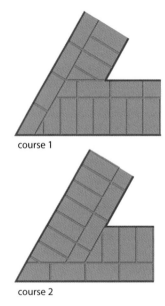

course 1

course 2

Figure 29.54 Bonding arrangement for 1½-brick thick wall in English bond

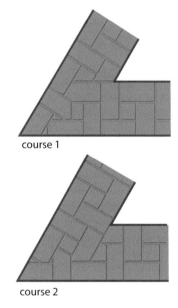

course 1

course 2

Figure 29.55 Bonding arrangement for 1½-brick thick wall in Flemish bond

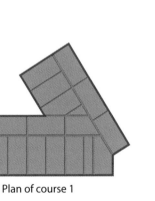

Plan of course 1

Plan of course 2

Figure 29.56 Bonding arrangement for 1½-brick thick wall in English bond

Method 2 – special-shaped bricks used to avoid sharp point at the corner

Where walls of more than 1 brick in thickness are constructed, a further alternative finish can be provided to the corner. In this method both the sharp point and the use of purpose-made bricks are avoided. This is referred to as 'bird's mouth' corner.

External obtuse angles

These types of angles are normally produced using purpose-made bricks known as 'squint' bricks on walls with 135-degree angles. Easy angle bricks can be used for other angles. Where angles are required which are not the normal ones covered by the use of squint bricks, then the angles will have to be produced by cutting the bricks on site (again a mechanical table saw will need to be used).

Figures 29.57–29.59 show a number of bonding arrangements used for producing obtuse angles.

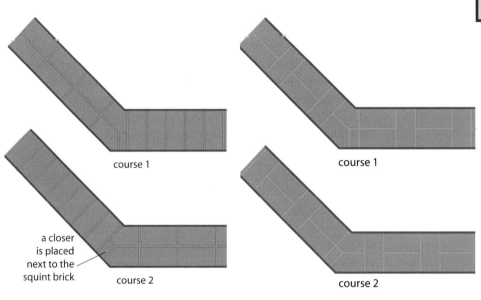

Remember

Whenever a squint brick is used at the corner, a closer brick will have to be positioned next to the squint brick in order to produce the correct lap for the bricks along the face of the wall. A closer is required in solid walling, but not in half-brick thick walling.

course 1
a closer
is placed
next to the
squint brick
course 2

Figure 29.57 Bonding arrangement for 1-brick thick wall in English bond

course 1
course 2

Figure 29.58 Bonding arrangement for 1-brick thick wall in Flemish bond

As with acute angles, an alternative method can be used at the **quoin** in order to avoid using costly, special-shaped bricks.

Key term

Quoin – the corner of a wall

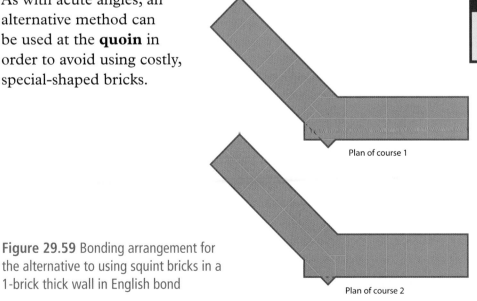

Plan of course 1
Plan of course 2

Figure 29.59 Bonding arrangement for the alternative to using squint bricks in a 1-brick thick wall in English bond

Internal obtuse angles

The preferred method of constructing internal obtuse angles is by using a purpose-made brick known as a 'dog-leg'. The dog-leg brick provides a much stronger joint at the intersection of the two lengths of walling.

Using standard, cut bricks can produce a weakness at the intersection of the two walls if the cuts are not accurate and are not lapped correctly.

Figures 29.60-29.61 show a number of bonding arrangements used for producing internal obtuse angles.

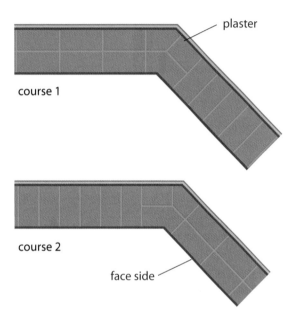

Figure 29.60 Bonding arrangement for 1-brick thick wall in English bond

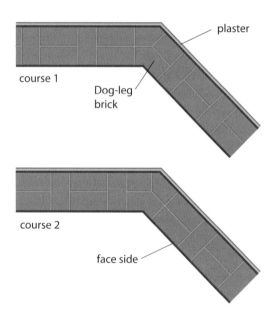

Figure 29.61 Bonding arrangement for 1-brick thick wall in Flemish bond

Find out

Search the websites of leading brick manufacturers to find full details of the varieties of special made bricks currently available.

Special-shaped or purpose-made bricks

We have already dealt briefly with a number of special or purpose-made bricks earlier in this unit – squints, dog-legs and plinths. However, there are many variations to these bricks and all have their own specific use. The following is a brief introduction to just some of the brick specials available.

Plinth bricks

These are used to reduce the thickness of walls vertically. They are most often used in decorative panels or to reduce external chimney breasts.

Figure 29.62 A plinth stretcher

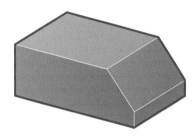

Figure 29.63 A plinth header

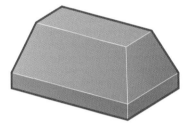

Figure 29.64 External plinth return

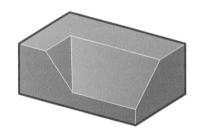

Figure 29.65 Internal plinth return

Squint bricks

These are used for acute and obtuse angles, mainly used on conservatories with angled corners.

Figure 29.66 Squint brick

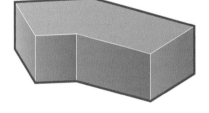

Figure 29.67 Dog-leg brick (used for internal angles)

Cant bricks

These are used where corners need to be chamfered. Single cants are used on brick quoins as well as corners on angled walls, such as conservatories and garden walls.

Figure 29.68 Cant brick

Figure 29.69 Double cant brick

> **Did you know?**
>
> Double cant bricks can be used as a brick on edge finish to a 1-brick wall.

> **Key term**
>
> **Cant** – meaning bevelled, sloped or tilted

Bull-nose bricks

These are used where the corners need to be rounded on brick quoins as well as a brick-on-edge finish to garden or retaining walls.

Figure 29.70 Single bull-nose

Figure 29.71 Double bull-nose

Capping and coping bricks

These are used to provide a weathering and pleasing finish to the tops of walls.

Figure 29.72 Brick coping (saddleback)

Figure 29.73 Brick coping (rounded)

Bonding bricks

These are pre-made standard brick cuts. They are normally made to prevent unnecessary cutting and save on wastage of bricks. These cuts are extremely accurate and are normally used where appearance of the finished article is required to be almost perfect.

Figure 29.74 Half batt

Figure 29.75 Three-quarter batt

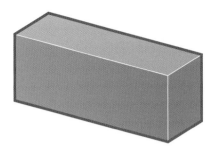

Figure 29.76 Queen closer

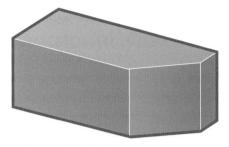

Figure 29.77 King closer

Arch and radial bricks

These arc used when constructing feature arches and curved brickwork.

Figure 29.78 Radial brick

Figure 29.79 Voussoir or arch brick

Slip bricks

These are used where a split course of bricks needs to be introduced into a length of walling.

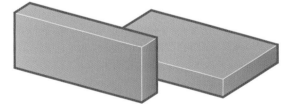

Figure 29.80 Slip bricks

Cill bricks

These are used to form window and door cills.

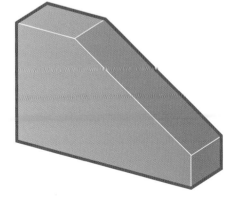

Figure 29.81 Standard cill brick

Remember

One of the features you may need to use are oversailing courses. The construction methods used for these are the same as those used for chimney stacks.

Did you know?

String courses can also be formed using specially shaped bricks, of which there are numerous types and variations.

Remember

Once the first brick has been cut at the correct angle (45 degrees), this can then be used as a template for all of the other cuts.

K6. Know how to set out and build brickwork incorporating features

There are several different types of decorative effect that can be used on brickwork. Good planning and setting out is essential, as there is very little room for error in decorative brickwork.

String courses

String courses are normally introduced towards the top of walls, particularly at eaves level or the last few courses of large boundary walls, as a decorative feature. String courses can be built using a variety of bonding arrangements. These include:

- soldier courses
- dog toothing
- dentil courses.

String courses are sometimes used lower down the face of the wall as a decorative feature. However, these are more commonly known as 'band courses'. The most common arrangement used for band courses is a soldier course.

Wherever string courses are constructed above normal 'eye line' the bricks used in these courses must be lined up along their bottom edge as opposed to the top edge. This ensures that the underneath of the feature, the edge that will be seen, appears straight and seamless.

Figure 29.82 A dentil course

Figure 29.83 Dog toothing (can be 60° or 45°)

Soldier courses

Soldier courses are bricks laid on end next to each other. However, unless great care is taken to ensure soldier bricks are laid both plumb and level across the length of the course, the finished wall can be unsightly.

When laying soldier courses, a line must be used along the top edge of the soldier course throughout the construction. In addition, a small spirit level or boat level must be used to ensure that the individual soldiers are kept plumb. Just one brick out of plumb will affect the line and result in a poor finish to the feature.

Figure 29.84 Soldier courses used as decorative features

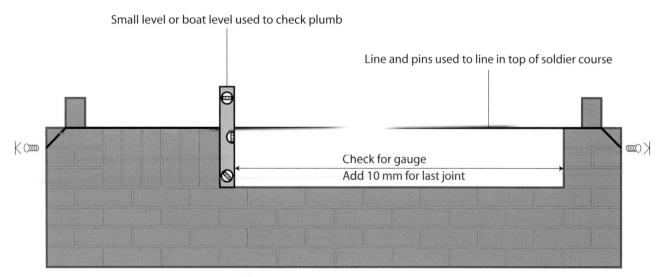

Small level or boat level used to check plumb

Line and pins used to line in top of soldier course

Check for gauge
Add 10 mm for last joint

Figure 29.85 Using a brick line and boat level to construct a soldier course

Soldier arches

Soldier courses can also be used in the bridging of openings, in the guise of 'soldier arches'. However, a soldier arch is not a normal load-bearing arch construction, and relies on additional load-bearing support systems to carry the soldier bricks, such as steel lintels – or, in masonry clad structures, relies on steel angles or brackets fixed to the structure.

Figure 29.86 Soldier arch

The method of laying the bricks of a soldier arch is the same in principle as that used to construct soldier brick string courses. Once the supporting lintel has been bedded in place, the reveals should be built up to three courses in height, to act as a support for each of the end soldier bricks as they are laid in position.

To ensure cross joints or vertical joints are kept to an even thickness across the span of the soldier arch, a 75 mm-gauge can be marked on the steel lintel. This gauge will need to be modified if the span of the arch does not work to standard gauge, to ensure that full bricks are 'worked in'.

As each brick is laid, it should be plumbed on the inside of the brick with the use of a boat level to ensure it is kept upright.

Weep holes

During construction, weep holes must be incorporated into soldier arch bricks. This allows any water that collects between the arch bricks and the lintel to escape.

The number of weep holes to be incorporated in the soldier arch will ultimately be governed by the size of the span, but there should be at least two weep holes above any opening. These can be formed either by using purpose-made, plastic weep-hole systems, or by removing the mortar from the bottom third of the soldier brick where the weep hole is to be formed.

Working life

You are constructing a soldier course above a window opening and you have four bricks left to lay. You have been ensuring all vertical joints between each soldier brick are full and that the surface being placed against the previous brick is fully covered with a 10 mm bed of mortar. However, you realise you only have sufficient mortar left to fully cover the surface of two bricks to form a solid joint.

Do you mix additional mortar for the two remaining bricks and lay the two bricks with full joints? Or do you make the remaining mortar spread for all four bricks by only applying mortar to the edges of each side of the brick, as there are only four to lay?

What are the consequences of both alternatives?

Functional skills

Working out the best mix for mortar will allow you to practise **FM 2.2.1a–h** and **FM 2.2.2** relating to applying a range of mathematics to find solutions and using appropriate checking procedures and evaluating their effectiveness at each stage.

Dog toothing

Dog toothing refers to a bonding arrangement in which the bricks are laid at a 45-degree angle to the main face of the wall. This type of bonding arrangement can either project from the main face or can be built flush with the main face. By building the edge of the angled bricks flush with the main wall, a recessed effect will be produced.

Remember

It is important to ensure that straight joints are avoided whenever possible.

When constructing a course of projecting dog toothing the projecting bricks must be lined in by fixing a brick line across the face of the bricks. The brick line will maintain even projection along the length of the feature. The use of a spirit level placed against the underside of the projecting course will ensure the 'seen edge' (the underside edge of the feature) remains straight and even to the eye.

Dentil courses

A dentil course refers to a string course where alternate headers in the same course are projected from the face of the wall. The same principles apply as for dog toothing when constructing a dentil course in that the underside of the bricks are to be levelled at eye line as the work progresses and the brick line is to be fixed across the face of the bricks being laid.

Both dog toothing and dentil courses should always be finished off with a course of bricks above them. These courses can either be laid flush with the feature course or project out past the feature.

This additional course is intended to finish off the feature and provide protection from the elements and possible damage to face and upper edges of the feature bricks.

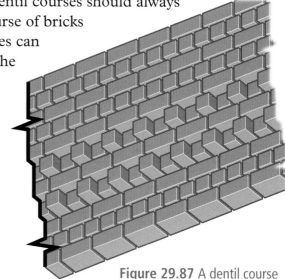

Figure 29.87 A dentil course

Diaper work

Diaper bond is quite simply the forming of diamond patterns within the face of a length of walling. This type of work provides no more than decorative value to a building.

The diamond patterns are formed using contrasting bricks to those of the main walling and incorporated as recessed, projecting or flush to the face.

There are numerous variations to the patterns which can be formed. Normally, patterns are formed using headers, as the use of stretchers is more difficult in relation to maintaining bond and does not provide the same uniformed diamond effect.

Whenever projecting diaper bond is used it is important to remember that all projecting bricks must be plumbed to ensure equal projection throughout the pattern. The projections should be plumbed both on the face and side elevations.

When producing a recessed diaper bond pattern, it is advisable to use a depth gauge or template to ensure that the recess depth is maintained throughout the pattern. These gauges can be made from timber notched to the exact depth required for the recess.

Figure 29.88 Diaper bond

Did you know?

Diaper work refers to the forming of diamond-shaped patterns.

Working life

You are forming a dentil course to the top of a solid wall and only have six projecting bricks left to lay, having already laid 30 projecting bricks, when the bricklaying line fixed across the face of the projecting bricks snaps.

What do you do? Do you repair the line and refix it to the face of the projecting bricks? Or do you leave the line off and judge the alignment of the remaining projecting bricks by eye? What are the consequences of both alternatives?

Coping

Weathering a wall

A protective finish can be added to walls that are likely to be exposed to weather such as rain and frost, which can weaken the wall and cause the top brick course to break up. Cavity walls do not require such protection as they are not exposed due to the roof structure covering the top courses. Garden walls, retaining walls and **parapet** walls will require finishing, however. A wall can be weathered with a:

- brick finish
- concrete finish
- stone finish.

Brick finish

Common bricks can be used to weather the top of a wall. However, it is advisable to use a hard stock brick or engineering type of brick, which is more resistant to water penetration and frost damage. The different finishes that can be achieved will depend on the thickness of the wall. On a half-brick wall there are two main ways to finish with bricks.

- The main way to achieve a brick finish is by using a brick on end, more commonly known as a soldier course (see Figure 29.89).

- Half bats can be used in the same way (see Figure 29.90), but they will need to be cut exactly in half (although this does not allow for the difference in brick sizes). In addition, the bricks would have to be cut by machine as cutting by hammer and bolster may not always cut squarely, resulting in variable back joint sizes, which gives a poor appearance to the finish.

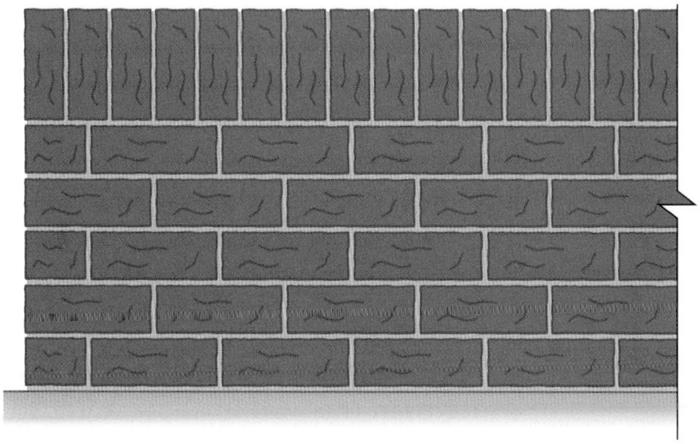

> **Key term**
>
> **Parapet** – a low wall that acts as a barrier where there is a sudden drop (e.g. a balcony wall)

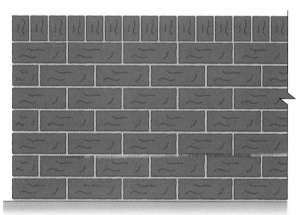

Figure 29.89 A soldier course brick finish

Figure 29.90 A half-bat brick finish

On a 1-brick wall, bricks are laid on edge to protect the top (see Figure 29.91). It is always best to use a hard water-resistant type of brick. Sometimes the wall may have what is called a tile creasing under the brick on edge. This is normally two courses of flat concrete tiles bedded on mortar and half bonded. This helps to stop rainwater penetration as water that would normally run down the face of the bricks is pushed away because the tiles are wider than the wall. A brick-on-edge finish can also be used on walls that are $1\frac{1}{2}$ and 2 bricks wide, as well as a finish to 1-, $1\frac{1}{2}$- and 2-brick **piers** (see Figure 29.92).

> **Key term**
>
> **Pier** – a vertical support structure that gives strength to a wall

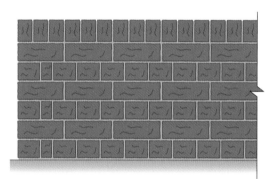

Figure 29.91 A brick on edge finish on 1-brick wall

Figure 29.92 A brick-on-edge finish on a pier

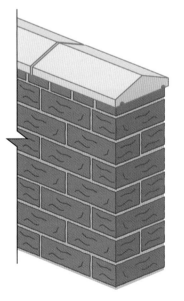

Figure 29.93 Saddleback coping

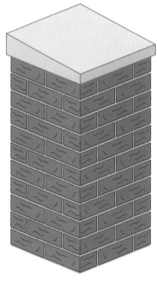

Figure 29.94 Feather edge coping

Concrete finish

Concrete can be used to weather a wall in the form of pre-cast sections called copings. These are usually factory manufactured and come in a range of width sizes to suit requirements but are normally 300 mm or 450 mm in length. Two main profile types of coping are normally used: saddleback and feather edged (see Figures 29.93 and 29.94). Copings are made slightly wider than the wall to allow water to drain past the face of the wall.

Stone finish

Natural stone cut to the desired size can be used to weather a wall in the same way as concrete (see Figure 29.95). Stone will give a more rough-looking finish as not all the pieces will be regular sizes. Stone is also a more expensive option for weathering due to the higher cost of the material.

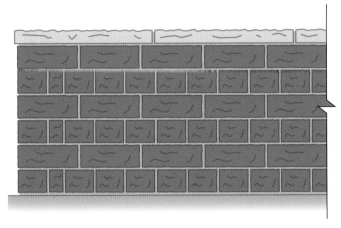

Figure 29.95 A stone finish on a wall

Tile creasing

Tile creasing is used as a form of damp-proofing as well as a decorative feature to the top of a brick or stone wall of 225 mm thickness. Creasing tiles are plain clay or concrete tiles without nibs or camber (flat). They are normally bedded on mortar below a brick on edge. They are laid in staggered courses and project from the wall on each side.

They can also be used as a finish to external cills, laid to an angle to allow water to run off. They are also used in corbelling as well as arch construction and chimneys, whether as feature work on the chimney breast or as decorative work to the finish of the chimney stack.

The recessed panel is only recommended for solid wall construction as the panel insert is usually recessed by approximately 38 mm and this would mean that in a cavity wall construction, the cavity width would be reduced due to the bricks being set back in the panel. This removes the minimum cavity width requirement.

Decorative panels

Types of panel

There are three variations to the way in which decorative panels can be presented. These are:

1. flush with the face

2. recessed

3. projecting.

Flush with the face

This is where the decorative panel insert is built flush with the face of the main wall.

Recessed

This is where the decorative panel insert is built back from the face of the main wall.

Projecting

This is where the decorative panel insert is built projecting out past the face of the main walling. The projection is normally no more than 25 mm.

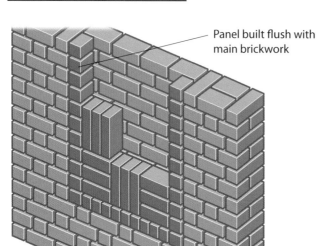

Panel built flush with main brickwork

Figure 29.96 A decorative panel insert built flush with the face of the main wall

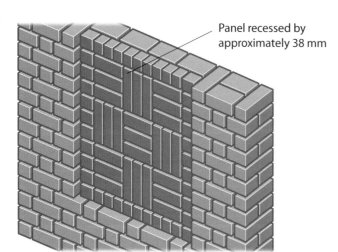

Panel recessed by approximately 38 mm

Figure 29.97 A decorative panel insert recessed from the face of the main wall

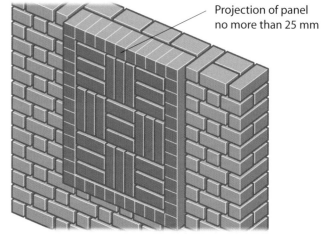

Projection of panel no more than 25 mm

Figure 29.98 A decorative panel insert projecting past the face of the main wall

Bonding arrangements for panels

There are three main bonding arrangements for use in decorative panels. However, all three have variations.

The three main bonding arrangements are:

1. basket-weave
2. herringbone
3. interlacing.

Basket-weave

This is the most straightforward of bonding arrangements as very little setting out is required in comparison to other arrangements used in decorative panels. As you can clearly see from Figure 29.99, basket-weave consists of three stretchers laid on top of each other, followed by three soldiers laid next to them and on top of them.

A variation to basket-weave bond is diagonal basket-weave. This is where the basket-weave arrangement described above is laid at a 45-degree angle to the base of the panel. This arrangement requires setting out and a large amount of cutting.

When setting the panel out dry, prior to cutting and laying the bricks, further variations to this bond can be formed. One such way is to use one of the main continuous joints as a diagonal joint passing through the centre of the panel in both directions (see Figure 29.100). This will give the impression of a diamond shape in the centre of the panel, which could be further enhanced with the use of coloured mortar around the border of the diamond shape and the bricks within the shape.

> **Did you know?**
> Where three stretchers are laid on top of each other, this arrangement is known as 'stack bond'.

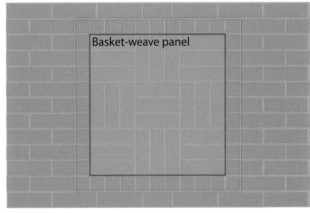

Figure 29.99 A decorative panel insert in basket-weave

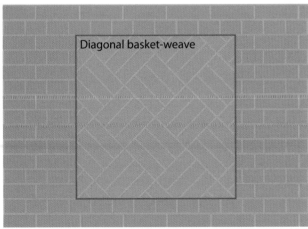

Figure 29.100 A decorative panel insert in diagonal basket-weave

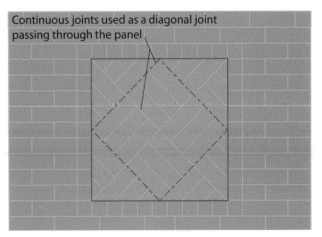

Figure 29.101 Continuous joints positioned centrally within a panel to form a diamond-shaped weave

Remember

As with diagonal basket-weave, vertical and horizontal herringbone bonding arrangements require accurate setting out and a significant amount of cutting.

Remember

Wherever possible, when constructing decorative panels, cuts should be made using a table saw/cutter or portable power cutter. This makes cutting more accurate and there is less wastage.

Another option is to use the centre of the middle brick of the panel positioned over the point where the 45-degree diagonal setting out lines cross (see Figure 29.102).

Herringbone

There are three main variations to this type of bond and they are:

1. vertical herringbone

2. horizontal herringbone

3. diagonal herringbone.

All of the above herringbone arrangements have one common factor and that is that the bricks forming the pattern are laid at 90 degrees to each other.

Vertical and horizontal herringbone patterns are also laid at 45 degrees to the base line of the panel.

Diagonal herringbone requires much less cutting than vertical and horizontal, and setting out is also minimal. This is because the herringbone pattern is laid in a similar way to basket-weave with bricks laid vertically and horizontally off the base line of the panel and not at 45 degrees as with the other two herringbone variations.

All of the above herringbone arrangements can be built using double bricks as opposed to the standard single brick arrangement. It is not surprising to learn that these are referred to as:

- double vertical herringbone
- double diagonal herringbone bond.
- double horizontal herringbone.

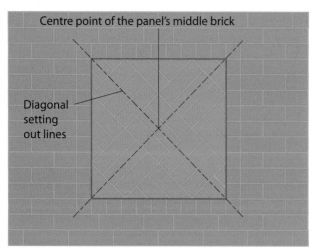

Figure 29.102 The centre point of the panel's middle brick is positioned over the point where the diagonal setting out lines cross

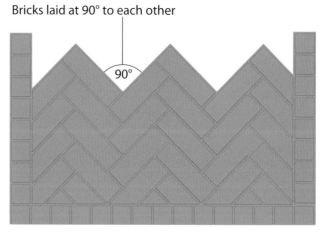

Figure 29.103 Bricks laid at 90° to each other to form herringbone bond

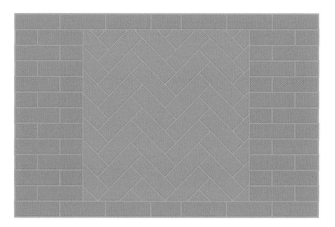

Figure 29.104 Vertical herringbone

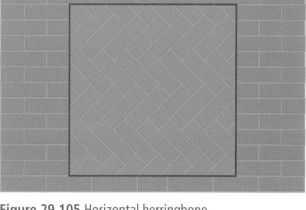

Figure 29.105 Horizontal herringbone

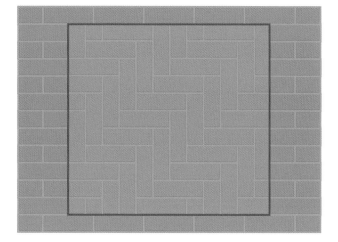

Figure 29.106 Diagonal herringbone

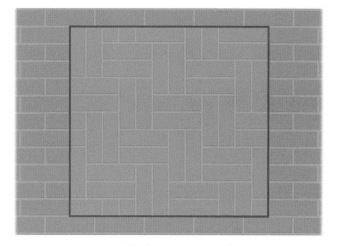

Figure 29.107 Double diagonal herringbone

Interlacing bond

As with all of the other bonds mentioned, interlacing bond can also be laid diagonally. The diagonal version of this bond requires more cutting than any of the other bonds.

As you can see from Figures 29.105 and 29.107, interlacing bond uses both $\frac{1}{3}$-brick cuts and $\frac{2}{3}$-brick cuts to achieve the interlacing effect. Diagonal interlacing also has the additional angled cuts around the perimeter of the panel insert.

The interlacing bond is the least commonly used of all decorative panels. This is because of the number of cuts required which make it time-consuming and costly (where the bricks are cut by hand).

Find out

Are there any other variations or types of bonding arrangements used in decorative feature work which have not been covered in this unit?

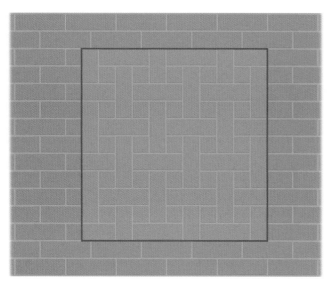

Figure 29.108 Interlacing bond

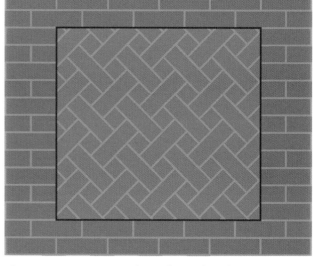

Figure 29.109 Diagonal interlacing bond

Did you know?

When preparing, it is of the utmost importance to ensure that the reveals of the opening are kept plumb and to gauge during construction. If accuracy is not maintained the bonding arrangement will not fit the opening size and have a flawed appearance.

Key term

Pinch rod – a piece of timber cut to the size of the opening and used to measure the distance between the reveals at various stages during their construction

Remember

If a concrete floor surface is used in step 1 you must ensure that this is an out of the way, unused area. This will prevent the dry bonded panel being disturbed during the setting out and cutting process.

Preparation

For all decorative panels, except basket-weave and interlacing bond, the opening in which the panel insert is to sit should be built first. As basket weave and interlacing bond patterns coincide with brick courses, this type of panel can be built as the work proceeds.

One method of ensuring that the correct opening size is maintained is by using a '**pinch rod**'.

Setting out

Basket-weave, diagonal herringbone and double diagonal herringbone are the only bonding arrangements which require little or no setting out prior to laying. However, care must still be taken during construction to ensure that each brick within the panel is laid plumb and to the correct angle.

The setting out process for diagonal basket-weave and herringbone bonding arrangements are much the same.

Step 1

Draw the outline of the panel opening on a suitable surface. This surface can be either a flat concrete floor or a piece of sturdy sheet material such as plywood.

At the time of drawing the panel on the flat surface you need to remember to draw the outline 20 mm shorter in its width than the actual opening size. This allows for a 10 mm mortar joint on each side, between the reveal and the panel insert bricks. You also need to deduct 10 mm from the actual height of the opening size to allow for the bed joint.

Functional skills

Setting out panels is a good opportunity to practise **FM 2.2.1a–h** and **FM 2.2.2** relating to applying a range of mathematics to find solutions and using checking procedures and evaluating their effectiveness.

Step 2

With the outline of the panel now drawn you need to mark out centre lines both vertically and horizontally onto the surface (see Figure 29.110).

From these centre lines you must now mark diagonal centre lines at 45 degrees (see Figure 29.111).This provides the starting point for the centre bricks of the panel.

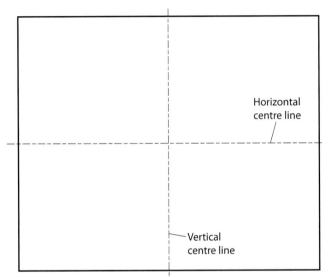

Figure 29.110 Vertical and horizontal centre lines marked on a panel outline

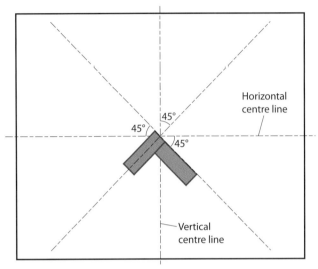

Figure 29.111 Diagonal centre lines drawn at 45° to the vertical and horizontal centre lines

Step 3

Once the position of the central bricks has been determined, position the remainder of the bricks required to complete the panel. At this point you must ensure that they are laid accurately at the correct angle and with the correct joint thickness between all bricks.

Step 4

Using the extended vertical and horizontal centre lines as a guide, you must now mark out the panel size, drawn on the flat surface, on top of the dry bonded bricks (see Figure 29.112).

Step 5

You now need to carry out all the required cutting.

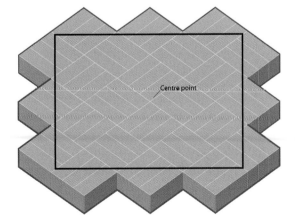

Figure 29.112 The panel size drawn on top of the dry bonded bricks

Remember

When drawing the vertical and horizontal centre lines onto the chosen surface, make sure that they extend past the outline of the panel. This ensures that, when the panel outline is covered by the dry bonded bricks, the centre lines can still be determined to aid the remainder of the setting out process.

Did you know?

In step 3 you are looking to produce the finished effect in terms of appearance. It is only now, prior to cutting, that any flaws or inaccuracies can be put right.

Construction methods

Ensuring accuracy when laying the first course of cuts at the bottom of the panel is essential in order to maintain the correct angle and gauge.

It is advisable to fix a temporary piece of timber across the face of the main wall, level with the top of the course from which the panel insert will be started.

This temporary piece of timber can be used to mark out the position of each of the cuts, including mortar joints, along the bottom of the panel.

When constructing flush or projecting panel inserts, it is important to use a line and pins to maintain the face plane of the feature. When building a recessed panel, it is difficult to use a line and pins so a straight edge which has been cut to fit inside the panel recess can be used (see Figure 29.113).

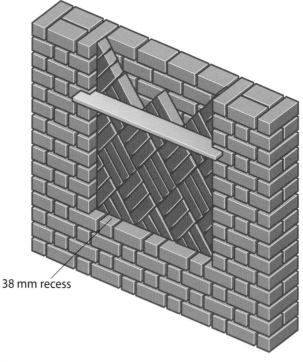

38 mm recess

Figure 29.113 A straight edge cut to fit the panel recess

When laying other herringbone patterns or diagonal basket weave, a boat level with an adjustable **vial** should be used to maintain the required 45-degree angle of the bricks. It is advisable to check each and every brick is laid at the required 45-degree angle. This will prevent the pattern of the feature becoming distorted and avoid unnecessary taking down and rebuilding.

Finally, providing the setting out and construction work has been carried out correctly, the cuts at the top of the panel should sit in line with the top of the reveals and there should be no need for further cutting.

All of the bonding arrangements covered within this chapter can be further enhanced in their appearance by introducing a border around the panel insert. This border is normally made up of bricks laid header wise and allowed to project or sit back from the main face wall, in line with the panel insert (see Figure 29.114). The use of coloured mortar in this border will further highlight the feature.

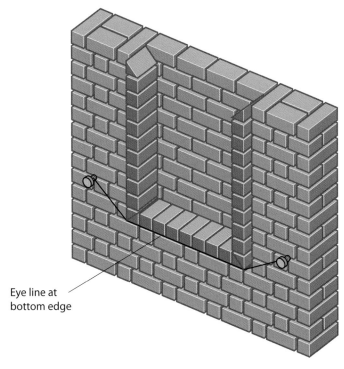

Eye line at bottom edge

Figure 29.114 A panel insert with a border

FAQ

Could a piece of string or bricklaying line, fixed at the pivot point, be used instead of a wooden trammel when checking or marking the face of a curved wall, either on plan or in elevation?

This is not good practice as there is a possibility that the line may stretch during use, giving a false reading, or if the line is not kept taut, again a false reading will be given.

Why not use a steel tape measure to check the width at varying points when building decorative brickwork?

There is always a risk of human error when reading the tape measure; a piece of timber cut at the accurate size required cannot be read incorrectly.

Why construct corbels in brick? Would it not be easier to use pre-formed corbels made from concrete or stone or even cast concrete corbels in situ using formwork?

It would be much easier to use pre-formed or cast in situ corbels. However, these do not always blend aesthetically within a structure where brick is required to be of a very high quality and may appear as an unsightly break in these types of structures.

Why is it best to make a template for the voussoirs and what material would be best to use?

The reason for making a template is so that each voussoir is exactly the same size. This will make the finished arch appear symmetrical. The best materials to make the template would be hardboard or thin plywood as the materials are reasonably priced and off cuts are usually available on site.

Check it out

1. Explain exactly what is meant by the term 'complex masonry structures' giving an example of each of the different types in situ. Use diagrams or photos to support your answers.
2. Prepare a method statement explain the techniques used to construct an arch using the axed arch method. Use diagrams and sketches to illustrate this, identifying any materials or equipment you will need to complete the work safely.
3. Explain what is meant by 'curved on plan' and describe the methods used to set this out and create this.
4. Describe how to construct a bay window, explaining the different techniques that will need to be used to create the opening for the window and the window itself.
5. Prepare a method statement explaining the bonding arrangements that can be used for Quetta bond, using diagrams and sketches and explaining the limitations of this bond.
6. Explain what the result of failing to plan effectively and following the requirements for bonding could be when building corbelling. Explain why you might tilt the front corbel bricks backwards slightly as you lay them.
7. Describe the special-shaped template used when tumbling in, and explain how to create and use this.
8. Describe, using diagrams and sketches, the method used to create a serpentine wall.
9. Explain the purpose of four types of 'special' brick, describing where these might be used and the benefits they would bring.
10. Explain what angle is used when forming dog toothing and describe how even projection is maintained across the wall.
11. Prepare a method statement for the construction of decorative brickwork, making reference to the different bonding arrangements that can be used and explaining how to create accurate measurements for cutting of bricks and components.

Getting ready for assessment

The information contained in this unit, as well as the continued practical assignments that you will carry out in your college or training centre, will help you with preparing for both your end-of-unit test and the diploma multiple-choice test. It will also aid you in preparing for the work that is required for the synoptic practical assignments. The information in this unit will help you to erect a large range of complex masonry structures.

Some of the material in this unit builds on techniques and skills that you may be familiar with from Level 2.

You will need to be familiar with setting out and building:

- arches
- brickwork curved on plan
- ramped brickwork

- reinforced brickwork
- obtuse and acute angle quoins
- brickwork incorporating features.

This unit will require you to practise a great number of practical skills. For all the learning outcomes you will need to be able to interpret drawings to establish locations and shapes required, accessing a range of information sources to do so correctly. You will also need to produce work method statements to establish all aspects of the building process as well as conducting risk assessments appropriate to the tasks you are carrying out.

Among the practical tasks you will need to carry out are:

- For learning outcome 1 – set out and provide templates for semicircular and segmental arches, providing temporary support for arches while cutting arch components, voussoirs and dry arch components
- For learning outcome 2 – set out and produce templates for brickwork curved on plan, cutting bricks and components to complete construction accurately
- For learning outcome 3 – set out and produce templates for ramped brickwork, cutting components and constructing ramped brickwork both curved and straight
- For learning outcome 4 – set out and construct brickwork incorporating both horizontal and vertical reinforcement, cutting components correctly and safely
- For learning outcome 5 – set out and produce templates for obtuse and acute quoins, cutting components and constructing, setting out and building these quoins
- For learning outcome 6 – set out brickwork features, cutting bricks and components accurately to construct brickwork incorporating features

Before you start work on the synoptic practical test it is important that you have had sufficient practice and that you feel that you are capable of passing. It is best to have a plan of action and a work method that will help you. You will also need a copy of the required standards, any associated drawings and sufficient tools and materials. It is also wise to check your work at regular intervals. This will help you to be sure that you are working correctly and help you to avoid problems developing as you work.

Your speed at carrying out these tasks will also help you to prepare for the time limit that the synoptic practical task has. But remember, don't try to rush the job as speed will come with practice and it is important that you get the quality of workmanship right.

Always make sure that you are working safely throughout the test. Make sure you are working to all the safety requirements given throughout the test and wear all appropriate personal protective equipment. When using tools, make sure you are using them correctly and safely.

Good luck!

Check your knowledge

1 When corbelling brickwork, the two most common measurements used for the overhang of individual courses are:

a) 25 mm or 52 mm

b) 32 mm or 48 mm

c) 28 mm or 56 mm

d) 15 mm or 28 mm

2 As each course is constructed the bricklayer must ensure that the corbel is square to the main wall. This can be achieved with the aid of a:

a) tri square

b) set square

c) building square

d) adjustable square

3 When constructing a curved wall, what types of joints have to be used in order to ensure the bricks follow the desired curve line?

a) straight joints

b) V-shaped joints

c) oversized joints

d) tight joints

4 A short length of timber, pointed at one end, is used to aid the production of curved brickwork. What is this construction aid known as?

a) traversing rod

b) pinch rod

c) gauge rod

d) trammel

5 An obtuse angle is:

a) less than 45 degrees.

b) more than 90 degrees.

c) less than 90 degrees.

d) 90 degrees.

6 The special-shaped brick used where corners need to be chamfered is known as a:

a) squint brick.

b) cant brick.

c) radial brick.

d) bull-nose brick.

7 Dog toothing is a bonding arrangement in which the bricks are laid at what angle to the main face of the wall?

a) 90°

b) 60°

c) 30°

d) 45°

8 In interlacing bond, which combination of cuts is used?

a) $\frac{1}{3}$ and $\frac{2}{3}$ brick cuts

b) $\frac{3}{4}$ and $\frac{1}{3}$ brick cuts

c) $\frac{1}{2}$ and $\frac{1}{3}$ brick cuts

d) $\frac{2}{3}$ and $\frac{1}{2}$ brick cuts

9 When constructing flush or projecting panel inserts, what should be used to maintain the face plane of the feature?

a) timber template

b) ranging board

c) line and pins

d) spirit level

10 Diaper work refers to the forming of:

a) triangular-shaped patterns.

b) circular-shaped patterns.

c) diamond-shaped patterns.

d) square-shaped patterns.

Index

abbreviations on drawings 38
accidents 5
acute angles 239–40
adhesives 10
aggregates
   codes 29
   safety 9
angle grinders 151
arches 209–21, 248
areas, calculation of 153–4
assessment preparation 59, 143, 179, 207, 263
axed arches 219–21

back boilers 158
bar charts 46–8
basket-weave bonding 255–6
battens 100
bay windows 225
beam and block floors 88–9
bill of quantities 43–5
blocks 9, 148
boilers 157–8
bonding 239–42, 255–61
bonds 187–8
bricks
   old/new 173
   repairing/replacing 204–5
   safety 9
   special-shaped/purpose-made 242–5
   types 126, 128, 147–8
brickwork. *See* complex masonry structures;
   repair and maintenance of masonry; structural
   and decorative brickwork
bridging floors 85–7
British Standards 29

calculations 152–5
cambered arches 221
capping 174
carbon footprint 63
cavity reinforcement 237
cavity walls 110–18, 120–1, 129, 132
cement 9, 149
chemicals, effects of 137
chimney breasts 162–9
chimney stacks 170–7
chipboard flooring 96–7
cills and lintels 199–200
cleaning 174–5
climate change 62–3
codes, material 29
communication 56–7
compaction of concrete 91
complex masonry structures
   arches 209–21
   coping 251–3
   corbelling 228–31
   curved brickwork 222–5, 226–34
   decorative panels 254–61
   dentil courses 249–50
   diaper work 250
   dog toothing 249
   features incorporated 246–61
   obtuse and acute angle quoins 239–45
   raking cutting 233–4
   ramped brickwork 226–34
   reinforced brickwork 235–9
   soldier arches 248–9
   soldier courses 247
   special-shaped/purpose-made bricks 242–5
   string courses 246
   tile creasing 253
   tumbling-in 231–3
component drawings 21
compressive loads 235
computer-aided design 22–5
concrete 29, 128, 130, 137, 140, 252

concrete floors 89–95
confidence in colleagues 56
construction methods. *See* methods of
   construction
Construction Skills Certification Scheme
   (CSCS) 4
coping 251–3
corbelling 228–31
critical paths 48–50
curing concrete 94
curved brickwork 222–5, 226–34

3-D dumb solids 24
3-D wireframes 23–4
damp proof barriers 79, 109, 111, 115, 136,
   150, 188–91, 200, 201
datum points 26–7
decorating equipment 10
decorative brickwork. *See* structural and
   decorative brickwork
decorative panels 254–61
delivery of material 155
dentil courses 249–50
deterioration of materials, prevention of 139–41
diaper work 250
dog toothing 249
door frames 182–3
drawings
   abbreviations 38
   accuracy of 39
   alterations to 56–7
   computer-aided design 22–5
   elevations 35–6
   floor plans 25–32
   hatchings and symbols 37
   projections 35–6
   scales 38–40
   setting out 32–5, 211–12, 258–9
   types of 18–21
   and work relationships 55
dry lining 124

eaves 106–7
efflorescence 135
electricity 13–14
elevations 35–6
emergencies 5
employer's liability insurance 53
energy efficiency
   in construction industry 63
   insulation 76–8, 97–8, 109, 110, 116–21, 133
   roofs 108–9
   walls 116–21, 123–5
environmental design 64–5
equipment
   power tools 151–2
   repair and maintenance of masonry 185–6
   safe working practices 8–10
   trammels 223–4
estimates
   added costs affecting profitability 52–5
   bill of quantities 43–5
   labour hours 51–2
   material/labour requirements 46–52
   plant, buying/hiring 45–6
   prices 42
   quotes 42
   resources 42–5
   tendering 41
extensions 200–3
external walls 110–21

fair-faced blockwork 123
felt 100
fibreglass 101
fireplaces and flues 156–69
fire(s) 15–16, 115, 138

firrings 100
fixing devices 182
flashings 101
flat roofs 100, 101, 110
flaunching 174
floating floors 88
floors
   beam and block 88–9
   components of 78
   coverings 95–7
   floating 88
   insulation 97–8
   plans 25–32
   restraint straps 87
   solid concrete 89–95
   strutting and bridging 85–7
   suspended timber 79–89
flues and fireplaces 156–69
formulae 152–5
foundations
   purpose of 66
   site clearance 68
   site investigations 67
   and soil 66, 67
   and sustainability 131–2
   trenches 69–72
   types of 72–6
frost, effects of 136–7
fuel 156, 157

Gantt charts 46–8
glass 129
glass fibre quilt 129
global warming 62–3
guttering 110

hatchings and symbols 37
hazards 5–7
header bonds 224
health and safety. *See* safe working practices
hearths 165–9
heat, effect of 138
heating systems 156–9
herringbone bonding 256–7
herringbone strutting 85–6
hipped roofs 104–5
hot weather 94–5
hydraulic lime 187
hygiene 6–8

I type joists 81
inductions, site 4
information
   checking 146
   material codes 29
   schedules 31, 32
   specifications 29–30
   See also drawings
insulated concrete formwork 130
insulated panel construction 130–1
insulation
   floors 97–8
   methods and forms of 76–8
   roofs 109, 110
   timber-framed construction 118–19
   between timbers 133
   walls 116–21
   water tanks and pipes 133
insurance 52–3
interlacing bond 257–8
internal walls 121–5
isometric projection 36

jointing 175–7
joists 79, 80–6

labour

Index

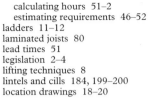

calculating hours 51–2
estimating requirements 46–52
ladders 11–12
laminated joists 80
lead times 51
legislation 2–4
lifting techniques 8
lintels and cills 184, 199–200
location drawings 18–20

manual handling 8
masonry. *See* complex masonry structures; repair and maintenance of masonry
materials
  brickwork 146–55
  deterioration, prevention of 139–41
  effects of water, frost, chemicals and heat 135–41
  estimates 42–5
  estimating requirements 46–52
  reclamation of 184
  repair and maintenance of masonry 182–4
  safe working practices 8–10
  sustainable 125–34
  weather, effect of on 141
metal 129, 135, 138, 140–1
metal stud walls 124
method statements 6
methods of construction
  and climate change 62–3
  in different structures 64
  environmental design 64–5
  sustainable 125–9
  See also floors; foundations; insulation; roofs; walls
mineral wool 129
monk bond 188
mortar 148–50, 187

oblique projection 36
obtuse angles 241–2
ordnance bench marks (OBMs) 26
orthographic projection 36
oversail 174

pad foundations 74
padstone 199
painting equipment 10
panels, decorative 254–61
parapet walls 238–9
PAYE 54
personal protective equipment (PPE) 15
petrol disc cutters 151
piled foundations 75–6
pinch rod 258
pipe ducts 156–7
pitched roofs 102–4, 108–9
plans. *See* drawings
plant, buying/hiring 45–6
plaster 9, 197–9
plastered blockwork 124
platforms 11, 13, 193–4
pocket reinforcement 236
pointing 204
power tools 151–2
prices 51
profit and loss, monitoring 54–5
projections 35–6
public liability insurance 53
Pythagoras' theorem 105

Quetta bond reinforced brickwork 235–6
quoins, obtuse and acute angle 239–45
quotes 42

raft foundations 74
rafters 99, 103–4
raking cutting 233–4
ramped brickwork 226–34
ranges, kitchen 159
rat trap bond 187
reclamation of materials 184
regulations 2–4

reinforced brickwork 235–9
reinforcement of concrete 90
repair and maintenance of masonry
  bricks 204–5
  damp proof barriers 188–91
  equipment 185–6
  extensions 200–3
  lintels and cills 199–200
  matching existing work 186–8
  openings in existing walls 196–9
  pointing 204
  reclamation of materials 184
  resources 182–4
  temporary support systems 192–5
restraint straps 87
risk assessments 6
roofs
  battens 100
  components of 98–9
  connection with walls 115–16
  coverings 107–8
  eaves 106–7
  elements of 98
  energy efficiency 108–9
  felt 100
  firrings 100
  flashings 101
  flat 100, 101, 110
  gable end finishes 105
  guttering 110
  hangers and clips 100
  hipped 104–5
  insulation 109, 110
  pitched 102–4, 108–9
  rafters 99, 103–4
  tiles 110
  ventilation 109–10
  water/damp proofing 109–10
rough ringed arch method 216–18

safe working practices
  accidents 5
  electricity 13–14
  fires 15–16
  hazards 5–7
  health and hygiene 6–8
  legislation and regulations 2–4
  materials and equipment 8–10
  method statements 6
  personal protective equipment (PPE) 15
  platforms and ladders 11–13
  risk assessments 6
  signs and notices 16
scaffolding 13, 193
scales on drawings 38–40
schedules 31, 32
sectional drawings 25
serpentine walls 228
setting out drawings 32–5, 211–12, 258–9
sheet materials 9
signs and notices
  drawings 37
  safety 16
site clearance 68
site datum 26
site inductions 4
site investigations 67
sleeper walls 28
softwood 95–6, 128
soil 66, 67, 68
soldier arches 248–9
soldier courses 247
solid bridging 85
spalling 136
specifications 29–30
stage payments 53
steel strutting 86–7
stepladders 11
stepped foundations 76
stock systems 50–1
stone 148, 253
string courses 246
strip foundations 73

structural and decorative brickwork
  calculations and formulae 152–5
  chimney stacks 170–7
  components, tools and equipment 151–2
  delivery of material 155
  fireplaces and flues 156–69
  industrial standards 160
  jointing 175–7
  resources for 146–55
strutting and bridging floors 85–7
suppliers 55
support systems, temporary 192–5, 212–15
surface finishes 92–3
suspended timber floors 79–89
sustainability
  methods and materials 125–34
  and water, frost, chemicals and heat 135–41

table mounted masonry saws 152
temporary bench marks (TBMs) 27
temporary support systems 192–5, 212–15
tender process 41
tensile stress 235
terms and conditions 55
thermal expansion 137
thin joint masonry 131
tile creasing 253
tiles 110
timber 135, 138, 140
timber codes 29
timber floors, suspended 79–89
timber stud walls 123
timber-framed walls 118–19, 121, 130, 231
tools. *See* equipment
toothing 202–3
trammels 223–4, 226, 227
travel expenses 54
trenches 69–72
triangles, area of 153
trussed rafters 103–4
trust in colleagues 56
tumbling-in 231–3
turning piece 216
tusk tenon joint 82

VAT 54
ventilation 109–10, 157
vial 260
volume 152–3

wall ties 112, 113
walls
  cavity walls 110–18, 120–1, 129, 132
  comparison of materials used 120
  connection with roofs 115–16
  damp prevention 115
  dry lining 124
  energy saving materials 123–5
  external 110–21
  fair-faced blockwork 123
  floor plans 28
  insulation 116–18, 118–21
  internal 121–5
  metal stud walls 124
  openings in existing walls 196–9
  plastered blockwork 124
  sleeper walls 28
  solid 119
  timber stud walls 123
  timber-framed 118–19, 121
  weathering 251
waste 8, 55, 155
water, effects of 135–6, 138
weather, effect on materials 141
weathering walls 251
weep holes 200, 248–9
wide strip foundations 73
window frames 182–3
windows, bay 225
wood 9 *See also* timber
work programmes 46–51
working relationships 55–7